MW01201255

AVID

READER

PRESS

ALSO BY HALA ALYAN

FICTION

Salt Houses

The Arsonists' City

POETRY

Atrium

Four Cities

Hijra

The Twenty-Ninth Year

The Moon That Turns You Back

I'll Tell You When I'm Home

A Memoir

Hala Alyan

Avid Reader Press

New York   Amsterdam/Antwerp   London
Toronto   Sydney/Melbourne   New Delhi

AVID READER PRESS
An Imprint of Simon & Schuster, LLC
1230 Avenue of the Americas
New York, NY 10020

First Avid Reader Press hardcover edition June 2025

AVID READER PRESS and colophon are trademarks of Simon & Schuster, LLC

Simon & Schuster strongly believes in freedom of expression and stands against censorship in all its forms. For more information, visit BooksBelong.com.

For information about special discounts for bulk purchases,
please contact Simon & Schuster Special Sales
at 1-866-506-1949 or business@simonandschuster.com.

The Simon & Schuster Speakers Bureau can bring authors to your live event.
For more information or to book an event contact the Simon & Schuster Speakers Bureau
at 1-866-248-3049 or visit our website at www.simonspeakers.com.

Interior design by Ruth Lee-Mui

Manufactured in the United States of America

1   3   5   7   9   10   8   6   4   2

Library of Congress Control Number: 2025932552

ISBN 978-1-9821-8258-8
ISBN 978-1-9821-8260-1 (ebook)

For Leila

I do not see in this night
other than the end of this night.
Mahmoud Darwish

Imagine you must survive / without running?
Ada Limón

The month is May. It is 1948. A girl named Siham is fifteen years old. Her village is al-Majdal, she lives in a seaside house with her siblings. Her father travels for months at a time, buying and selling textiles and garments to other coastal towns and villages.

Two hundred miles to the north, in Damascus, a girl named Fatima lives in a house with marble floors and a courtyard filled with basil and oleander plants. Fatima is the middle daughter, the daughter of a sheikh, a man of God who will stop speaking with her when she elopes with a stranger in twelve years. Fatima wears her hair short and bobbed, speaks French, will have three daughters, but only two will live. She will leave Syria in a decade.

Siham will leave al-Majdal this month. This week. Tonight. What does she pack? A dress? A notebook of dried flowers? Her family will live in a house in a new town, in a neighborhood in Gaza, Haret el Daraj: the neighborhood of stairs. They will be the lucky ones. When Siham marries, it will be a man from the camps, she will have son after son after son, an army of sons, six of them, and only one daughter, the second to last. Siham will leave al-Majdal tonight. She will leave and there will be a crescent moon or half-moon or no moon. She will leave and the soldiers' voices will fill the street and sea and sky. She will never stop hearing them.

✦

They brace themselves to leave. For the length of a dirt-packed road, the burning rubber of airplane tires, a new city, then another. These two women, not yet mothers, not yet my grandmothers. It will be thirty-eight years before they meet in Kuwait, their adopted home, their children marrying, the wedding in the banquet hall of the Holiday Inn hotel in Kuwait City, both the groom and bride wearing white, another five years before all that too is gone, before one stays, the other leaves. The Palestinian one will be buried in Syrian soil. The Syrian one in Lebanese soil.

◆

More than seventy years later, I wake from anesthesia. I am in a white hospital room in Manhattan. The nurses have apple juice, crackers, news of an incoming snowstorm. I tell one of them she's beautiful. I tell the other I'd been dreaming of green mist. *It's gone, right?* I ask, but nobody answers.

There is a pandemic. I have to walk myself to the elevator. Outside the building, Johnny is waiting in an Uber and I get inside. I don't say a word, just watch the skyscrapers, then bridge, then river. At home, there is Gatorade and soup. There is a daybed, a window, a money plant. I am supposed to sleep. I am supposed to watch bad television, take Tylenol, not make any big decisions. Instead, I wait for his office door to shut, then open the laptop and search my inbox for "surrogate." I make the choice like so many others: hotly, impulsively. I email the coordinator a single line: *I'd like to proceed.* There is an application they'd sent me months earlier, before I'd decided to try again: two more attempts at carrying, at the blue cross of a positive test, the sour gummies for morning sickness, the blood tests every three days.

In as much detail as possible, tell us about your infertility journey.

◆

I am still woozy from the drugs. I keep misspelling words, clacking the wrong letters. But I don't stop writing until I'm done, until it's all on the page: the last two years, the doctors, the surgeries, the blood work, the frozen eggs, the tiny embryos, the bleedings. There is a story and I tell it. It will be circulated among surrogates. I will be matched with someone in two days.

◆

For as long as I can remember, I've been obsessed with the *you*. The *you* in songs, the *you* in poetry. The *you* that—even unaddressed—exists, folded inside any writing. Every book written, I remember realizing as a child, had an audience in mind. "Artists are people driven by the tension between the desire to communicate and the desire to hide," D. W. Winnicott once said. There is a *you* even when we pretend there isn't.

◆

Winnicott also famously said: "There is no such thing as a baby; there is a baby and someone else."

◆

There is the self and there is audience. There is the self and there is *you*.

◆

It was the second March of the pandemic and, on the daybed of my living room, I emailed the Canadian surrogacy agency. For years, I'd gotten pregnant. I made recordings in the early weeks. I ate lentils. I prayed. Then the spotting would start. The doctor's tight voice. The cycle would begin again. But this last one had been different. I'd heard the heartbeat. I'd heard it fast. I'd heard it slow. Then I heard nothing. There was just the slow breath of the doctor, then her still face in the darkened room. I'm so, so sorry, she said, and she was, I could tell, and for a second, she looked at me and I looked at the assistant, and then I cried, but I didn't feel anything. I just cried because that's what the moment called for. I was an almost-mother, my legs askew, relegated back into not-mother. The doctor looked at me like I should cry and so I did.

♦

I played Scheherazade in high school. It was my junior year and there is a tape somewhere that I cannot for the life of me find. I remember I wore red. There were sequins. It was some sari thing, culturally inaccurate, but the theater instructor—a Mexican American woman with beautiful hair—clapped when she saw it. I was the frame of the play. It was a reimagining of *One Thousand and One Nights* and I would come in and out between scenes.

♦

"For Scheherazade more than anyone else represents the ancient frame-tale tradition," writes Heide Ziegler. The archetype of Scheherazade is centuries old, called upon in film, literature, visual art. In some ways, it is a cop-out, the easy framing device, the story outside the story, the nose pressed upon the windowpane. The reassuring maternal voice lulling us into imagination. It organizes, it streamlines, it grounds.

♦

The school was in Brummana, a mountainous town in Lebanon. Some students boarded there, and I was always a little jealous of them, how adult they seemed. Some evenings they were allowed to leave campus, alone, like grown-ups, with plans and dinners and monthly budgets. There were different sections for the girls and boys, but it still seemed scandalous to me that they all slept in the same building, mere floors from each other. It was my eighth school, fifth city, and third country in ten years. The campus was gorgeous, a fact I didn't appreciate until much later, founded by Quaker missionaries in the 1870s, and there was a meeting hall, and a gathering once a week, where we would sit in silence for several minutes. The buildings were red-roofed, and we were perched on a mountain, the city and sea in the distance. After the small town in Maine, this was my favorite school, the one where I felt most like a person. My closest friend was half-British, and I loved her fairy-tale blonde hair, her accent, the way I felt younger with her than I had in my childhood. I reinvented myself in that high school; I wore thick eyeliner and band shirts and started listening to Nirvana and Soundgarden and Hole. I smoked cigarettes, made up a boyfriend, and had the kind of friendships teenagers on American shows did.

+

There was a terrible king named Shahryar who learned his wife had been unfaithful. He then resolved to marry a new virgin every day and have her beheaded by the time dawn came. This, his logic assured, meant he'd never be dishonored again. Enter Scheherazade. In some versions, her father—vizier to the king—offered her only after he couldn't find any more noble-blooded virgins. In others, she volunteered. Then, night after night, she told the king lush, intricate stories about lovers and sailors and genies and birds. She cleverly timed a cliffhanger with each dawn. The morning would arrive and her tale would stop. The king, eager for resolution, would keep her alive for one more day, to hear the rest of the story that night. *When does she sleep?* I remember thinking as a child. This stressed me out. Then, rereading it recently, I realized that she'd borne him three sons during these years. *But really*, I thought, *when the* fuck *does she sleep?*

+

At some point during the play, someone missed their cue. I was alone on the stage, my line lobbed and nothing returned. I waited. The audience waited. I could hear my heart pound in my ears. I repeated my line. Nothing. Finally, I started to complain to the audience about how unreliable the character was, about how you had to do everything in this life yourself. The audience laughed. The magic of the moment endured, the suspension of disbelief unbroken. It mattered so much to me that I was able to keep them believing.

✦

The king kept her alive. Day by day. Night by night. After one thousand stories, on the thousand and first night, she told him she had no more tales for him. By now, we are made to believe, he'd fallen in love with her. She'd become mother to his children. She's told him every story she had. He let her live.

✦

There was a stone courtyard in the Brummana school. It was where people loitered during break, a cafeteria stand at one end, cedar trees surrounding. There was a large handball pole and every now and then, the cool guys would get restless and hoist someone up like they were crowd-surfing them, only there was no crowd, no surf, only the poor guy being lifted, his legs gripped apart by the other boys to meet the pole. They would do this in front of everyone, a dumb peacocking for the girls, and we would watch, even dumber, giggling and sometimes letting out fake cries of protest. One afternoon, they did it to one of the quieter boys, and he fought like hell, thrashing like a shark, so hard they swerved and banged his head against the metal. We all saw it. Later, the principal interviewed each of us individually. We all lied. We said he'd fallen. We said the guys—the cool ones, greasy haired, druggy—had had nothing to do with it.

That same courtyard, when I was a few months into the school. I don't remember what I was doing, probably telling some story, laughing at something too hard. I'd made friends, adjusted to their temperature, to what they liked, what they wanted. This was my spiel. It was my playbook. This guy Elie watched me for a minute before saying, so only I'd hear, *You try too hard*. He said it nonchalantly, casually, like commenting on a bird.

✦

After the play ended that night, the director hugged me hard. She laughed. You did so good, she said. I don't think anyone knew it wasn't on script.

✦

Sometimes, when I'm being bad, overspending, overpromising, I'll tell Johnny, *That's future Hala's problem.* Weeks later, faced with the consequences, an irritated friend, a credit card bill, I'll say aloud to myself, *Goddammit, Hala.* I don't know when this started, this bifurcation of self, the overt naming of it. There is the Hala who acts and the Hala who pays, and they somehow seem discrete, some hyperbole of dissociation. I've always spoken aloud to myself, since childhood. Not words or admonishments, but full conversations, in distress, in excitement, when puzzling through a particular overwhelm. I speak in full sentences, like I'm on a late-night show, trying to dazzle even my dumb self with wit and insight.

✦

For my prom, I found a lavender dress in one of the only thrift stores in Lebanon. It was long and floaty and I had to get the top hemmed in. When I tried it on for my family, my sister, Miriam—still a toddler— made a little house of it, hiding behind my legs, flouncing the tulle in awe. You can wear it someday, I told her, and she laughed and danced around the room. Years later, my cousin Layal wore the same dress to her prom. We filled it out differently and I felt a little jealous seeing it on her body—boobs where I had none, flat where I was hippy—like seeing an ex on the arm of a new woman. I asked her to save it for me. I had a vision, for a long time, of dissecting it into its beautiful, wispy parts, of making something with the tulle and silk: curtains, wall hangings. The last time I asked my aunt after its whereabouts, she looked at me blankly.

The houses have been emptied. The storage rooms have moved. There have been two wars. The elders are dead. I was as stupid as my question.

✦

But what of that first night in the king's quarters? In the myth, it is Scheherazade's sister Dunyazad who asks her for a story. This allows Scheherazade to begin spinning her tale in the king's presence. He becomes spellbound and she gets to live to see the first morning. But there are no accidents. It is a set-up, the first of many. Scheherazade had asked her sister to join, and perhaps it is this detail I love the most about the tale. This little subterfuge, the confidence behind it. The whispering of femme voices behind male backs. The plotting that demonizes women and saves their lives.

✦

Nobody understood my grief over the dress. I'd wanted it saved as a memento, yes, but I really wanted it for the tulle itself. I wanted my sister to take it apart, reconstruct it; I wanted a daughter to find it and make it her own.

Everything we had was lost, my mother would say of the invasion in Kuwait.

She meant the furniture, the clothes, my toys, all but a handful of photographs and pieces of jewelry. This refrain made me miserly with objects, a burgeoning klepto: everything could disappear and so everything became contraband. I'd love a library book and hide it under my pillow for months. I'd steal neon erasers from classmates, hair ties, holographic stickers. I'd sometimes look at photos of our life in Kuwait, my first birthday party, my parents' wedding, and think to myself, *this is gone, this is gone, this is gone* about the pale blue couch, the red majlis cushions, the ridiculous hat I wore. I felt owed, as though I could call an army—Israeli, Iraqi, American—and demand reparations. Where are my mother's pearl earrings? I'd imagine myself asking. The ones she wore at her wedding. Where is my grandmother's brocade? Where is that wooden armoire, those cream-colored curtains, the archive of our lives?

+

There is another reading of the Scheherazade archetype: "the first female psychotherapist in history."

+

I moved back to America after college to become a psychologist, to train for thousands of hours with children, asylum seekers, substance users, immigrants, incarcerated men. I sat on seven-hundred-dollar couches, in school offices, in hospital clinics, took notes, nodded, asked, fumbled, as people talked about their lives. Look what a story can do, those years showed me. Look how it can keep you stuck—patterns of longing, heartbreak, addiction—and look how it can liberate you.

+

Scheherazade transformed the passive female listener into a storyteller, catharsis-bringer, therapist. She told and her telling rehabilitated, or we are asked to believe: the bloodthirsty king subdued, healed, even capable once more of love and trust.

+

Since childhood, I've been aware of audience. We moved constantly—from Kuwait to Texas to Oklahoma to Maine to the United Arab Emirates to Lebanon—and this allowed new stages, tabulae rasae. I was a girl who fucked even when I didn't. A girl who dated even when I'd never kissed. But I loved the invention of that high-school self best of all: that girl of sixteen, seventeen, who'd learned from her previous subterfuges. She asked a grungy-haired boy to prom. She made an art film and left the room when it screened. She was magnificent: sly and muted, she lied better, stole better, learned what it was that people wanted and gave it to them. Often what they wanted was something to do with *themselves*, a mirror smuggled in the form of a story.

✦

Nobody knows where the story of Scheherazade originated. It has roots in Sanskrit, Persian, Mesopotamian tradition. The earliest tales are traced back to India, with conjecture of an Arabic translation in the eighth century. Stories kept getting added on, decade after decade, century after century, city after city, the ultimate game of telephone, an exquisite corpse of epic proportion.

✦

That high school kid Elie was right. I was too keenly aware of audience. I made other people my kings. I experimented selves on them: this red-clad girl in the spotlight, this teenager dragging lavender tulle in sand after prom. I studied them. I learned their desires. The only thing I liked more than power was giving it away, being at its mercy. This was the tableau I was most comfortable with: performing for a king, awaiting my sentencing. Tell me I'm loved. Tell me I'm enough. Tell me I nailed the part. Tell me I'll make it to the morning.

✦

The thing about reinvention is it has, as its precondition, erasure. Something needs to be erased to be replaced with a shinier, reinvented version. Only a self can't be fully erased. It just gets buried, a grave beneath a grave, a skeletal hand poking through the dirt of your own interment. Never gone. Never disappeared. Just dormant.

✦

The myth of Scheherazade is anonymously authored. In 1948, the scholar Nabia Abbott discovered handwritten fragments of the Arabic manuscript. She dated it back to the early ninth century. It was titled *Kitab Hadith Alf Layla*.

◆

What do I want to know? I want to sit with Siham and Fatima, my grandmothers, on a park bench in Brooklyn or the marina in Beirut or Kuwait. These women who were once young, who are now dead. What I want to know are the stories they told themselves. What they told themselves to survive, to keep going. What stories they told their daughters, so that they might do the same.

◆

Of course I loved Scheherazade. She'd studied her shit. She was quick on her feet. She'd prepared for the role of her life before it started. She saw the world in terms of cliffhangers and incentives, what would hold others' interest. She knew what people wanted before they did. She understood the stakes of an untold story.

◆

And she was the best fucking liar around.

◆

The lies were necessary. They were how she survived, of course. What I'd like to know is: what stories would she have told if she wasn't trying to survive, but live? What is it to tell a story not out of fear but of love? Not to have to improvise to get through the night, but to tell a story—which like all stories is thousands of stories—steadily, unurgently, to an audience that isn't even here yet, but who you hope against hope is coming.

Preconception

Levantine; n. (Textiles) a cloth of twilled silk; adj. (Placename) of or relating to the Levant; n. (Peoples) (esp formerly) an inhabitant of the Levant; n. Anything pertaining to the Levant, the region centered around modern Syria, Lebanon, Israel, Palestine, and Jordan.

It once meant anywhere in the large swath of land between Greece and Egypt. The word narrowed. The word sucked its waist in.

✦

It rains the last night I'm in Beirut. This is 2019. It is spring and, by the end of the year, there will be a thawra, a revolution that lights downtown with hundreds of thousands of protesters. A year later, the pandemic will have started and, two years out, my grandfather will die in this very apartment, on a plot of land he devoted his life to. I'm a decade into living in New York. Each trip back feels stranger and sneakier, like I'm getting away with something. The city is unpleasantly rearranged year to year, a thief in the night closing DVD stores and opening glassy cafes in their place. This trip has been melancholy at best. My great-aunt is dying, the family spending each afternoon in the ICU. Her daughter, torn about the Islamic ruling on DNR orders, has finally thrown her hands up, saying, *Someone else needs to tell the doctor. I can't.* That someone else is me. These are the moments I shine: crises, emergencies, a near-pathological calm slinking over me like a slip. I like being needed. I like the attention, but there's something else to it—the calm that reminds me of sharply made hotel beds, the satisfaction of order, a knife slicing cleanly into fruit. If I do something myself, I don't have to wonder how it was done.

◆

In French, *le soleil levant* means "the rising sun," "levantine" being a geographical reference to the east. By the nineteeth century, the word meant anywhere in the Ottoman Empire.

◆

The hospital overlooks the sea, though the ICU rooms have no windows. The building has recently been remodeled, all glass and sleek corners, and it reminds me of an airport. I haven't been in the sea in a long time. You don't swim, I remind myself as I wait for the doctor. My mother is asking him if we can move her aunt. She should be buried in Syria, my mother is saying. It's what she would want. *Mama couldn't be,* my mother tells me. *But we can get Nadia there in time.* Numbers are exchanged. A price named. There will be an ambulance in a few days. It will leave in the morning. It won't stop until Damascus.

◆

The word got a facelift in the mid-1800s. It took on a connotation. The Levant wasn't just a place; it was also a people, and a certain *kind* of people at that. A fickle kind of people. An in-between kind of people. The French knew where the sun rose, but they also knew where it settled.

This was more than astronomical: it was the natural progression of evolution, of civilization and culture. Everything, eventually, came west. To be Levantine was to be stilted, half-colonized, not quite there.

♦

It isn't just Nadia's dying. Beirut feels all wrong this time, a sweater too tight in the armpits. I keep trying not to cry. The trash is worse, a heavy smell in the air that nobody else seems to notice. I feel frantic when I go out at night. There is a bar from my college days, completely unchanged, and I'm jumpy the whole time. I keep thinking I'm going to see someone I know, and finally, unnervingly, I realize I'm afraid I'm going to run into *myself*, nineteen years old, torn shirts and bad bangs. That night I call Johnny and he is depressed and I tell him something to hurt him. I tell him I wish I'd never left this city. The rest is unspoken: to wish this is to wish never to have met him. The electricity cuts while we're speaking.

♦

Nadia wakes up while I'm in her room. I have missed her twice: months earlier during a trip to Beirut when she left for Syria suddenly, and this very week. The day before I landed in Lebanon, she'd fallen unconscious. I had a voice note from her that very morning, saying we'd get lunch when I arrived. I'd never hear her voice again.

But she wakes up and the nurse coos and I take Nadia's hand. I take it and I tell her to squeeze if the nurse is hurting her. She squeezes. *Can you stop*, I ask the nurse. She kindly tells me she can't. *New plan*, I tell Nadia in my inconsistent Arabic. *It's going to hurt, but I'll be right here.* My mind sputters like an engine. She will be unconscious again soon. What can I tell her? I'm exhausted from jet lag, half-tanned from Doha, where I've just done a reading, my coat still smelling of my detergent in Brooklyn. I feel like a cutout, something collaged onto the moment from another one. Her gnarled hand in mine.

✦

In the end, I tell her what I'd want someone to tell me. I tell her not to be afraid. I tell her she can go if she needs to. I tell her we'll take care of her daughter, even though her daughter is forty. I tell her she doesn't need to worry about her daughter, or my mother, or anyone. I tell her she lived such a good life. That she lived it so well. I tell her that Allah is waiting and she was His all along, so there is nothing to be afraid of. I tell her we will speak her name for as long as we live. I read the Fatiha. I don't cry. At some point, her eyes flutter shut again, and I keep talking and I know I'm doing it for myself.

✦

Afterward I clack down the hallway to the doctor's office.

The family decided, I said. I—great-niece, not daughter, not sister. *If something goes wrong, we don't want her resuscitated.*

The doctor nods. *The family's decision?* he asks. I say yes. *Good.*

It's the best hospital in the country, but this is Lebanon. There are no papers to sign. No questioning of who I am, no request to see my ID. The doctor holds my gaze for a second, then nods. That night I dream we kiss.

✦

I first heard the word in college. It was a poli-sci course—my doomed major—and I wasn't the only blank face in the room. Only the thing is— that room was in Beirut. We were *in* the Levant. The pudgy white professor told us. He said it with finality and so it was so. I liked him. I'd run into him at an expat bar later in college. He was perfectly appropriate. He bought me a beer and told me I wrote well. He tapped my elbow, and said urgently, like we were being overheard, *I heard some things about.* He stopped himself. I buried myself in the beer mug. I knew what he'd heard. I knew what everyone had heard. *You should maybe leave when you graduate*, he finally said. *To the States or something? I think you'd be happier there.* I could see how much he meant it. His red-cheeked face, lit up with a vision of me, a smooth new reputation, strolling the streets of Chicago or Oakland. No vicious rumor chasing me from year to year. No terrible ex. I don't know what the Levant was for him. A career move, a passion project, a sea of Arab faces taking notes while he told us about ourselves. Beery Fridays in Gemmayzeh, the beauty of that campus. He didn't speak Arabic. He was a good professor. He got to be abroad and not abroad at the same time; Beirut's great appeal. His face shone with earnestness in that bar. I was smart and I was hurting and this city wouldn't protect me. Not even with all its rising suns. He wanted something for me. I was used to that. I was a faux-broken bird, not as sick as I seemed, and somehow sicker than I realized. People wanted things for me all the time. And what they wanted for me wasn't here.

◆

I dreamt of the professor the other day. Fifteen years later, I am thirty-six, and he returns to me, someone I haven't thought of in a decade. He stood under an archway and said, *Why did you come back*, and as I opened my mouth to answer, he dissolved.

◆

But there is no Beirut this year. I'm older, in America now. I'm years into infertility. There is only the same thorough erasure of self, like a canvas painted over. There is only one wriggling amoeba of a truth: what I want for myself isn't here. Even if I'm not sure what *here* even is. The uneven floors of my Brooklyn apartment? The siren-filled blanket of the pandemic over the city? That smell of antiseptic soap and peppermint in the fertility clinic? It's more like time itself has become the trap and I don't know how to emerge. Days trudge by like aimless elephants, gathering around the watering hole of my one sad, tiresome goal: to lie on my back, to wait for semen, to have matter meet matter. To emerge transformed.

◆

It is March. Then April. Then May. The year after the pandemic began. I haven't been to Beirut in over two years.

◆

I grew up with elders. I grew up at their dining tables, drinking their soup, hearing their stories, speaking with their accents, wearing their perfume. My grandparents were everything to me. Fatima—who we called Meimei—with her soft hands, her soft voice, and her sister, Nadia. Salim and his earnest temper.

I'd seen my father's parents less growing up. Teta, as we called my father's mother, died when I was sixteen, in a hospital bed in Homs. We'd seen her weeks earlier, visiting her in Syria as she died of lung cancer. I'd asked her questions about her childhood, then forgot the answers. It was her hands that would linger in my memory. Smooth and unlined, pale, they seemed so young. They held themselves as she spoke. *Did you love him*, I remember asking about her courtship with my grandfather, and she laughed. *Do you hear this question*, she'd said playfully, though there was nobody else in the room.

I cried when Teta died. I cried for the young woman I'd seen in photographs, for my father. But I couldn't grasp the vastness of the life she'd lived: the girl she'd been in Gaza, the lands she'd been driven from, the wars she'd lived through, the life she refused to leave in Kuwait, even after soldiers and tanks came. She was a woman who'd raised mostly sons, men who became doctors and engineers and fighters, who went to Egypt and Beirut, fought for Palestine, designed airplane engines in Kansas.

But when Meimei died, when Jiddo, my mother's father, died, I was an adult, could locate myself in their deaths. I'd spent years with them in Lebanon, thousands of meals, so many New Years Eves watching glitzy Beiruti singers on TV, kissing each other at midnight; I'd listen to my grandfather talk politics, talk writing, I'd cry over heartbreaks to Meimei. Then—in rapid succession—Meimei and her sister died. I was thirty, thirty-two. The loss was the kind that filled, not drained. The kind that filled my mouth with sour when I woke in the middle of the night, remembering. I'd left Beirut promising Meimei I'd return. Instead, I stayed, choosing America, a white man, a life veneered with ease. I watched their illnesses from continents away, their disappearings, their deathbeds and burials missed. Their bodies fell and, in some weird way that felt prophetic, otherworldly, their cities fell too. My grandmother's dementia echoed the wreckage of Syria. My grandfather—born in Turkey, childhood in Akka, a believer in Arab unity—fought for Beirut all his life. Then came the failed revolution, the pandemic, the port explosion. He became a different kind of infected. He became sick with a failing city. I'm certain of it. Two weeks after the D&C—the only pregnancy that reached a heartbeat—in the spring of 2021, my grandfather died.

✦

In as much detail as possible, tell us about your infertility journey.

✦

For years, my life has been an endless carousel of paperwork: the emergency room, the hospital after the ectopic, the fertility clinic. Everywhere, there are forms. My age changes on them: 31, 32, 33, 34. They want to know about preexisting medical conditions. Allergies. Family history. They want to know if I sleep well, if I have anemia, if I urinate too much or too little. They leave little blank spaces for some questions. *Number of times pregnant.* Five. *Number of live births.* Zero.

✦

But there are different forms for surrogacy. Different questions. There are no binary yes-or-noes. You have room for hundreds of words. They want details, an arc, a story. Your story is what will match you. It is what will find you someone to carry your child. *I am thirty-four years old*, I write. *I am the daughter of two living parents. I am the eldest of three, a brother four years younger, a sister almost thirteen years younger. I have wanted to be a mother for a long time, longer than I've ever admitted.*

✦

My story is what matches me. In two days, I Skype with a woman. Dee. In three, we are filling out paperwork. During the video call, I catch glimpses of Dee's life: a blonde toddler, a small dog, a wooden chest of drawers. Why did you want to meet me, I ask. She says it was because of my story. Because I was a writer. Because of the way I spoke of wanting motherhood. Because of how honest I seemed. We talk about our lives, the weather, how we found the agency. Neither of us has done this before. Whenever there is a silence, we smile at each other.

✦

Everything needs my signature. The embryos must be shipped to Canada, and I keep imagining cartoonish scenarios where they get lost. The emails from the agency are dotted with exclamation marks, winking faces, prayer hands for the first embryo transfer. The surrogate is kind and petite, with two girls of her own. Her hair is the color of sand. She sends me emojis too. But there is a joylessness to my mornings. I wake up and I remember: this is my life. This clump of hair I twist into a bun. This flattening belly.

✦

I am Palestinian American. My father was born in Palestine. My mother was born in Kuwait with Lebanese citizenship. My maternal grandmother was Syrian. I spent my childhood between the United States and the Arab world. I returned to this country for graduate school and fell in love: with this city, with a man. I thought I would go back, but it never seemed like the right time. Then it became less possible. I hope to be paired with a surrogate who is comfortable carrying for someone with my background.

◆

I'd gone feral after the last miscarriage. I spent three hundred dollars on thrifted clothes, dresses the color of Lisbon and citrus fruits that I wore once and later felt nauseated at the sight of. I got Botox and Lasik and fake lashes all in the same week. None were planned. I visited one minimalist waiting room after the other. They had fiddle-leaf figs in the corner, lemon-flavored Pellegrino. I was their target audience. I was the target audience for everything: Marlboros, ads for meal prep services, mani-pedi specials. Afterward, I squinted in the sunlight and walked to First Avenue, even though Union Square was closer. I smoked a ton of weed. My body was mine, only mine, and there was a vindictive pleasure in that. I had planned for sacrifice. The benevolent mother at four a.m. with rock-solid, lactating breasts. I had planned to give my body over. To make eyebrows and toenails with it. Instead, it was no one's except mine. While I sign paperwork readying another woman to carry the embryos Johnny and I have made, my body unmothers me. It is like time-lapse photography in reverse: my breasts unswelling, no longer sore, my sense of smell settling, the bile in my throat gone. I have been released of something; it is a terrible and unasked-for freedom.

◆

Spring, two years since Nadia's death. Spring, one month since the last miscarriage. I am surviving on matcha lattes and snooping on Johnny's phone. Our apartment has turned into a mausoleum, a place for ghosts to graze. I kept losing track of the ghosts. Every lost embryo—ghost. Every heartbeat—ghost.

"What would've happened if I'd told you first," he'd said once, when

I first learned about my infertility. We stared at each other. I kept my face blank. "If I'd said, I don't think I want a child. If I'd asked you to make a choice between that and this."

I knew what he meant by *this*: he meant our life, a marriage fraught by our histories, the ways we'd been hurt, the ways we'd learned to hurt. He meant one-way tickets to Mexico and Barcelona and Chile, our adolescent lifestyle, one that we'd speak of sheepishly but a little proudly to other people. He meant himself, solo, unadorned, a man, not a ticket to somewhere else.

My throat tightened. I had no response. It was a fair question, but my love for him had become embossed with fear: of his leaving, of his retracting his promise to have a child. There was a clock in every room of the house and a clock on my wrist and they tattled on the day of the month and the year. They told me I might run out of years. They told me he might run out of patience.

♦

The last time I see my grandfather, that month Nadia died, he is in the doorway of his house. The house Meimei died in. The house I will not see again. He'd bought this plot of land in the 1950s, a neighborhood called Mazraat Yachouh, mountainous, north of Beirut. It is the spring before the virus. The spring a man was taken to an embassy and murdered. Everyone is talking about it, my mother repeating, *Can you imagine, can you imagine.*

My grandfather is crying in the doorway. I am crying. We shouldn't be crying, I want to tell him. I will be back. I don't know there will be a virus. I don't know I'll miscarry and miscarry and miscarry. He says my name. He says, *When you have a child, I'll put her right here,* he pats his shoulder. *Just like I did with you.* My entire life I'd been retold this story: how I loved knafeh so much as a child in Kuwait, that when I'd ask for it late at night, he'd hoist me on his shoulders and we'd set out into the dark, my little voice babbling with excitement.

✦

On the phone with Meimei once, in the final year of her life, she asked: *Keef ibnik?* But there was no son. She was in the grips of her dementia but sounded tremendously lucid asking the question. *Tell me, tell me,* she said, a lilt of anticipation in her voice. I'd had the ectopic already; the miscarriages were awaiting me. I froze with choice: to correct her gently, to speak my shame aloud. Something I had no blueprint for. There is no son, Meimei. Instead, kindness was a lie, one that relieved us both. And I was so good at lying by then. He's well, I told her. He's so calm. He's already crawling. Can you imagine? We marveled together, at this miracle, at how time flew.

✦

"I'm sorry, Hala," Johnny would say after every miscarriage. He'd kiss me. He'd order me sushi and tell me to pick a movie to watch. That was care, too, but it was straining, then barely there. I'd been possessed. For years, my whole life, each preoccupation replaced the one prior to it—obsessional rituals to alcoholism, tequila to anorexia, thinness to codependency. I wanted and wanted, and had turned Johnny into a tool of my wanting, and he'd eventually responded by disappearing. We shuffled past each other in rooms, eyes barely meeting, discussing roof leaks and travel and vet appointments like strangers. These were my pregnancies. And so they were my griefs. My ghosts. We barely mentioned the surrogate. We spoke with the fertility lawyer separately. I signed paper after paper for him, the large, hooking loop of his *J*.

✦

In February 2018, I was diagnosed with a cornual ectopic, which left me with scarring. At the time, they also discovered I had a completely septate uterus; there was a surgery where much of the septum was removed. During that laparoscopic procedure, the surgeon accidentally punctured my uterus, leaving me with more scarring. Soon after, we tried without any medical involvement for over a year, then—due to my history—were referred to a fertility doctor at NYU Langone. We then went through three rounds of IUIs. One worked and ended in a miscarriage. After that first miscarriage, one round of IVF yielded seven PGS-tested embryos. The first transfer resulted in a second miscarriage, and the second transfer ended in a third miscarriage. The fourth and most recent miscarriage has been particularly difficult, as I was farther along than the others, and had heard the fetal heartbeat during a couple of visits before the heartbeat stopped.

We had a long conversation with my reproductive endocrinologist, who explained that, due to the operations, the puncturing, and the miscarriages—not to mention the lingering septum—my uterus will struggle to carry a child to term. It was a hard conversation. I am tired. My body is tired. Five times, I've felt my heart rise at the sight of those two blue pregnancy lines, and five times I've felt it break. We are very committed to having a family and raising a child in a healthy, creative, loving home, but it seems as though my uterus (while lovely in many ways) is having trouble carrying this out. I think we need help. I believe strongly that it takes a tribe to raise a child, and there's nothing wrong with it taking a tribe to make one.

✦

Scheherazade's gambit succeeds—with the Sultan and with readers everywhere, Michael Austin writes, *because it taps into a very deep human need for literature.* Narratives create a distance between the listener and the story, and in that distance there is freedom: to create links, to see connections, even to see the self, plain as a penny at the bottom of a clear fountain. In narrative therapy, this is called externalization: the mere fact of the story means you are outside the story.

✦

I need this story out—I can feel it clawing my neck, tightening my breath. But how do you birth something before you know what it will be?

My friend, when I pose this question, blinks at me: *But that's exactly what birth is.*

✦

I matched with Dee a year after the pandemic began. Everything had stopped during lockdown: the day the ambulances began shrieking through Brooklyn, that strange smattering of applause at seven every evening.

✦

Meanwhile, clocks stopped in every room. The alarm clock suddenly stopped working. The clock on my laptop forever told me the wrong time. I couldn't get it fixed. Throughout the day, I would check the time in Beirut compulsively. To check the time in Beirut was to check it in Syria, in Palestine, in Iraq, in Jordan. The Levant lived in the same hour, hour after hour. I could mark my cycles around the land thousands of miles away. The first miscarriage: weeks after the port explosion that brought Beirut to its knees. It is one of the largest non-nuclear blasts in the history of the planet. I watch the men hurling their beautiful fists against the sky in protests, the women erupting into song. I bleed through a pair of shorts, a nightgown, two sets of sheets. I watch the explosion over and over, from different angles, different shaking cell videos, different shouts, different voices cursing the same people.

There is one explosion video taken from a balcony, a man idly asking what that smoke is before that enduring booming sound. *Say Bismillah,* he shouts at someone off camera and a woman, shakingly, obeys. I feel the ripe word in my own mouth. I say it too, then feel disgusted with myself. This isn't mine. What's mine is the fat pile of pads on the bathroom sink, the estrogen pills, the quiet man in the second bedroom. But still—I marked my body around these disasters.

✦

The truth is I don't know what makes me deserving of motherhood, aside from the fact that I deeply, deeply want it. I have wanted it for as long as I can remember, and I remained invested throughout this journey in not turning against my body. I have felt my body try so hard, over and over, to create a home for an embryo, and despite all the sadness I feel at times, I continue to have love for this little ecosystem I inhabit. It's done its best. And I believe there are other bodies that can take on this task with less toil and heartache. I don't ask for a surrogate lightly. I recognize how immense of a gift it is: the sort of giving that simply can never be repaid. It's hard to make a case of "us" over another potential intended parent. We deserve parenthood no more and no less than anyone else. All I can say is there is a tremendous amount of love waiting in our household for a child, and we are already humbled at the mere prospect of someone helping us in this way.

◆

Suddenly, there was another woman, another womb, a smiling face on a screen telling me she'd started taking her prenatals, because it was important to begin early. Her name was Dee. I sleepwalked through the weeks. Sometimes I found myself blinking mid-session or on the 6 train, as though I'd stumbled onto a set.

◆

In May, I watch a bulldozer split into a house like teeth. It happens thousands of miles away in a Palestinian village, and I can't stop dreaming of it. I feel the heave of the earth. The embryo transfer is a week away: when they will take that spitlike bundle of cells—mine, his, millennia of our ancestors and recessive genes—and sluice it through a catheter into another woman's cervix, into the final mouth of her uterus.

The bones of that house crumble, then another, then another. It has been all over the news: the Palestinian activists handcuffing themselves to their grandparents' doors, the news anchors reporting in front of prisons. Still the bulldozer has continued its clawing. When it ends, there is the wailing of a woman, several women, cursing, crying. I cannot make out the words, so I imagine them: This was my father's house. This was my house. This was my child's house. May you never know rest. How could you. How could you. Where will we sleep now. What will I tell my children. What will I leave my children.

✦

This is not how I want to enter motherhood. I finally write this down. Not in a journal or document. I write it on the inside of a brochure in one of the waiting rooms. I leave it on my seat when my name is called.

✦

My final appointment with the fertility doctor is the same month as the bulldozers. I tell her about the surrogate, how in the other country they won't let me choose the gender of embryos. *Then you'll be just like the rest of us,* she says kindly. I like her eyes, the way they crinkle when she is thinking. *This time next year,* she says, undoctorly, a risky kindness, *you could be a mother.* My breath catches as she examines me, but what I'm thinking of is Nadia. Years earlier, I'd had an ectopic. That Mother's Day, she'd sent me a voice note from Syria. She told me to read a particular sura. Then she wished me a happy day. *Next year,* she'd said, *you'll be the most beautiful mother in the world.*

✦

The terrible consolation of the elders' deaths: they no longer had to watch their countries fall. Only the living are left to watch, those remaining, those not yet born, the not yet here.

✦

That last trip to Beirut, I returned to my college campus for the first time in years. The security guard recognized me. It was like seeing someone from my dreams. Where have you been, he asked, as though I'd missed curfew, as though I was just a few hours late.

America, I said. As though that word could explain it all. And here's the thing: it did. He nodded. He nodded like he'd seen it all: the night-clubs, the blackouts, the twelve-step meetings, like he knew the long winters of New York, the rumbling subways, the American husband, the American headlines, the American small talk.

It's a shame you all left. You lot, he says. You were troublemakers. I remember you.

We laugh. We laugh at the trouble we made, at the children we'd been, unchecked in a city like this one, a city flanked with cities like it, to the north, to the south. We laugh at the time I was caught going into the boys' dorms, the time I'd tried to climb the gate, the time I was car-ried into campus.

And when will you be back, he asks as I'm turning to leave, and we both shrug at the exact same time. As though we both know something without knowing it, an explosion that hasn't happened yet, a virus that hasn't begun yet, a husband that will leave, a daughter that will or won't come. We shrug and we laugh and we say soon, soon inshallah.

◆

The sura Nadia told me to read is my favorite one: Surah al-Nas. It is only six verses, used to seek protection against jinn and evil eyes. It is to be read before sleep, during illness, after other prayers. It guards against possession, wayward influences, bad intentions. There is a line in the sura: *They who whisper into the chests of humankind.*

Chests can also be translated to heart. Or breast. I love that imag-ery. A bad mouth whispering against a breastbone. Not the ear. Not the neck. Into the ventricles of a heart, the heart of the machine that is a person.

◆

In Arabic it is: اَلَّذِى يُوَسْوِسُ فِى صُدُورِ ٱلنَّاسِ.
al ladhī yuwaswisu fī ṣudūri n-nās

◆

I love all the slinky, rich *s* sounds. Whisper, whisper. *Waswisu.* It is the final chapter of the Quran. It is said to be the final imploring, the last reminder to ask not only for guidance, but for freedom too. You speak syllables and an evil spell breaks. A possession ends like bad weather.

◆

I want to welcome the *you*—baby, daughter: both the possession and the thing that breaks it—but it's not time yet. You are still sleeping at this point in the story. The *you* is still just a hunger, a thundering one at that. A concept, a desire, a thumbtack holding a to-do list in place. The *you* is still something I'm afraid of not having, more than an actual person I can imagine.

◆

There is a meeting with the surrogate, the agency representative, and the lawyer. We smile at each other on the screen. The conversation is full of half-starts. They are all white women. Everyone I've interacted with is a white woman, except for the man who handled my embryo shipment. He is Israeli, and keeps referring to me as his cousin. I smile then too. I smile everywhere now and for some reason people still keep asking me if I'm okay. This confuses me until one day I catch a glimpse of myself in a mirror mid-smile and wince; there is something frozen in my face, more grimace than anything.

"So," the lawyer chirps, "we want to make sure we have all our bases covered." She's talking about all the things that go wrong. Unsettling ultrasound scans, disagreements about birth plans. The meeting is long and thorough and we all shift uncomfortably in our respective chairs, in our respective cities, in our respective countries: it is occurring to us why these rules exist. It means things have gone wrong. It means there have been disagreements, while having to continue to be connected in this most intimate of ways. The prospect is unthinkably awful, and Dee and I text each other jokey comments throughout the meeting. I already know I will be hands off, the perennial Cool Girl, because I will have no choice. I will have to trust her. We are too far apart, the pandemic isn't over. In some ways, her distance helps with this: we would never have crossed paths otherwise. She is from a small town in Canada. She has never left the country. I've heard of women using their friends or sisters as surrogates, stories of things turning sour, unrecoverable rifts. But this woman and I are blank slates to each other, no history to project anything on, no shared divot in the lives we've lived. Until now. Until this. I imagine it like a final, black knot in the lines of our lives. Even if we never speak again after this, we will be bound.

✦

I keep smiling in the subway. I smile in the waiting room at the clinic. I smile in Zoom meetings. The surrogate sends me a countdown to the transfer with emojis. Six weeks! I smile at strangers on the street. Inside, I churn with worry: the embryos, my marriage. My body has started to feel unsettling, dishonest. I see one doctor, then another, then another. I obsess over the blood work. I can't stop checking my body for bumps. I lose weight, abruptly, swiftly, and am certain this means something sinister. Five weeks! We go to Mexico on vacation with friends.

During the other pregnancies, I would walk around Cooper Park speaking into my phone. There was nobody on the other end. I'd record my own voice, a trove of recordings, an audio-diary, a *you* and my voice rising to meet it. The *you* was the pulsing between my hipbones, my new pregnancy, my third, my fourth, my fifth. I was talking to the pregnancy—I knew it was a *her*—about the winter, how I'd come to love the cold, but how she'd soon meet the heat.

And now here we are, in the bright streets of Mérida, Valladolid,

Holbox, only it isn't the *we* I'd meant. It is Johnny, a few of our friends. They drink cold beer on the beach and taste each other's margaritas, and I keep sneaking into bathrooms to catch my breath. I keep googling symptoms. *Runny nose two months. Uneasy feeling in chest.* My clothes hang off my body, like I'd borrowed them from someone else, and maybe I had. Everything about Mexico feels confusing, my brain sluggish: it takes me too long to laugh at jokes, to answer questions. When someone points out a sunset or storefront, I am the last one to look. We stay in Airbnbs, large stone villas built around courtyards with towering plants and crystal-clear pools. Everywhere we drive, the highway is dotted with little shacks, stores filled with handmade ceramic pots and bowls, scarves the color of water, fruit, gems. I am convinced I am dying. When I think of the spit of cells in a Canadian freezer, my stomach knots. There's a refrain that starts to tap at my consciousness like an intruder: What kind of mother spirals. What kind of mother can't get out of bed. What kind of mother gives up so quickly. I'd been pregnant five times. Some women got pregnant ten times. Twelve times. Sometimes it worked the fifteenth time. Why aren't I on the examination table right now? Why am I ducking my head under this perfect water, reaching for its surface like a reverse anchor, reluctantly breaking for air, my sight sparkling with salty water.

◆

I smile at the mariachi bands. I smile at the women who speak with me in Spanish, who shrug and continue speaking when I shake my head and point at my throat, as though I'm without voice, not just language. That sleepwalking sensation persists, a pane of glass between me and the salty air, the constant music. Then, one day, I'm in a textiles shop in Holbox with my friend Sahar. We're flicking through the hangers of robes, dresses, swimsuits. Sahar finds a beige-colored skirt and disappears into the dressing room, a long white sheet at the corner of the shop, hanging from a large tree branch. She slides the sheet across and a sob rises from my throat. My body shudders with it as I push the door of the store, outside onto the warm, humid, sea-salty night air. It takes Sahar several minutes to find me; we make our way onto the beach. The farther from town we walk, the darker it gets, and we stumble over the rocks and sand, the water slapping the shore to our right. I am trying to explain: I'd been so good. I'd been so *fine*. I'd smiled at dinner. I'd spoken patiently and practically about my infertility: my body couldn't do it. Would I be mad at my liver for not producing bile? I would not. I'd found a solution. I was grateful. I was so grateful. When I stop crying long enough to speak, I'm as curious to hear what I have to say as Sahar is.

They're all gone, I say. She thinks I mean the pregnancies, those apple seeds, those wishes. I do. But I mean something else too. The clock—the real clock—has run out. The redwoods are gone, and there will never be a crossroads: no sweet babbling in the crook of an aged arm, no shoulder ride into a city night, no shoulders, no city. They are all gone. The enormity of the losses, that lineage, the cascading matriarchs. Those smooth unlined hands. The questions I never asked. My grandparents, their cities. There are things only they could've taught a child, and now those things are gone too. The time is up. I have failed. It doesn't matter that I'd recoil from anyone else if they said that. It doesn't matter that I understand the imprecise logic. I've failed to bring them a child. I've failed to bring a child to them. If a child were to come, she'd be left with only my stories of them. My stories of their cities.

◆

Three weeks! Prayer hands emoji. Two weeks! Clock emoji. One week! Fireworks emoji. One day! Cat emoji, party hat emoji, kissy face emoji.

◆

On the first day of July, the surrogate sends a picture of a strip of white. There is a pink slash on one end and, above it, another. This one fainter, but persistent. I sit for several moments in my bed, blinking in the new morning light. What kind of mother. And the story, ready or not, changes.

✦

You, the imperative you. Fine then, finally, I'll invoke you. It was for you anyway—the waiting, the pre-waiting, what came after.

✦

I invoke you: the shell of a tiny ear to whisper Surah al-Nas into. To kiss the air around a scalp with my fingertips, a blessing. To adorn text photos of you with the emoji of that blue evil eye. I invoke you in dreams and waking hours and so invoke the near-year that is about to unfurl, and so invoke a night, my voice whispering against a temple, hushing a *you* back to sleep.

✦

This story is about waiting. I was terrible at waiting but used to it, or so I'd thought. But those pink lines meant a different kind of waiting. Suddenly waiting had a purpose, a goal; the waiting became tolerable because, ostensibly, it had an ending.

I'd become consumed with leavings—Johnny's, my body's, death, the way places became inaccessible—with what wouldn't stay. No bulldozer cleaved my life in two. It had been just one noiseless departure after the other, and beneath that pulsing loss, an echo of all the vanishings and takings that had come before.

But now there is something coming. There is a waiting that matters: how I use my time, what amends I make. The stories I gather, what I'll tell you and how. Stories of the people you'll never know. Of the places of love and wreckage, in equal measure. My entire life, I hungered for stories more than anything else, the story inside each war, each arrival. I'd lie in bed as a child and imagine myself a time-traveler, returning to my mother's childhood, my grandmother's youth. Back even farther:

all the women and houses and births and burials, the prayers, the wedding ceremonies, the armies. I was determined of one thing: I'd put my waiting to good use. I'd wait myself to reclamation: a self, lost all these years; a land, split and arranged like bread. This is your true inheritance, your true birthright: these histories, these migrations. Yours to reject or keep or burn. But it hinges on the stories, on their capacity to reclaim and resolder in these coming months. It hinges on their wild and honest telling.

Month One

Your baby is the size of a grain of rice! Blood cells are taking shape and circulation will begin. The embryo is only two layers of cells, making it microscopic. But by the end of the month, a little poppy seed will already have grown.

I dreamt of a lyrebird once, before I knew it existed. I was walking through an empty grocery store—that fluorescent lights find me even in dreams is the truest symptom of late-stage capitalism I can think of— and there was a strange shape at the end of the aisle. It looked like a shadow eating itself, some frenzy of smoke. As I got closer I saw it was a bird, a tail fanned out and trembling. The bird opened its beak and the sound of a siren emerged.

✦

I don't tell Johnny about the pink lines right away. I wait until the first blood test. Then the second. The beta numbers, as they're called, doubling. Then the third, one week later. Johnny travels early in the month and I hold those pink lines to myself. For two weeks, it's my secret. It feels like an affair almost, something thrilling and a little sickening all at once.

✦

Perhaps I'd seen it before, some clip clinging to my memory like lint. But to my memory, it was years after the dream, watching a nature documentary with Johnny. On the screen, a dark bird hops and shakes, its feathers quivering. The voiceover tells us to listen. The bird can mimic the call of other birds, a perfect replication of sound.

Later, I watch David Attenborough's *The Life of Birds*. We are shown a lyrebird imitating the motor of the camera. An alarm. A chainsaw. Lyrebirds in captivity can mimic hammers, chains, even—in one famous instance—the human voice.

✦

There is a D. W. Winnicott quote: "It is a joy to be hidden, but a disaster not to be found." This is the true devastation of exile. One hides, but is never found. The new country doesn't care to find you. Often, it would rather not.

✦

For years, I'd learned a mimicry. The mimicry of the pivotal scene in movies, the turning point in sitcoms, the punchline, the second act, those two words: *I'm pregnant*. For years, I'd rehearse them. I'd turn the words in my mind like twin stones. Then I spoke them. I'd see the words glide across his face. I'd see his breathing change with them. I'd see him look stunned, then smile, then slowly nod. Then—like an actor being asked to run the scene one more time, I'd speak them again. The second time it was clunkier, a question mark at the end. Then again. *I'm pregnant*. The words became rushed, embarrassed—how many times does a person need to get pregnant to get pregnant—an afterthought. Don't bother reacting. Let's wait. Don't believe this to be true yet.

I don't remember the final time before the surrogate, only that it must've been in January. I might have waited until the first blood draw, my doctor's voice excited. *These numbers look so good, Hala,* and I could feel my overachiever's heart rise like bread. I'd gone to a pastry store in the Village, bought an éclair, eaten it so quickly I'd ripped a bit of the paper with my teeth. Then I told him. I must've. I just can't remember.

◆

The month of July is hot and sticky, marked by little returnings to myself. I go to a concert alone, screaming at the top of my lungs in the first row. I wear my hair up, old dangly earrings I thought I'd lost. They are yellow, worthless beads of plastic, but I love them. I feel beautiful and embarrassed: a woman in her mid-thirties dancing alone. I am free to dance. I am free to smoke cigarettes and stay up until dawn. I have been replaced. What would the overachiever say now? I feel like a girl who failed her math exam, an actor tapped out for the understudy. I turn to my usual machinations: stoic quotes, poetry, metaphors. Surrogacy as that which carries another. Surrogacy as code for relief. Surrogacy as code for ministration. I dance, the secret of Dee's positive test in my throat.

◆

In Aboriginal culture, the word "Dreaming" also signifies origin tales of creation; how the world came to be. In one account of the lyrebird, it is said to be the only creature able to communicate with all others. In another, its singing moves a spirit so deeply, the lyrebird brings it into animal form—frog—and then teaches it how to sing.

◆

In 1798, Napoleon launched a campaign in Ottoman-run Egypt and Syria. His much-hyped Armée d'Orient—thousands of men on foot and horseback—were eventually defeated, and the French left the region.

They would be back briefly in the 1860s. Then again after World War I, after the Ottomans had fallen, the French would be given mandates over some of the land.

✦

While Johnny's away I throw a Fourth of July party and when the sun begins to set, we all walk to the pier, watching the fireworks worm their way across the sky. The booms scare me at first, the way they always do, but eventually I am enthralled by the light and color, how the sky seems to sizzle in the aftermath. I remember something almost violently: A decade earlier, a Fourth of July I spent walking the darkening streets of Eighth Avenue alone, hearing but not seeing the fireworks, dazed. I'd woken that morning to a stranger in my bed. I was still a ways away from sobriety; I still had worse and worse to tunnel through. I'd finally found my friends and their picnic blanket. The show was almost over. My stomach roiled the whole time, and the only thing that kept me from crying was the thought: *Next July won't be like this.* It wasn't. It was worse. But the next July I spent in France, cheering at soccer matches, my cheeks painted with a foreign flag. And now, so many Julys later, I sipped my sparkling water and joked with friends. Remembering that girl steadied me. It was bad, but it wasn't that bad. This is how it always is to remember my drinking days: at least I'm not also doing *that*, I'd think, and something in my spirit would lift. Next July won't be like this, I think to myself watching the bright lights. I can't yet conjure a child.

✦

For the first year of our life together, I told Johnny I didn't want a baby and this is perhaps the worst lie I'd ever told.

✦

When I was almost thirteen, my sister, Miriam, was born. For years, I'd hold pillows and dolls to my chest, murmur soothing words against fabric. Then there was a baby: Miriam, actual, mewling, reddish hair, impossibly small fingers and toes. I was practically a teenager. Her hands curled into themselves. Her lips pursed while she slept. I picked her middle name. I made up stories about a mermaid named Jewel. I changed her diapers, rocked her for hours, walking the length of our family room, singing an Arabic song about her hair, about doves, about who loved her best.

✦

When Johnny returns, I finally tell him. "She's pregnant," I say, and there it is: the anticlimactic reveal. There is none of that same gravitas to the moment. A woman hundreds of miles away from here, a woman right now tucking her children into bed, a woman neither of us really knows: that woman is pregnant. It is not my body. It is not my hand on my abdomen. I tell something about someone else's body and he says, "Okay." Just *okay*, almost a question, like he is waiting for me to tell him what to do with that information. There is nothing to do. He has to finish coding something. I take a shower, then stare at my phone for an hour. We watch a dumb movie that night and barely speak of Dee again for weeks.

✦

It is like learning a word, then hearing it everywhere. After Dee, I see ads for surrogacy, a billboard for egg donation, a TV sitcom plot about infertility, a podcaster talking about her surrogate. The metaphor concretizes. Surrogacy as metaphor for rescue. Surrogacy as metaphor for exile.

✦

The first thing to go are the fruit-colored dresses from the spring. The ones I'd thrifted, imagining their former lives, unable to imagine my future one and so pouring myself into their lacy or velvet or tight contours. They would tell me who I was, as I ran errands and attended birthday dinners. But now their beaded waistlines feel gaudy. I look like a melted cupcake in the pink tulle. I'd never wear the silvery bodysuit, which looks like it's been tipped over my limbs. I may not know my self, but I know she isn't this. And so into an enormous K-Mart bag they all go, trudged down Driggs Avenue to another thrift store, on their way to their new, actual lives, not the pit stop of this one.

◆

In twelve-step programs, the fourth step involves taking inventory. There can be a grimness to this, a necessary kind of excavation. "You get home, that's when you notice the mold," so goes the Louise Glück poem. "Too late, in other words." Too late. My inventory is bleak. Who has been living like this? I think, looking around our apartment. I'd blinked three years away. I frittered away entire weeks on one obsession or another, trying to avoid the core fear. Sometimes people have to repeat themselves, once, twice, before I hear them. My husband and I barely speak. When had this happened? How could these things sneak up on you like this?

◆

Napoleon's doomed campaign shook the Ottoman Empire and its Arab constituents. Western inventions and ideas started to spider through the region, from liberalism to modernization to nationalism. Meanwhile, there was the Tanzimat—a period of Ottoman reform—and the Young Turk Revolution. Suddenly, there was a press, and a true one at that, literary salons, reforms at community and economic levels. Figures like Ahmad Faris al-Shidyaq resisted "Turkization" and promoted writing *in* Arabic, having salons *in* Arabic. Intellectuals argued for women's rights. Religious figures like Jamal al-Din al-Afghani advocated for Pan-Islamic solidarity against colonial forces. Arabic poetry and literature proliferated, led by writers like the dubbed "Poet of the Nile," Hafez Ibrahim, and Kahlil Gibran. Egypt fought and won independence. Arab armies studied Western tactics and implemented military reforms.

This became known as the Nahda. The Arab Renaissance. They were invaded, and then they learned.

◆

Nahda. A word that means waking up. Eyes blinking open.

◆

Dee's pregnancy wakes me up.

◆

I start making lists. I've long thought my mental health can be assessed by two things: am I making lists and have I baked a boxed cake in the last month? If the answer to both is yes, then things are *great*. A list is a magnificent thing, all that future in one place. It is the concretization of hope, not only that something will get done, but that *you* will be the one to do it. Sometimes, if I realize I've completed a task without having put it on the list, I'll go back and write it, just to cross it off. The pathos in this seems sweet, childlike, a delight in both archiving and putting to rest.

Here are the things I need to complete. Here is what I'll do with my waiting. Afterward, I admire my handiwork: the neat blue and green letters, the geometric circles and arrows across the page, my way of connecting one goal to the other. Here it is, my map.

◆

Albert Hourani said of being Levantine, "It is no longer to have a standard of one's own, not to be able to create but only able to imitate."

◆

The lyrebird is considered a symbol of poetry. Of songs. Of the stories we tell. Of what we mimic back.

✦

In 1986, my mother arrives in an airport in Illinois from Kuwait. She is eight months pregnant, tells the security officer she is visiting her brother. This is technically true. He lives in Carbondale, and my mother is in Carbondale. But so is the Memorial Hospital of Carbondale, where I will be born. So is the U.S. Consulate office, the clerk who will fill out the citizenship papers, the doctor who will write down my birth time, the nurse that will check me for jaundice. My mother has a vision when she lands in America and it has nothing to do with America. She doesn't want to stay here; we will be back in Kuwait within two weeks of my birth. But she knows I will inherit more than my father's eyebrows and temper and curls; if I am born in Kuwait, I will also receive the passport he has, which is no passport at all, just the laissez-passer papers for Palestinian refugees, the no-man's-land of citizenship: you belong nowhere, you are allowed somewhere, always as a guest. My mother is uninterested in America as a place; what she wants for me is to have its cloak, the protection of its name. What is an American daughter, she thinks, if not safe?

✦

It turns out, I tell anyone who will listen, *everything is a surrogate*. I ask Siri if she loves me, when the next full moon is, which herbs cure insomnia. *Are you a kind of mother*, I ask. I'm not sure how to answer that, she says, not unkindly. I watch dozens of videos online, then interrupt Johnny's workday. Has he heard of brood care? Has he heard of allomothering? Does he know that when the mother emperor penguin hunts for food, the father incubates the egg? Does he know that worker bees are usually infertile? That they feed and take care of the larvae? So that the queen bee can reproduce? So that the colony can survive?

✦

The lesson of performing Arabness comes young. I am seven or eight. It is summer and I am at the YMCA pool. I am my mother's American daughter, only we're in America now. There is a woman, white, American, probably in her twenties. Maybe she is a swim teacher or lifeguard. She is asking me about my parents.

"And when did you come here?"

I remember saying, "A long time ago." Not because anyone had instructed me to, but because somewhere, somehow, I knew that was the correct response. I remember the wet swimsuit wedging in my butt; I didn't want to fix it. I hated how it made you look like a waddling duck. Children understand dignity, too.

She asks what language we speak. She has pretty hair, blonde and in a ponytail. I tell her.

Her eyes light up. "Is Arabic the one with the stars and moons? In the alphabet?"

I understand her question to be ridiculous. It awakens something angry in me, but also a little mean, like I want to punish her. "Yes," I say. She asks me to wait here. She comes bouncing back with a notebook, drying her hands against her bare thighs before holding it out with a pen.

"Can you write my name for me?"

Her name. It could've been anything. Emily. Jessica. Amy. She tells me and I take the pen and glide it across the page into nonsensical curlicues. I draw two five-pointed stars above the scrawl, then a shaky crescent moon in the middle. Do any alphabets have moons in them? I wonder. She beams at what I've done.

✦

The French campaign failed, but the imperialism inherent in it stuck. What they took back west with them was a story. The story of civilizing—a mission narrative that would trail European colonial forces in the coming century.

✦

What did she do with it? That nonsense scrawl of a child. Did she show it to her boyfriend? Doodle it on the corner of a college notebook? Did she get it tattooed on her forearm? And what is the name for the glee I felt watching her, as she beamed at the notebook? A revenge I didn't even understand I was taking, but took nonetheless.

✦

Many immigrants come to America already well versed in their erasure. They bring what they've learned, and what they've learned is to hunger for the West. For Europe's Messianic complex, America's exceptionalism. In the Levant, the fingerprints of colonizers are everywhere: French street names, European architecture. It's like this around the world: Vietnam, Colombia, Morocco. Albert Hourani said, "[T]o be a Levantine is to live in two worlds or more at once without belonging to either." This is well-trodden territory. I'm tired of it. I'm tired of talking about my own in-betweenness, living in an empire that has called itself by another name, and behaved like the old one. That empire has launched "forever wars," has eroded countries and people of their borders, their dignity, their children, has created the conditions under which people seek shelter within *her*. What a trick, this empire. Like a drug dealer: creating the fix by creating the problem. There's no mystery to it. Forget the why. Ask *then what*. What is landlessness that takes root, turns inward, what is it to carry that lack, that undoing.

✦

I have never not been Palestinian. That has never not been written upon my body. In Lebanon, in Kuwait, in Oklahoma—I am what my father is and my father is a man who was once a boy who was born to a woman in Gaza. Who speaks with the accent of that place.

✦

The lyrebirds don't choose what sound they hear, which is to say they don't choose what sound they carry.

✦

And me? Now absent a poppy seed or almond, what do I carry? Klonopin. Night terrors. A note app on my phone filled with half-finished letters to women that are dead, and men that aren't. Beirut in every dream. The vocal fry of a white girl. There is a video of my brother and me in Maine, where we are talking a mile a minute, our drawls impeccable. We sound Oklahoman. When we moved to Beirut, I was fourteen. I had to sand my Arabic down, get rid of its rough Palestinian edges. My green eyes granted me a certain leeway; my father's *G* rang out in public places. I learned the soft vowels of the Lebanese accent, how to bleat out curses. I learned to carry the country in my mouth, my hand gestures. The Lebanese hairdresser beneath my grandmother's apartment would always say *Na'eeman* after washing my hair, a blessing, and I'd rehearse for hours in advance to reply *Merci*, instead of the more Palestinian response. I'd always forget.

✦

I love the bard symbolism of the lyrebird, of course. I love dreams and fortunes and conjecture. I decide the lyrebird is the perfect archetype. I write *lyrebird as symbol for the Levantine* on an index card and tape it on the wall of my new studio. Then: *lyrebird as metaphor for surrogate*. Because isn't it? It carries what it hears. It returns it to the world. Days later, I find another article, this one about a male lyrebird trick. A study found that when female lyrebirds try to escape males trying to mate with them, the male bird will mimic the sound of a "mobbing flock," a signal that a predator is nearby. Not the sound of a single bird. A *flock*. A whole damn flock. I know it's ridiculous, but I am angry at these rapey, dishonest birds. I am angry at what they've done with their gift.

◆

I tear the notecards up. I misspoke earlier. Landless is a misnomer. It is the adjective of the unlucky, the passively determined. But a border isn't passive. Nor is its erasure. There's a way history teaches rearranged maps that can sound inert. Polite, even. A housekeeper who moves the knick-knacks while you sleep.

◆

In Arabic, we say: Do you have no mother, no father? The implication being that to have no mother or father is to have no name, and to have no name is to have no anchor, nothing to claim you. This was how I'd come to feel, unclaimed, dislocated from the places that made me, the places I'd sworn I'd return to but hadn't. I made home with the scraps, with the almosts. I'd forgotten what I belonged to. It was like the first few weeks after Meimei's death. I kept thinking of things to ask her, things that only she could've answered. The questions were like fishbones scraping my throat. They had nowhere to go. And now: there were pink lines. A doubling beta number. The Canadian nurse's chipper voice on my cell: "We'll have the gender for you in a few weeks!"

◆

There is an evolutionary reason for vocal mimicry—a skill driven by sexual selection or self-preservation. It can be used to attract a mate, to call the attention of others in case of a threat, to alert one another about food or other resources. I feel my anger wilt. It's an old story: survival.

◆

In Arabic, the Levant is *blad el-sham*. The Greater Syria. I prefer the simple *blad*. Countries. When an Arab says it to me, I know what they mean. I know which ones.

✦

Dee tells her daughters about me, about the baby. *I'm like an oven*, she tells them. *I'm like a little house.* I think of a land mass dismantled by white hands, borders drawn and redrawn. I think of the airport in south Beirut, how during the civil war in Lebanon, tens of thousands of Lebanese sought shelter in Syria. I think of the Palestinian camps dotting southern Lebanon. How each place became a surrogate for the other. One carries when the other can't.

✦

Is it tiresome to say I lie at night and feel exiled from her body? Her body inside another? I imagine it bopping around like a little red dot on a map. And mine? Hundreds of miles away.

✦

"Every day we are engaged in a miracle which we don't even recognize," Thich Nhat Hanh wrote. The recognition comes from presence, the state that cures what meditation practitioners call being "unconscious" or "unawake." We do terrible things in non-awake states. We hurt. We get hurt. We see the other as an obstacle, a checkpoint between ourselves and what we want. We skirt the truth, mostly to ourselves. "Being entirely honest with *oneself* is a good exercise," Sigmund Freud said. This from a man who recanted a wide swath of research on female trauma because of societal backlash. Still, he was right about that. Waking means honesty. It means finding the right voice and the right song.

✦

I tape a notecard back up. I scrawl in the margins: *scarcity*. I scrawl: *persisting*. Another notecard next to it: *Forgive the birds.* In smaller words below: *They were surviving.* Next to *they*, an even smaller word in parentheses:

♦

(we)

Month Two

Your baby is the size of a raspberry! Human features are starting to develop: eyes, a nose, a mouth, and ears are growing on the outside, while lungs and nerves are growing on the inside.

My clients are all heartsick in August. Everywhere I turn, people are talking about resolutions. Phantom exes. Men who leave and never return. *You have to let people sleep where they want to sleep*, I tell a client, *no matter what they've promised you*. I omit the part about following Johnny down to the basement. Banging on the door. Listing all the things he owed me.

♦

When they came to America, my parents had to adjust to wanting it. This is the well-trodden immigration narrative: the hunger to go to the West, the better life. But my parents had been happy in Kuwait. Their life had been upended by Saddam's army in 1990; their exit was one of grudging necessity. They had no plans to move to America, no scheming for its dreams or futures. They arrived defeated, barely any dollars, their whole life scattered like sand throughout the globe. My father's sister stayed behind. My mother's brother was in St. Louis. My father's brother in Kansas.

◆

It is August in Brooklyn. The year after the pandemic began. The year after the Beirut port disaster, when a stockpile of ammonium caught fire and exploded. The argument begins like so many others: stonewalling, accusations, my voice reaching a strident pitch. We are arguing about the dog, which is to say about everything and nothing.

"Can you at least look at me?"

"There's nothing left to talk about."

"You can't say you're mad about something and then stop talking."

"Okay, I'm not mad. Are you happy?"

It goes on for a while. We are eight years into our relationship and I've devoted so much of it to the why: why did he retreat, why did I get so panicked, why did we so mimic our respective parents. I'd done everything differently: chose New York, married a white man, lived a life that would've been unrecognizable to my grandmothers. And yet here I was, my voice an echo of my mother's: demanding attention, answers, my due.

"If it's *so* hard to do something you don't want to, then don't," I say bitingly. I am thinking of protesters, tear gas, one-way flights to the West. I am thinking of Beirut. The explosion had happened after a year of protests, and now there was so little left of the revolution, no more bodies marching in Martyrs' Square, no more chants and songs filling my newsfeed.

My sarcasm doesn't register. Instead, something goes flat in his eyes. "You're right," he says almost searchingly. "I don't have to." He rises, starts reaching for his backpack, his phone, his charger. "I don't have to do anything." His voice is dull, dreamy. "I don't have to be here."

✦

It isn't the first time. It won't be the last. This is the crux of our dynamic: one fears abandonment, one leaves. It's never the right one who does either.

✦

When I next speak with Dee, he has already left. Where has he gone? He has gone to Mexico. This is to clear his head. This is to give us space. We will not speak for a month. *I need a break. I need to be alone for a few weeks.* This isn't his life, he'd said with certainty, with a kind of wonderment at finding himself here. If I hadn't been so panicked, I would've felt a kinship: that dissonance, that dis-reality. He'd handed a plastic cup to a nurse, he'd understood I was trying to get pregnant, he'd agreed to something without really wanting it. But we'd both gotten used to the false alarms, and he must've come to believe it would never happen. That we'd live in limbo forever, caught between our wants. Only now something was happening: a woman, a test, an apple seed.

✦

I tell Dee everything. I start to apologize, start to cry.

"I just wanted you to know." The shame lumps my throat. "Because you chose a couple and . . . we . . . may not be a couple and—"

She interrupts me. "I chose *you*," she says. It's true. The phone calls, the Skypes, the emoji texting: it's me and her. "We started this together, we'll continue this together."

✦

My outrage and grief at his leaving become somewhat rehearsed. The surrogate is *pregnant*, I hear myself repeating to friends. He disappeared to *Mexico*. But the truth is trickier: we both have vanishing acts. I'd married someone who always lusted for a break from himself. He was the flight in the trauma response. I was the fight. I lusted for something to pour myself into. I overdid everything: drugs, love, even abstinence. During our wonderful, fiercely connected periods, we are exactly what the other is looking for: I an antidepressant, he an escape hatch into something that isn't myself.

◆

The cockroaches come back mid-August. He has been gone ten days by then, and they skitter across the floor whenever I turn a light on. This is the month of insomnia. I don't bother laying out traps. The sink is leaking. The dog ruins the new sapling in the backyard. The roof needs repair. I compare paint chips. Run every day to the water and pant at its side. Tell more people what has happened, the story changing with each telling: he's abandoned me, I didn't see this coming, he'd seemed *fine*. There's a dream I keep having. I am walking across a lawn and something is rustling behind me. It's the train of a dress, or it's an animal; I can never tell which.

◆

This is when I start speaking aloud to my grandmother. Meimei. Fatima. She has been dead for five years. I make eye contact with her photograph and ask advice. She is younger than I am, wearing a blouse with dark buttons in the grainy photograph, her gaze slightly to the left. *Did you ever want to leave Jiddo?* I ask. *Should I text him?* I ask. *Tell me again about Yaffa?* I ask.

◆

You're not supposed to tell a story without first knowing its ending. A writing teacher once said that. I was in college and I remember how the sun fell across the table we all sat around. I remember the lesson unsettling me: how was I supposed to know the ending before I knew the beginning? Wasn't the ending something that would announce itself?

Or—more precisely—wouldn't the ending be made *through* the telling? And isn't there sometimes no ending at all?

✦

Here's one story: The first thing I ever knew about Johnny was that he was leaving. I'd just given a talk at the Brooklyn Bowl. It is December and we bounce on the balls of our feet to stay warm, as we smoke cigarettes outside. I am two years into my sobriety; he is about to move to Barcelona. We both say we don't want children. I spend those cold months thinking of him in Spain, stamping the spine of Manhattan with my daydreaming. He sends me photographs of bright flowers peeking through stone, an unruly sea. I send him back a line of poetry, a lacquered wooden heart. Months later, he chooses Manhattan over Barcelona. We move in. In this story, we pick a red couch and a Midtown apartment and we string lights from the curtains. These are good years, or we decide they are.

✦

Here's another: A year after we meet, I am pregnant. There is something wrong with the sac. I am spared from having to make a choice. I cry for weeks. During the procedure, he holds my hand. Afterward I go back to work. That same afternoon, I bleed through three back-to-back sessions in the forensic unit of a hospital before I can change the pad. I am different after that pregnancy: I want a child now. I want a child as badly as I want Johnny. It's worse than that. I want a child *because* I want Johnny. I've gotten a taste for love and I become crazed for more.

✦

I hated being apart in those early days. I loved being apart. I wanted the courtship, but not what came after. I disliked sitcoms where characters got married, had children. Things stopped *happening*. I was newly sober, but here was something I could toast to, this great unraveling, this pouring out of self. I'd never forgotten what it was to tip my neck back, to drink, to obliviate. But now I could do it in the sunlight, out in public. We were our best in new worlds, trips we'd save up for, Barcelona and the Dominican Republic and Nashville, the glittery evenings of Feria in Seville, the crowded lines at La Xampanyeria, New Year's Eve in Beirut, riding the back of his scooter in the eerie, still-lit midnight of Reykjavík. For years, I'd wanted things in secret, without ever admitting I wanted them. Here, finally, was a convenient excuse for my own fear of proximity: he pulled away. He retreated. He needed solo time. And I, patient wife, always seeking, always pursuing, always leaning in. I was granted the illusion of never having to confront a cumbersome truth: that my obsession with connection was maintained by the fact that I never really had to contend with it.

✦

As a child, I'd read. The stories I was drawn to were about lost women, drinking, bad love, tousled hair. They were a distraction from my usual vigilance. I read stories too old for me: *Anna Karenina* at twelve, Greek myths in elementary school. The gory versions. I loved stories of waiting and error: Orpheus' glance back, Demeter's scorched earth as she searched for her daughter. I loved Anna Karenina stepping into her death. The women I admired were undone by their devotion, but there was something noble about it for me. The idea of love began to twinkle like a distant lighthouse. Love so pure it ate into you like fire. "[There are] . . . two kinds of people," psychotherapist Adam Phillips wrote, "those who can enjoy desiring and those who need satisfaction." I loved the former. Longing. Even that word, the croon of it, the bay window of its soft *o*. It was a new kind of watching, a new kind of vigilance, one that promised a released self. I started young: loving from afar, fast and dumb, the kind of love that winces from closeness, a cockroach scattering at light. I'd create soap operas out of middling crushes, versions of them far better than the reality, and fall in love with that. In this way, it was always my own imagination, my own sorcery I loved best of all.

✦

During traumatic events, time wobbles. It splinters. This happens to me abruptly in these weeks without Johnny, with Dee. No matter how many times I whisper to myself *You're safe*, my heart leaps into my throat upon waking. My amygdala believes I am reliving an earlier story. I am living two timelines simultaneously: I am nineteen and I am thirty-five. It is the dying of a season. My clothes drape off my body. There is a man and that man is hurting me. I forget things mid-sentence. This is the hallmark of trauma: the mind going suddenly blank. Is it Thursday? What was I just saying? I forget who I've told about the baby. One day I tell my friend, *Probably by the due date*, and he gently responds, *What due date, Hala?* I sob on the subway. I wake up and think I'm in Beirut. There is a man and that man is hurting me. But which man? Which city? Which year?

✦

Some evenings, I wait for nightfall and jog through Williamsburg, down Graham Avenue, until I reach Frost Street. This is where I always end up: the peach-colored building, the top floor, a studio apartment I'd lived in before Johnny. I'd just gotten sober. The Italian landlady would only turn the heat on after multiple phone calls. I could hear any music the neighbors played. There was a small balcony, cheap wooden floors, a bathtub I never used. I'd strung mosquito net above the bed and whenever I woke in the middle of the night, it was like being at sea, in a cloud, a continuation of dreaming. This is where I run when he is gone, to the past, to the last person I was before him. I pretend to stretch in front of the building, wait for the light to come on, wait to see the outline of a figure. I never do. And what would I do if it appeared? The waiting is a pretense. There is a part of me that believes *I'm* still there, that if I called my name, I'd emerge.

✦

Do you remember my wedding? I ask Meimei. She'd sat blinking at the crowd with a slightly awestruck expression. When I caught her eye, she'd smile hesitantly. She had wed in Beirut, her father remaining in Latakia. He didn't speak to her again until after my mother was born. What had it been like? For Meimei to sit across from her new husband, call his name. To leave a country with him. To give him everything. For years, she'd told me, *I'll dance at your wedding. No matter what.* Even after she fell and broke her hip. Even after her memory started to go. In the end, she'd sat and smiled. She'd watched a woman dance in white and in moments, at certain songs, she'd shut her eyes and swayed her head a little to the music.

✦

Melissa Febos describes the fear of abandonment as "the great nothing." For me it is a contamination. How to explain that sense of ruining? He leaves and he takes the light. Now everything I touch is soiled. My life is a fine silk and his leaving, his absence, his departure, is an inkblot.

✦

Our last night with Meimei, I overheard her talking to Johnny. He was using google translate. *I love your granddaughter,* the tinny sound said in Arabic. *It was so good to meet you,* it said. Meimei smiled politely. Perhaps she thought he was a neighbor's son, a handyman, a nurse. He was being kind and so she smiled and nodded. *We will see you again soon.* The next day we left. I never saw her again.

✦

When Johnny leaves, the to-do lists are swiftly rendered useless. The bright jewel-toned ink is a mockery. There is no map, no box to be checked. What kind of mother . . . ? For the first time in memory, I am suddenly glad, ferociously, that I am not a mother. Not yet. Not in this moment. The self that emerges is a wolf, hungry, wounded, limping through the city with arms folded across her solar plexus. There is nothing to take care of and that is the biggest relief of all. When I think of the surrogate, the little almond of life in its amniotic sac, for the first time I don't feel jealous. I feel grateful. Good. Keep the almond away from me. I'm glad the baby isn't inside me. I have a timeline for this destruction: I have until March. And then: I would have no choice but to stop.

♦

My wanting did this, I write in a journal. The surrogate wants to do another Zoom. She politely avoids the topic of Johnny. She says she'd rather not know the gender, asks if I could keep it a secret. We'll be finding out soon. I don't tell her what I know—I'm certain it's a boy. In the Langone clinic, I'd used two of the female embryos on myself. There were five left, mostly male. I knew their rankings—the elasticity of their expansion, their cell composition, their fragmentation. It was illegal to pick gender in Canada, but I knew.

♦

Another story. This month last year, I'd been pregnant. I'd been pregnant when Beirut exploded. I'd been pregnant when my grandfather was alive. Johnny and I were in Maine, in the gorgeous sprawling estate by the sea that his family bought nearly a century earlier. The spotting started our second day there. I went to the mainland hospital alone, taking the boat across the icy water. I waited in the little hospital chapel with plush red cushions and a pretty stained-glass window. *Do not lose hope*, someone had scrawled in a little book at the altar. I couldn't think of anything to add, so I'd underlined it and drawn a heart. They took my blood, and I returned to the port, back on that boat slicing the water in two. I'd barely landed on the shore when my cell rang. It was a New

York number, my fertility doctor. She'd gotten the results. *Hi dear*, she said quietly, and I started crying.

When I get back to the house, I start packing. The vibrant sprawl of the island feels suddenly overdone and oppressive: all that green, all that sky. I want concrete, antiseptic soap, the hush of waiting rooms. I'm miscarrying. Johnny holds me, then starts to fold his clothes. We'll leave in the morning, he says. I can hear the little latch in his voice, the question. No, I say. No. I'll go alone. We just got here. I insist. I'll stay another night and leave in the morning. His eyes go sweet and wide and grateful. I'd promised him, I say. I'd promised his life would still be his, even with a child. That it would remain open, unfettered. These were the promises of desperation, but I still feel bound to them. Are you sure, he finally asks. I am, I am.

✦

That last night in Maine, Johnny takes me out on the motorboat. We bring the dog and she watches in delight when the seals come out, the sun glittering their sleek coats. Johnny envelops me in his arms. His heart thumps fast and hard through the fleece. I wanted to say, he starts. He clears his throat. *I wanted to say thank you. For this. I won't forget this, Hala.* I close my eyes and see not a heart, but a clock.

✦

The car ride back to New York, I cry into my mask for the first hour. I am afraid and cramping. The taxi driver keeps asking if I want tissues. At some point, he pulls wordlessly into a Burger King and I follow him inside. We order fries then trudge back into the car. We eat without saying a word, licking the salt from our fingers.

✦

A year later, it is also August. The surrogate is pregnant and I'm alone. While Johnny is in Mexico City, I repaint the living room. I buy an

Egyptian side table at a thrift store. I go to a boutique and buy red taper candles. I ask the woman at the counter what herbs help with fear. *It depends on what you're fearing*, she says intently. I don't say everything. I don't say a man. I don't say the absence of a man. Instead, I ask for a love spell.

What is a story that forgets its origins?

✦

The first month we met, Johnny gave me a notebook. He inscribed a single line: *Don't ever let anyone take this from you.* He meant the writing. Every time I entered a room, he said, *You take my breath away.* He wept at flamenco music. He argued about God, never spoke about his father, loved rooftops and sunsets and guitar. We'd stay up all night, talking so quickly we'd dissolve into laughter, as though there was a clock, as though someone would usher us out of the restaurant, the street, the bedroom. He wanted to open a brunch place in Barcelona. He didn't call his mother enough. He'd wanted to leave his childhood city and so he had, and now only returned as a visitor. He begged me to gain weight. Once, watching me move a piece of branzino around my plate expertly, he knocked the table with his fork, wouldn't stop until I looked up. When I did, he said sharply, *Stop.* I asked what he meant. He shook his head. This time his voice was soft enough to cut through. *Just stop. Please.*

✦

There is a slight, barely perceptible thrill in my solitude now, my righteous rage: the stoned nights, the flirting with bartenders, the way I gather myself every morning like a bouquet of wilted flowers and run around McCarren Park until I wheeze. I feel entirely, unapologetically sorry for myself. I long, ridiculously, for last year, when I had returned to Brooklyn alone from Maine, miscarrying in the hot hours of August, getting sushi and watching *Crashing* with Sahar. She'd taken me shopping and I'd bought a beautiful green lamp, then dropped it steps from my house. The glass shattered magnificently, and I kept seeing green twinkles on the pavement when I'd walk the dog. I bought a large, leafy, pilea peperomioides plant that reminded me of a carnival ride, got a manicure the color of mango skin. I was not happy, but my sadness had a shape, a container for it, a reason, and so it felt luxurious. *I bought a miscarriage plant!* I texted friends. *I got a miscarriage manicure!*

◆

But—he'd tried to leave last year, too. I keep editing this out of my memory. This is what it is to have blinders on: to keep handcuffing yourself to the same story, even when it has rubbed its wrist raw trying to escape. He'd returned from Maine glum. My body was cramping in earnest by then and I resented his unhappiness. Couldn't my misery get its own week? Its own day? We argued and it ended with the open mouth of a suitcase, my weeping, his relenting. I'd cried, *You can't leave. I'm miscarrying*, and he'd tilted his head, as though I was talking about the Asian stock market, as though what I was saying had no place in my mouth, in this room, in this conversation. *You'll get through it*, he said. We clocked in another year.

◆

The psychotherapist Harville Hendrix writes of Imago Therapy, "[W]e choose partners who can help us heal our childhood wounds." This hinges on a central concept: in order to resolve a past hurt, we first have to re-create it. But what happens if we re-create, then never resolve? A wound, reopened, angry, weeping. What then?

◆

How else to say it? We were hurt. We forgot the other person was hurting.

◆

One night I see an old friend in a bar. *You look like shit*, he says cheerfully. I laugh. I've lost weight and there's something hunted in my eyes that spooks me when I catch my reflection. But suddenly the world is full of men. They crawl out of the L train. They hold doors open. They ask me to dinner. One walks two blocks by my side at one in the morning, holding his phone out like alms. Put your number in, he says. Come on. Please.

Another pulls a car up to me and says, *I'm sorry I'm late.* What, I say, startled.

For our date, he grins.

And for a brief second, I imagine getting in the car. Shocking him. Saying, Can we go to the Cloisters? I've never been.

✦

I tell my friend everything and he listens. He is one of those neutral friends, annoyingly fair-minded, an American I met in Beirut years ago. The bar is cramped, our knees knocking under the table. We speak of the explosion anniversary, the failing economy in Lebanon, people bringing guns to gas stations. The country is nearly out of petrol. I tell him that when I chose Johnny, I chose America. I chose not Beirut. And now Beirut is gone.

"What is he saying?" my friend asks. "About Beirut?"

I say I haven't heard from him since he left for Mexico. This was what he'd asked for: a month apart, a month of no contact.

His face changes. "But he knows what's happening there?" he asks quietly. I nod. "And he hasn't checked in?" I shake my head.

He lets out a whistle before he can stop himself. "He really doesn't get it," he says, more to himself than me. That's all he says about it. That whistle, those words, ring in my head for days.

✦

Once I start speaking, I can't stop. I talk about inevitability, the ways I'd seen this coming, all the signs of unsturdiness, of a person who would never stop leaving. Afterward, my friend doesn't speak for a minute. Then he says, "I don't know if that's how it works." "What do you mean?" I say. I'm already annoyed, defensive. "I think when something ends," he says carefully, "there's this tendency to work backward. To cherry-pick all the signs that it was always going to go this way. But when you're living it, you couldn't possibly know."

◆

I pretend not to, but I understand what he is saying: The narrative impulse to write toward an ending. That in some ways, to know an ending is to curse the telling, because you retroactively tell everything through that prism, pick through it like a meal.

◆

Could you remind me what your father's name was? I ask Meimei. *No, of course I know it. I just forget. No, I don't want to ask Mama right now. If I ask her, she'll ask about Johnny, and then—well, you know what happens next.*

◆

The morning after the bar, I wake to an email in my inbox. It is from Jill, the nurse at the Canadian clinic. CONGRATULATIONS, the subject screams. I open it. *IT'S A GIRL!*

◆

Will I love her even though I didn't carry her? I ask my grandmother. *Will she love me?*

◆

The weeks pass. Johnny and I do not speak. I smoke minty cigarettes and promise myself I'll stop. I dream a couple of times of the other man, who was really a boy. A teenager like I'd been. Saif. It was in Beirut, he'd been hurt and he'd hurt me back. I dream that Saif is in my backyard with the yellow eyes of a lynx. I dream that Johnny and Saif are drinking together in our kitchen, their hands so ordinary against the marble counter. I wake with my heart beating like a drum.

◆

Meimei's dying took years. The last time I spoke with her, it was two years after my wedding. The Skype connection was terrible. I was upstate at a writing residency, in a room Sylvia Plath had once used. The window overlooked pine trees and the roof of a nearby house. My grandfather was holding up the phone. He kept repeating my name, as though she'd remember me.

"It's Hala," he kept saying. "Do you see? It's Hala."

I imagined what she saw with her fading vision: a cluster of colors, a female voice trying not to break, saying her name, saying she loved her. Jiddo looked so scared. He'd been impossible to be married to, with his quick temper, his finicky nature. But when she died, he'd wept like a baby. I wish she'd been there to see it.

◆

One evening, I walk to the Williamsburg pier. The water glitters. I buy tacos on the way over, and the vendor wants my phone number. He asks if I'm married and I look at him so dumbly for so long, he frowns. I can't find the language. So I finally hold my left hand up, the diamond visible in the dark. He shrugs out a devastating smile. *Could be any ring.* He won't let me pay. I leave. I leave with my phone number and my any ring.

◆

I miss Beirut. I miss the stupid neon sign of the pharmacy under my grandparents' building, the smell of hairspray in salons. I miss hearing Arabic. I think of my watching, my waiting. For what? For a child. For a man. For a city. For a way to bring all three together. For a way to have all the lives at once, to resuscitate the lost. To have Beirut, and Johnny, and an apple seed–turned–cantaloupe in my womb. To have America when she was tender, to leave when she was not. To finish what my grandparents had started: to find a land, to break it open, to nestle something in it and watch it grow. To have something to show her. Her. Her. Her.

✦

There are stairs near the Williamsburg water, bleachers for the spectacle of dirty river. My hands smell of salsa. I have bitten every nail down to the nub. It's the water that does it to me. In the dark, the glint of waves could be anywhere and my body longs. It is muscle memory. I walk down and I am walking down Hamra Street. I feel split, revving in all directions. I sweat through my shirt. There is no wind. There is nothing to break the heat but more heat. There is no home to go to, no truth but this truth.

I have been left: to my own devices, to my own story. That night, I can feel the story of Johnny leaving heave beside me like an unloved pet. I look at it for a second. I touch its fur. It is all I can bear, that one second, but it is something. I catch a glimpse of something flimsy and untrue about it. I face the river. *It is entirely possible*, I tell the water, which is also America, which is also Brooklyn, *that I've left myself.*

Month Three

*Your baby has fingers and toes, and is starting to
grow nails. Your baby is the size of a lime!*

✦

The women in my family have powers, or say they do. My mother dreamt of lions prowling the gates of the city in the weeks before the invasion.

♦

When Johnny is away, I rearrange the house. "Nice power move," my friend Lola says when she visits, but it is more about exorcism than revenge. I couldn't keep looking at the Gaudí painting he'd bought me. The photograph of us kissing on a beach in the Dominican Republic, the outline of our lips making a little heart. I let myself be a little petty: the hoodie I bought him goes on our stoop, vanished by the morning. I spend an ungodly amount of money on a cactus the size of a child, and spend hours trying to find the least cursed place in the house to place it.

"Good luck with that," my mother says. She's made me wary of cacti, her conviction they bring bad luck. But I love the sturdy ridges of their bodies. Their spines.

◆

I place the cactus in front of a window, the first visible thing upon opening the door. Arab folklore says cacti are repellents, prickly, unwelcoming, bringers of wounds. Let it be the first thing anyone sees.

◆

Growing up, I heard of the powers. The great-aunt who could speak the future. The distant cousin whose brother fell ill; that evening, she'd prayed for one of her children to be taken instead. She couldn't bear losing her brother. In the morning, the brother was clear-eyed and speaking, his fever broken, his body healed. Her second-eldest son had died in his sleep.

◆

What is the lesson here? That love will recover or dismantle, that everything has a price, that you must understand what you are willing to give before asking for anything.

◆

The women that raised these women believed in Allah. They believed in ritual: the right time to cut hair, the right month to marry, the right foot to enter airplanes and new houses. They believed in the power of incantation, suras, the evil eye. And they believed in luck.

◆

My mother sees my father first. It is 1981 in Kuwait City. She is eighteen years old and they meet on a boat. They are all university students, and my father wears his thick glasses and smokes his thin cigarettes and barely makes eye contact. He is the son of a Palestinian schoolteacher, one of seven siblings. My mother immediately has questions. She asks about his family. She asks about his classes. What do you want to be? she asks him. After all this? He finally looks at her. They have the same eyes, dark and curious. My father exhales smoke into the salty air. I'm going to be a prime minister, he says.

◆

My mother saw something and wanted it. She had a vision for a life, and that life came true. A husband who wanted degrees and a view of the sea. A husband who would never leave, at least not in the way other husbands did. There would be an American daughter, an American son, another American daughter. There would be houses next to water, next to desert, next to cornfields. My mother saw a life or—my mother was that life. She stepped into it.

◆

In Arabic, "once upon a time" is *kan yama kan*. There was and how much there was.

◆

There was. My mother and my father met on a boat in the Persian Gulf, off the coast of Kuwait City.

◆

And how much there was. I was born a Palestinian because I was born to a Palestinian father. I was born to a mother who boarded a plane at nine months pregnant, and disembarked in Illinois. I was born in an American hospital, with English brochures and nurses who told my mother where to sit, when to push, when to stop. Everything was American: the accents, the anesthesiologist who numbed my mother's spine after hours of labor, the surgeon who cut her open to save both of our lives. It was an American doctor who proclaimed my birth time—5:22 in the afternoon, late July—who said to my mother, *She's almost blonde!* My mother crossed a border and worked magic in that crossing. She landed and made us all American. She left a country with a placeless daughter and returned with an American one.

◆

There was and how much there was.

◆

I buy mirrors, two of them. I place them in front of each other and suddenly the light in the room goes berserk, hungry for itself, filling the space. A ceramic mug. A money plant. A string of bronze moons, from a store with stuffed llamas and stylish plastic necklaces. I've forbidden anyone from buying baby things. A cactus is one thing. I'm not about to tempt fate. I ignore the baby section.

◆

The women in my family wait and wait, and then they make things happen. This is a kind of power, too, isn't it?

◆

In the glorious *Annotated Arabian Nights: Tales from 1001 Nights*, translated by Yasmine Seale, the introduction by Paulo Lemos Horta reads, "Magic [is] understood as the ability to understand and manipulate the hidden forces that lie behind the visible world." Even more magical than my mother's lions was her ability to place those lions in the context of what happened next.

◆

I go to a twelve-step meeting while he's gone. I never went when I was quitting drinking, but this one is about love, codependency. I'd gone faithfully the first year of COVID, but my intentions always felt suspect, an atheist praying out of desperation, because her back was against a wall. I'm not sure what my resistance is. The people are kind and honest. They are unflinching toward themselves, willing to be wrong. But there is something formulaic about it. I like to palm my healing quietly, sneakily, without anyone knowing. The barista who poured me green tea every morning for months when I was doing exposure therapy for panic. I'd drink caffeine to elevate my heart rate, to face that discomfort, and every day she'd pour more panic for me in a cup, without ever knowing it. She healed me. My clients who spoke of their eating disorders while I was confronting my own. The open mics I went to my second year in New York City; I'd gone every Friday night for a year. Nobody knew about Daniel. Nobody knew someone I'd loved had died, nobody knew I was getting sober. The bartender, a tall Russian man, would make me virgin mojitos, ask me out, and shrug good-naturedly when I said no. I'd enlist people to be part of my healing without them ever knowing, and in this way their presence felt authentic, organic, spontaneous. Unrehearsed.

✦

I grew up with three mothers. Hanine, Reem, Fatima. Mother, aunt, grandmother. Mother, mother, mother. And so my cousin is also my sister, my mother is my sister, I am my sister's mother. We are like a tangle of gold necklaces, impossible to tease apart. We are filled with fire, quick tempers, easy laughs, a love for bad gossip. When I think of my mothers, I think of them on Meimei's couch, collapsed in a heap of laughter, that same swelling cackle, the slap of my mother's palm hitting the other, once, sharply, the Arab woman's gesture for stolen delight. As a child, I wanted to live in that joined laughter. I wanted to move through it like water.

✦

I go to a meeting one hot night in early September. I dutifully share my name. I listen as a woman describes a breakup that's destroying her. I listen to a man, clearly an old-timer, talk about his ex-wife. He speaks in twelve-step vernacular: let go and let God; progress not perfection; it works if you work it. I share after him. I talk about Johnny leaving, about his return in a couple of days. I talk about how hurt I am, how I'm trying to remember I've played a part here, but it's hard when he's the one that fucked off to Mexico, you know? I can feel myself shaping the story as I tell it: I share about the surrogate, say I'm worried about what the baby will be born into, say he owed us all better behavior, himself included. I'm nearly out of time. "But of course," I rush to add, "I can't control him. So. You know. I'm just. I'm focusing on myself. It's all I have control over."

That's it. My time is done and another person is talking. Nobody gives advice. Nobody tsks. This isn't a conversation. It's a place to be witnessed but more importantly, it's a place to do the witnessing. But I'm miserly today. I want commiseration. I want pity. I glance around, trying to catch someone's eye. The woman next to me notices. She's older. She pats my hand and leans in. *Careful not to martyr, honey,* she whispers, then turns her attention back to the speaker.

◆

I grew up on stories of wayward women: women who disobeyed their fathers, women who took what they wanted, who could build new lives at the drop of a hat. I heard about luck, how it wove its tendrils down generations. There was one story told over and over, at the knee of my great-aunt Nadia, whispered from Meimei to my mother, declared by my mother over and over: *The women in this family have no luck in love.*

◆

In Arabic, you don't necessarily say "bad luck." You say *beedoon 'haz.* Without luck. The absence of it. A pool emptied of water.

◆

In *The Odyssey*, Penelope's defining characteristic is her ability to wait. This becomes conflated with loyalty, fidelity, womanhood. She keeps her hands busy while she waits. She weaves, she unweaves. She is patient. She is still as a statue otherwise. I wait the way fire waits. My waiting burns what it touches.

✦

Abandonment by a lover won't kill us, Melissa Febos writes. *But it awakens the parts of us that remember when it could.*

✦

My parents waited. They waited in immigration offices. They waited for asylum lawyers to call them back. They waited for America, even while they were in America, and slowly it began to infect them. This new, strange land, the cornfields stretching out farther than any horizon, farther even than sand dunes could. The fluorescent lights of Wal-Mart and Albertsons, all those aisles, all those anticipated wants. America told you what to crave and it told you to crave everything: shopping malls and cookouts, the camaraderie of white men who stopped at the gas station where my father worked, Braum's ice cream sundaes, extra sprinkles, the Cowboys, the Sooners, highways from your town to your sister's, the only person you trust for thousands of miles. It told you to crave its praise, its embossed navy passport, its *approved*, red letters like soldiers stamped across my parents' application.

✦

My father's leavings were into himself. He would lapse into silences. We have, twice, gone unbearable stretches without speaking, each of us more stubborn than the other. Growing up, I was afraid of my father, but I loved him more than I feared him. He was leveraged, like so many Arab fathers, by my mother—an instrument of discipline, of fear and threat. *Wait until I tell your father*. After a bad grade. After my brother and I

70

were caught imitating the moves of professional wrestlers. It wasn't until later that I realized he likely hated being used in this way. He worked long hours in my childhood, at a gas station, then as an adjunct at a university hours away. He'd always been playful, goofy, at heart.

And anyway—the worst thing I could imagine wasn't being hit or yelled at. That happened, and then it passed, and then I'd forget. I feared something more primal: that he would forget who I was. That I'd wake up one day and he would blink at me without any warmth or recognition: just another girl, nobody he loved. I feared him leaving, though that never happened. What had happened was him being left behind, briefly, a story I could barely stand telling.

✦

I wait for the missives from Dee. I wait for Johnny's return. Dee sends me a video of the baby's heartbeat. In it, you can hear the doctor asking if she has started recording. Then—nothing but the deep rumble of something making itself. One afternoon, I buy a bagful of expensive cobalt-blue yarn and start a blanket. The click of metal against metal, the rows of yarn eating itself, becoming looped around its own bristly body. Dee describes a metallic taste in her mouth. The next morning, I wake tasting pennies. But there is nothing when I open my mouth in my new mirror: just pink and then, farther back, too dark to see.

✦

The story of the women starts with the land. The story of the women starts with the men. It is the men whose names make their way into textbooks, on plaques, on street corners, it is the men who name the land and fight for the land and lose the land, it is the men who meet in secret rooms, the men who decide what is surrender and what is resistance, the men who marry women, then take them from Syria to Lebanon, from Palestine to Kuwait, from Jordan to the West. What is left for the women—amid all these men, all these new lost places—except stories?

71

♦

If a man can't love himself, I ask Meimei's photograph, *can he love any-thing? Can he love a daughter?* I don't need to meet her eyes to know they're admonishing. I don't need to ask the question to know the answer.

♦

This is a surrogate too, I know. This glossy photograph of a dead woman. Her lively eyes. A surrogate for the real thing. When I was younger, I'd confuse her with Quran verses, fables, heroines in stories. She was what I understood of love, where I forged my image of it. A woman who kept her hands busy, who raised children, then raised their children, who had devoted her life to that care. A surrogate for god.

♦

In America, the women worked as babysitters and bank tellers. They dressed us in each other's clothes, waited for sales and two-for-ones. They raised us as siblings: my cousins Omar and Layal, my brother Talal, interchangeable, taking turns visiting each other in Oklahoma and Texas. The women wore their hair curly and frizzy. There are photos of us in the Norman mall, dressed as witches and clowns for Halloween. There are photos of us in the park, the one by the lake, feeding geese, the long-legged fathers jokingly reaching for the monkey bars. Sometimes, the women would gather with other women, from Syria and Lebanon and Palestine, women who'd found themselves in this country too. They would drive to Oklahoma City or Dallas, cook elaborate meals, gossip about people back home, laugh at stories of their husbands. Once, someone put on Arabic pop music and I snuck away from the rec room, from watching *The Lion King* with the other children, to watch the women's bodies move to the music, dancing, taking turns clicking their hips and shimmying and clapping for each other. I watched in awe. This magic trick of delight, what they were able to do with music in another country.

◆

Once, when I am in the midst of a miscarriage, and my cousin Layal is mired in her own grief in eastern Germany, I text her: *I send you my heart.* She replies: *It's already here.*

◆

You become defined by what you wait for. Giovanni Gasparini writes, "This . . . can lead to reclassification and possibly, or ultimately, a social role." My role, then: not mother. Not wife. Not mother.

◆

It is early September when Johnny returns. He enters the rearranged apartment, hugs me lightly. He won't look me in the eye.

"Hi, Hala," he says quietly.

The past month lies between us like a carcass. I try to smile. The rage in my body wakes; I can feel the buzzing in the roots of my teeth. You left me, I want to scream. What had returned him to me? Love, perhaps, but also fear: fear of being the bad guy. What story about fear isn't also about love? A self at its most primal, young, unwilling to lose anything else. When that part thinks of the grainy ultrasound, of Johnny's closet emptied, of my life sagging like a used mattress under the weight of nothing, I cannot breathe. I am feral with that fear: there is nothing I won't do not to feel it.

Which means I am fated to keep feeling it. Watching him pour himself water, take off his shoes, I am overwhelmed by it, I can see nothing but it: the being left. I am left in a way that feels boundless. There is no bound because he always returns. The rage comes with a kind of seeing: how his eyes dart around the room like a trapped animal. I watch him take off his dusty backpack, the front pocket gaping open. He'd forgotten to zip it. The leaving will be endless, and I suddenly see that purgatory as something preordained, like a punishment by Greek gods.

He finally looks at me, for a second. His eyes are elsewhere. Then he looks past me.

"Is that a *cactus*?"

I welcome him home.

◆

My adoration of Baba never wavered as a child. I still remember the visceral shock of hearing an American classmate speak of her father. The girl called her father a deadbeat. She said it casually, matter-of-factly. "But," I said, desperate to have her unspeak the word. It felt sacrilegious. "You still think he's the best father in the world, right?"

She'd looked at me strangely, then sympathetically. "No," she said slowly. That was it. No. I was stunned. I felt embarrassed for her, embarrassed for her father. This lack of loyalty, of devotion.

◆

When the women in my family want something, it multiplies like seeds or bacteria. It infects them. It becomes an obsession. They become blinded by their desire: for a desert or accent, for a man, for a child. Their desire, soured, turns into rage; the women in my family wear their resentments like bracelets. They will tell you all about them. They will ruin dinner. They will tell you about your father's family, how they are less cultured or more arrogant, how they never liked them. They will blame their misery on the men. *Our women*, Nadia once shook her head, *always choose men who are no good*. My father nodded good-naturedly. Nadia loved him, but she loved that story more. It was her mother's story, it had become her daughter's story. Her niece's. One story played out over and over again; we get called to the stage hastily when the other bows out, understudies for a part we never auditioned for.

✦

The surrogacy agency tells me to start making recordings. I am not the vessel and so I am not the chamber of sound. She must learn my voice. I download the app, upload recordings that Dee plays for the baby. I believe her. In her surrogate application, she'd written her biggest regret in life was *Not saying I love you to my grandmother on her deathbed.* This made me love her a little, this unnecessary truth.

There is something familiar about the act of recording: I have an audio diary. I regularly swap voice notes with friends around the world, especially after the pandemic. My voice-note friendships are exclusively women: Olivia in Beirut, Alexis in New Jersey, Dalea in San Diego, Kiki in Boston. They are meandering soliloquies, the background noise of our lives in them, interrupting our stories with different stories.

But I don't know what to say in these recordings. I keep greeting the lime-sized embryo with "baby." I talk about the weather, like we're on a bad date.

"Oh baby, this heat just won't break."

✦

What did you tell yours? I ask my grandmother. *When they were in the womb?*

✦

One afternoon, I start to tell her a new story. "My mama and baba lived in a desert." I keep stopping, rerecording. It feels risky: I've invited others into the narration. It's like one of my favorite photos of myself, how the person who took it has a shadow in the shot. It's impossible to unsee it. I am not alone in the photograph. I'm not alone in this room typing. I'm not alone speaking into my phone's recorder. I'm not alone.

✦

My mama and baba lived in a desert. It wasn't their desert, but it had opened its arms to their families years earlier. They had houses in different parts of town, fathers who were journalists and schoolteachers, mothers who raised children, cooked maqloubeh and kibbe from scratch, spent afternoons watching Syrian soaps. It wasn't their desert, but they planned to live there forever.

✦

Johnny and I find a therapist. Then another. Then another. The one I like he doesn't. The one he does is too expensive. We find a woman in upstate New York, our sessions via Zoom. During our first session, she asks us to tell her how we met. Within minutes, we are interrupting each other, laughing, our shoulders relaxed.

"You were late to that bar," Johnny reminds me.

"I was trying to find my lipstick."

"You never told me that!"

For a moment, we are transported, admiring our younger selves, their bravado, their red lips. The way they stepped into a life without a hesitation. Is there any story more ordinary than falling in love and thinking it extraordinary? I can see Johnny's face on the screen in front of us, even though he is right next to me. What is a story you tell over and over again? Does it become prophecy, memory, truth? His face is luminous and young and for a second I remember what it was like not to know him, how he'd seemed so enormous and free, undaunted by the things that scared me: oceans, illness, drugs. He didn't care about dirty floors or annual physicals. He lived out of suitcases for months at a time. When we traveled, he'd trust vendors with fifty-dollar bills and, when they didn't return, he'd shrug and say, "I guess he needed it more than I did."

"I was moving to Barcelona," Johnny says. "And then I met Hala."

He loves this story. We both do. It was so unlikely. We were both so afraid and then we weren't. It was like discovering alchemy. *I'll never be alone again*, I'd written in a journal entry from that year. Johnny tells the story like he is eating something delicious, syrupy and slow. All past and hope.

His face in front of that Brooklyn bar. I met him a year into my sobriety. It was still a performance, a loud order of green tea at every dinner. Our first date, we met at a bar across the street from my studio apartment and my lips were bright red. My anorexia was raring and I felt that familiar dizziness as we swallowed cigarette smoke. His smile in the Barcelona airport when I landed to visit him several months later. Gaudí's artwork, bright red sculptures, plazas flanked with palm trees, the impossible blue of the freezing ocean. I wrote in outdoor cafés while he sipped cold beers. In the evenings, starving, I'd sneak into the shared kitchen of our rental and eat olives and crackers. He was moody and inscrutable, boyish and whimsical. He was a chaotic traveler, reveled in small inconveniences, was prone to long silences. What is a story you tell over and over again? A prediction, a recounting, an accountability. He stayed in things too long: jobs, cities, relationships. He was afraid of hurting, and so he hurt, afraid of regret, and so he became resentful.

✦

Here's what I remember most of that trip: not the trip itself, but a visit to Forever 21 right before, an afternoon spent trying on dresses, envisioning Seville and Barcelona. If I could stay in any moment, it would be this one—all anticipation, the promise of who I'd be in the spangly black dress, the knit yellow cardigan. This is the quintessential exile craving, only transferred to love: the anticipation of the trip. After—it would be the memory of it, the nostalgia for it. All I knew of love was longing, and longing requires absence. I am like my mother. I am like my mother's mother. I decide I want to marry him. I do.

✦

My parents arrived in the United States on a Tuesday. My mother was pregnant, I was four. We landed in New York, then flew to Oklahoma, where my aunt and uncle picked us up. Gone was the desert, my grandfather's library, the friends and cousins they'd known since birth. The restaurants, the marina, the houses they'd grown up in. *I spent nearly thirty years there*, my father tells me later. *It wasn't Palestine, but it was the place I knew best. And suddenly, it was gone.* In its place—a strange land. Megachurches, grocery stores the size of villas, diners, tornadoes. White men and their God. It was hard to locate ourselves in this new place. We were pale enough, but clearly other, dark-haired and accented. My father wore Sooners baseball caps. My mother wore her hair with honey highlights.

◆

After Kuwait, my father says, *every place was just a place. When we'd leave, it stopped existing for me.*

◆

"We do this interesting thing," the therapist says at the end of the session. "Most people. We try to find the person who can help us have a different ending. But the problem is that a different ending usually needs us to be different too. It needs us to tolerate what will help us heal."

I'm irritated. I don't want a therapist. I am a therapist. I want a fortune-teller. I want someone to read my palm and say yes, say no. I want crystal balls, a forecast. I want to know what the future will look like. I don't care if it's the right question. It's the one I have.

"In that sense," the therapist continues, "you are, in the best and worst ways, perfect for each other."

◆

The curse of the eldest immigrant daughter is to be painfully observant. I saw things the adults did not see. I saw how they stumbled over their words. I saw the ways people looked at them. Once, my mother and I ran into a girl from my class at the YMCA, popular, blonde. She'd never spoken to me. My mother, unaware of the intricate social norms of my elementary school, began to chat with the girl.

"You should come to our house and play sometime." She squeezed my thin, tense, perpetually hunched shoulders. "Holly would love to be your friend."

The girl was not unkind. She smiled at my mother. I think she was rattled by her oblivion. The next time I saw her in class, she nodded benignly. We never spoke to each other again. I spent recess in a quiet panic, shoving my mother's food in my mouth, pretending to be preoccupied by clouds, or else making small talk with the stray friend I'd make here and there, our companionship always marked more by our common outcast status than any affection. I hated school tremendously. But the memory of my mother's open smile made my heart constrict for weeks. I couldn't bear the pain of all the things my mother didn't know.

✦

I got a new name, I tell the seed, her, you. *It was all anyone called me for years.*

✦

We renamed ourselves in America. My father had loved my name: the name Saddam Hussein had given his youngest daughter. It had nothing to do with the man. It was the throaty *H*, the singsong of the vowels. *Abu Hala*—father of Hala—a chant sung in the streets of Baghdad, and my father knew what he named me. Then Saddam invaded Kuwait and my parents left. He arrived in America, Abu Hala, Hala in tow: this new land. I became Holly. My father Nick, my mother Janine, my brother Timmy.

✦

Immigrants are often made to disavow where they come from. If you can melt into whiteness, you can become something else entirely, a ghost in the census. In *Minor Feelings*, Cathy Park Hong writes, "In our efforts to belong in America, we act grateful, as if we've been given a second chance at life. But our shared root is not the opportunity this nation has given us but how the capitalist accumulation of white supremacy has enriched itself off the blood of our countries." I am grateful to this country, for what its passport enabled: asylum, shelter. But what of this country funding Saddam a decade earlier? What of oil siphoned off and at what cost? What of the bankrolled dictators, the misleading headlines, the allegiances that displaced my father's family to Kuwait in the first place, decades before that? What is it to demand devotion at gunpoint?

✦

At home, my waiting changes with Johnny. I am vigilant. I watch him like a wolf. I circle him. I am tense. Even my forehead is tight. I have to keep unlocking my jaw. I am a creature waiting for thunder.

"Please," he says one day. "Don't look at me like that."

"Like what?" We have just finished a therapy session. There was no fight. We'd talked about our mothers. Love always came with the risk of annihilation for him; he panicked in the face of need, and I panicked in the face of retreat. He'd grown up alternately punished and idolized. Growing up, I'd fantasized about attention, stages, spotlights. He longed to be invisible.

"Like I'm something about to *combust*." He stops. I see his hands are trembling.

✦

Every story is a retelling of another story. When I tell the story of Johnny, I am telling the story of America. When I tell the story of America, I am telling the story of Palestine. None exists without the other. I come from a people that were dispossessed of land and its archive, and in that dispossession they clung to whatever came their way. I learned that clinging, learned that hungry reach. But the trick of America is the wanting only dislocates you further. The story of America is the story of Midwestern public schools, my name re-ordained, a teacher asking me how to say "mosque" in Arabic, then saying, *We don't do that here, honey.*

✦

I've always been confused by the stories of luck. Because I couldn't see how luck had anything to do with it. We'd been given the warnings, the admonishments. We were the ones doing the choosing. We were the ones fighting for what we wanted. But perhaps it is easier to tell a story of luck than one of powerlessness.

✦

What happens to love in exile? What happens to the exile in love?

✦

There is a fantasy in loving what cannot love you back. It is the fantasy of entry: an avoidant man, an unfriendly nation. It is the fantasy of a border trespassed, access through stamp or lovability, to be granted entry to what others are not, to be the winning number on a visa lottery.

✦

When we moved to Lebanon, the women changed again. They wore their hair straight, sat for hours for keratin treatment. They smoothed their brows, wore bright lipstick, bought stylish outfits. Their voices changed, became softer, new, unrecognizable.

✦

Whenever we audit the past—long circular debates about who let who down, who made what promises, who broke which—my first impulse is to fawn. *A trauma response in which a person reverts to people-pleasing and appeasing behaviors to diffuse conflict and reestablish a sense of safety.* This means I don't contradict Johnny. I don't ask necessary questions. I let the stories lobbed at me stand. When he talks about leaving, I plead and reason and spin futures. I remind myself of our dog: when she angers us, she immediately goes belly up.

◆

It matters what you do with power, I tell Meimei's photograph. *It matters.* My voice echoes back to me, my grandmother's dark eyes gleam.

◆

I lay my power at Johnny's feet like a wreath. Unasked for. An unwelcome offering. But I find that—like any habit—I've been doing it for years, that once I've started, it feels impossible to stop.

◆

When the fawn doesn't work, the wolf arrives. A darker impulse kicks in. The wolf flings herself at people. The wolf demands things she knows the other cannot give. The wolf revels in the no, in any possible cruelty. This is a kind of power too: the wolf can break her own heart whenever she wants. Look at these long teeth.

◆

There's a saying in twelve-step programs. It's my favorite one. It's about not going to the knife store for bread.

◆

Attaching to what cannot reciprocate—man, country, mother—is a kind of perverse protection. It keeps you from true connection.

◆

But what if you aren't really looking for bread? I ask the photograph one afternoon. Meimei considers this. *What I mean is,* I rush on, *what if you're looking for knives but saying you're looking for bread? To prove to yourself that all you'll ever find in this life are more knives?* My grandmother doesn't have to speak for me to know she's calling me an American.

✦

As a child, I watched the women vigilantly. I learned about their fear. I learned it is bottomless: it has no end, no edge to it. It is a kind of hunger, an ocean, an enduring horizon. I learned that it cannot be helped, cannot be stopped. It is a wound without staunching. The women could be undone like a knot, and when it happened, the undoing didn't stop. My mothers were afraid of highways, of elevators, of germs. One afternoon in Oklahoma when we first arrived, a tornado siren screeched, and my aunt was alone with us. She gathered my baby brother and cousin into the bathtub, yelled at me to follow. She piled us with blankets, dragged a mattress into the room. She wept the entire time, the way women in movies do when their lovers leave. *This country*, she kept panting. *I can't. This country, I can't.* The words became jumbled. This country can't. I can't this country. She hyperventilated and laid the mattress on top of us, and I listened to the cries of my brother and cousin, felt her trembling arms above the mattress. I felt her panic in my teeth, felt her trembling become my own, felt her fear enter me until it became my own, forever, for life. I understood something that afternoon: when fear found you, there would be no egress, no way out. It was just you and the bathtub. You and the terrible wind. I learned that to wait in fear was a terrible thing, an unacceptable thing, an unbearable thing, the thing expected from you all the same.

✦

The hudhud is native to Palestine. It is a bird of dispatches. The sky is its jurisdiction, as is the water, the sea. In the Quran, the hudhud spoke. The bird carried messages between a prophet and a queen. It was a bird of communication, a bird of information, a bird of messages. Trained to gather missives, to bring them across borders. A bird of unity.

✦

People told me things when I was a child. They whispered about their lives. Their regrets, their dreads, their missteps. A relative once told me about an affair. I was blank-faced and barely a tween, a perfect receptacle. I was still a good girl then. I would listen well. My mother told me about her sorrows. I listened. I nodded. I was the eldest grandchild, my grandmother's fifth child. A little adult. I knew how to keep people talking. I learned you always agree with the speaker, always soothe their guilt. Everybody was doing the best they could; everybody wanted to hear that. If you are indispensable to someone, I understood, it was almost as good as love. It was a kind of love. It would have to do instead of love.

✦

Like the hudhud, I sometimes did not keep secrets. I shuttled lives back and forth from person to person, from ear to ear. I brought tell of scandal from one to the other. This, I learned, was another way of getting attention, of being needed. Being the person who had access to information, to the lives of others. Like gold or emeralds, their currency was higher in value when traded.

✦

There is a dream I have during the lime-sized month. I dream Dee tells me the baby is coming, and we are suddenly in a queenly bedroom, surrounded by brocade and candles. It's just me and her. There is a fur blanket and I'm telling Dee to lie down, but she is no longer there. Instead, there is a bundle on the fur: a baby. I suddenly know this is the son my grandmother believed I had, the child I'd pretended to have. I hold the baby and suddenly remember I have no milk. I don't know how to swaddle. I look over and Dee is touching her naked belly: white, white, still bulging. The skin is so white it starts to become transparent and I can see the pink of her uterus, the steady drum of her heartbeat. It gets louder and louder. It's going to wake the baby. This first and only sound the baby has known for nearly a year. "I never got to hear it," I tell Dee. I'd heard the baby's. But I never heard hers. Dee smiles. "That was a secret between me and her," she says. I wake up.

◆

The first scientifically documented case of surrogacy was in 1985. It's known as the Baby M case. A woman in her twenties became pregnant after being implanted with a woman's egg and inseminated with the woman's husband's sperm. But when the surrogate held the newly born baby, she decided she wanted to keep the child, that *this was her child*. She returned to the couple the next day and threatened to kill herself if she didn't see the baby. When they agreed to visitation, the woman fled with the baby. A legal battle ensued. The surrogate threatened suicide and threatened to kill the baby. The court ruled in favor of the couple. The baby grew into a girl. The woman who had birthed her saw her less and less frequently. When Baby M entered adulthood, she gave an interview in which she said her parents are her parents. She called herself lucky. She called one of the women her mother, and it wasn't the one who'd carried her for all those months. I cried reading the interview. I couldn't say who I was crying for.

◆

"Here's another question," the therapist asks us during a session. "Why are you fighting for this marriage?"

◆

I answer the question with a question. What is the point of a vow? I start talking about the morality of waiting. The woman staring out of a window, riding a train, counting days, waiting for her life to begin, or to end. The archetype of the damsel in distress, the woman in mourning, the woman waiting for a war to end, for a husband to return, for a child to arrive. The woman who waits and in her waiting lights candles, grows her hair, cuts her hair, checks the clock, talks to photographs. She is submerged in time: in the loss of it, in the monstrosity of it.

The woman who waits is lauded, beloved, a symbol of endurance, of virtue, an object that travels between past and future. Her waiting is not to be fretted over, or grieved. It is adored. She is valuable because she waits. She is valuable because of all the things she doesn't do in the name of that waiting. The more passive she is, the more loyal. The more she sacrifices, the more she has loved.

✦

America taught me to want, and my mothers taught me to fear, but nobody taught me what to do with things when I got them. I am still often possessed by wild, useless desires: linen stationery, teacups, sea glass, indigo pigments from centuries ago. For a beautiful woman to look at me twice on the L train. I made Johnny drive us four hours to a black beach in Iceland once, just to steal a stone from the icy waves. I put it in my mouth when he wasn't looking. That cold oval. It is so unsatisfactory, to feel such acute want and then have no way to assuage it: a forever itch, a hallway of mirrors and no doors, no way out.

✦

One night, I dream of Johnny standing on a balcony. He tells me his flight is nearly here. He will call when he lands. I weep, ask him to stay. But the sun is already setting, I can't make out his silhouette anymore, his voice melting into the honks of a city below me. I am alone.

✦

The next morning, I am dialing Mama's number before I realize what I'm doing.

I tell her the two dreams. I tell her how people kept vanishing, how alone I feel. I ask her if she still believes in love. She asks if the sun was rising or setting in the dreams. It was nighttime, I say. *Mmm*, she says. She sounds bored. She is cleaning something. I tell her to focus. I ask if she thinks the war changed her, if it made her love differently. Her voice sharpens. *You better not be writing about me.* I tell her I'm not. And *anyway*, can she focus, did the war change her. She asks which one. I launch into a rant about invisible costs of displacement and she tells me not to be dramatic. I ask her to define gaslighting. She tells me I'm so sensitive sometimes. I explain the plot of the movie that coined the term gaslighting. She reminds me not to forget her Tupperware this weekend. She's already lost three of them. And anyway, she reminds me, I don't have the gift of dreaming that she has. *You should try to stop if you can.* I hang up without getting an answer about anything. My dreams mean nothing.

◆

I record my voice as I walk to the water. I answer the therapist's question to nobody, to myself, to a heartbeat. A missive: one that will never leave my phone.

◆

Because I don't know how not to fight. Because I want the lighthouse, the beach rock, the sea glass. Even if I don't know what to do with it. Because I thought love was the cure for fear, but the only path I know to love *is* fear. It's become mixed like ink in water. Because I can't fathom walking away from love, even if that love hurts. I don't know abundance like that. I'd grown up idolizing women who longed to be left as much as they feared it, because to be left was to have something concrete to fear, to defend against, in a world of vague, intangible threat. Women who told stories about luck because they couldn't tell stories of loss. Here's what nobody ever tells you: erasing yourself, sinking yourself in someone, drink, obsession, is a powerful thing. An unmet need is a powerful thing. It can become a command, a superpower, something that turns everything you touch into a wish.

Month Four

*By the end of the fourth month of pregnancy, the baby is
roughly the size of an orange or avocado. Her skin is still mostly
translucent, so you might be able to see her blood vessels.*

Autumn comes suddenly, abrupt and welcome after the endless heat.
The trees costume themselves in fiery red and orange, and the days
shorten. I'm hungry for the dark. I walk the early dusks through Williamsburg, under the bridge, toward the water, toward the park. There
is often the smell of something ashy, like a faint burning. It smells of
adventure, newness, something about to happen. There is a particular
smell of fire—rubber and garbage—that reminds me of youth, of trouble, the fire of protests, the fire that arrives as a warning, the first sign
of danger. Once upon a time, this was the season of destruction. Once
upon a time, this was the season of blackouts, one-night stands, remorse.

◆

When I first met Johnny, he asked if alcohol made me uncomfortable.

"Not at all," I said. "I don't mind." It was the truth. I'd been intentional about remaining close to alcohol. The first three months after I quit, I lied to everyone about why I wasn't drinking. "I'm on these dumb antibiotics," I kept reciting. This meant I kept going to nightclubs, bars, house parties. I became inured to its presence, the *ah* of a popped beer bottle, the clank of ice against glass. It wouldn't rule my life, I swore. I would heal myself. I wouldn't be someone who made my sobriety its own kind of addiction. I was twenty-four.

Our first year dating was a whirlwind: travel, bar after bar after bar, in Spain, in Manhattan, in Boston and Providence and Oakland. I was finishing up my doctoral degree in clinical psychology and he was learning how to code. We stayed up like teenagers, slept past noon, woke bleary-eyed and disoriented.

◆

In twelve-step meetings, there's the same saying of alcoholics and codependents: *They don't have relationships, they take hostages.* What is addiction but wanting gone awry? What is the story of addiction but the story of a longing you have to disavow? Leaving when you want to stay. Stopping when you want more. The addiction to the substance can become the addiction to another person. The continued thump of another heart. To burn yourself at the altar of the other, and to call the burning love. In Arabic, my favorite expression is: *What is coming is better than what is gone.* All addiction is the same in this way: the delusion of a better tomorrow, the delicious waiting for that turn. You wait because there is the promise of what will come, that kryptonic hope. Whether it's the next hit, the next drink, the next lover—the addict is the quintessential archetype of the hopeful.

◆

I'd always sought out drinkers, even after I stopped. But Johnny was different. I drank to destroy. He drank medicinally—like a chemist, not a gambler. His drinking was a constant and so it was like background noise. I poured whiskey into cut glasses. I lingered at the mezcals in the store. By the time I met him, I never drank. I never touched it. It didn't have to be my lips touching alcohol, just so long as there were lips on it. There was a proxy delight in his drinking, the adventure without the consequence, my nervous system relaxing with his, the long exhale I felt at his eased body, the rush of serotonin. I loved his hangovers, the way I entered them like a room. Like this I found a way to keep drinking without drinking, a way to cheat the years.

◆

Waiting can be an inherently hopeful act. You wait because you believe—even on the faintest level—that something is arriving. There is something to wait *for*. Against all odds, Penelope genuinely believed Ulysses would return.

For years, I rarely thought of drinking myself. If I did, I envisioned it like visiting a faraway land that I used to live in. I wanted to see if things had been rearranged. I wanted to check in on the gardens.

◆

There was and how much there was. Kan yama kan. How many narrators. How many endings. When there is deep trauma. When that trauma has taken root. A technique in narrative therapy: asking the client to tell the story in third person.

◆

In Beirut, she never knew mornings. Instead, she'd sleep past noon, stay up until sickly sunrises. She sucked her stomach in. She threw up in the bathroom. She lied. The city felt like a playground. Then a prison. The city grew around her like a tree. She drank. She sloshed around like liquid in a dirty glass, she spilled into booths and taxi cabs, she rolled around in beds with strangers, she woke up in unfamiliar places, her neck hurting and her mouth dry. She visited emergency rooms: the time she cracked her head, the time she woke her friends hyperventilating from too many drugs, the numerous alcohol poisonings. Afternoons spent flirting with the cute doctors as they unsnaked IVs for fluids and antiemetics. The dreaded hours of solitude: the hangover, heart palpitations, nothing to armor against the truth. Every day she seemed to get farther and farther from herself. A self built from bluster and duct tape: *You try too hard.* She tried too hard. She drank too much. She ate too much. She wanted and wanted and wanted and the bottom would never bottom out.

The first time she drank, she was sixteen and visiting her cousin in Amman. Studies show that an indicator of later alcoholism is whether someone's first experience involves inebriation. She blacked out for five hours. She cried on the hood of a stranger's car and told stories about love and nonexistent breakups. That was the thing with her and alcohol. Other people got drunk and told the truth; she drank and lied. She lied and blacked out and forgot the lies. The second time she drank, it was at her friend's house in Lebanon. They drank Bailey's straight from the bottle, and she remembers how the air in her room seemed to vibrate, the carpet, the electric tingles in her fingertips, all that unbridled potential. It was a feeling she'd chase for the next eight years: the promise of something happening. She could imagine small revolts, her crush appearing at the house, taking a flight to Paris. Never mind it was two in the morning. Never mind they were high-schoolers. When you were drunk anything could happen.

✦

"A blackout doesn't sting, or stab, or leave a scar when it robs you. Close your eyes and open them again. That's what a blackout feels like," Sarah Hepola writes. I'd found the best way to disappear. A blackout is the most spectacular magic trick of all. You erase yourself without anyone knowing it. You are absent only to yourself; to everyone else, you are still laughing, still moving, your mouth opening and closing, words fall out like stones. You still order another beer, tug a body against yours. You are a marionette, a hijacked engine, possessed. I never knew who took over when I blacked out. Maybe it was a stranger. Or maybe it was me, the actual me, the truest one.

◆

The year I graduate high school, my family moves to Qatar, a neat bit of luck that means I'm the rarest of creatures in Beirut: a single young woman, still a teenager, living in her own apartment, with her own roommate, without curfews. Beirut is fourteen years out of its civil war, an era that partitioned the city, brimmed the country with sectarian ties and violence. People rarely speak of it, and when they do, it's like something of a bygone era. I start drinking right away: at the orientation event at university, with friends after classes. It begins like something fun, a little naughty, an adventure that never ends in a city that seems boundless. In this way, what I knew of Beirut I knew of drinking—I became fluent in the city at night, its alleyways and tiny bars and the sea glittering under the moon. The drink and Beirut became similar things, magical and terrible at turns. I became the confidante of taxi drivers. I befriended middle-aged bartenders who'd tell me to go home. I danced on boats, beaches, tabletops. One night, my friend nearly got taken by Hezbollah men—we'd drunkenly wandered into their tents in Beirut's downtown square—and I, plastered, flirtatiously begged the man in Arabic to leave my friend alone. *Take your Americans and go*, the man had finally said, hesitating before adding, not unkindly, *and sober up, sister.*

◆

Whatever I do tonight, I write in a bad poem during this time, *will be outdone by tomorrow.*

92

✦

The truth is I lived in Lebanon for nearly a decade with only a hazy grasp of its history. I was a tween, then a teenager, then a college student. I parroted what I heard adults say during dinner parties, and drank my way through a political science degree. I chose the major because I couldn't think of a better one, but my brain was always unable to hold all the dates and politicians. By the time I moved to New York for graduate school, I could barely explain anything. It was like trying to explain grammatical rules of Arabic, my first language, the first I knew of this world, but didn't learn to read or write until age twelve. It meant I understood the sinews of it, the syntax, intuitively, but had no way to explain why. In America, Lebanon was seen as safer ground: the refugee camps, the Sabra and Shatila massacres, the oligarchical politicians, the corruption were overlooked. The West loved to tut over Lebanon. Creased brows. A country of French speakers. A country of bikini-clad women with dark eyebrows on postcards. The Paris of the Middle East, did I know they used to call her that?

✦

I don't send a voice recording to the avocado-slash-orange baby that week. Or the next. Or the next. Instead, I wait until I'm alone in the house, and rant to my grandmother's photograph. She's looking more solemn these days, more tired, a little older. I can almost make out her *mmm*s. My soliloquies are becoming more deranged. She was right. I should've never stayed in America. I'd married America. Did she know that? I'd married it and I'd missed her death and I'd never forgive myself. And anyway, what was the point of leaving a place, when that place became a euphemism for every other place, when it became the reference point, when it superimposed itself on everything?

✦

One morning in Beirut, I'd woken hungover.

"Get up," my friend Karam said when he called me. "Let's *go* somewhere."

"I think I might be dead."

"It's Valentine's Day. You can die after."

We decide to go to Saida with another friend. It's the third largest city in Lebanon, on the Mediterranean coast in the southern part of the country. In the days of the Phoenicians it was a major trading port. That day, we take a bus and I'm the only girl, flanked by my two friends. We walk through the cobblestone streets, the ruins and their distorted reflections in the sea, the streets filled with people and hawkers. The day is unseasonably warm, the air smelling of salt. We buy ice cream, then argue about which restaurant to go to. There are small stores everywhere, with men inside them: electronics, fruit, nightgowns.

There is a way that air rearranges itself in disaster. The ruins remain still. The water keeps lapping at the coastline. The people get in and out of their cars, the traffic worsens. But the voices start to seem louder. One man calls to another from across the street. A woman hurries by with a child. A man plants both his hands on the hood of a car, bracing himself, his head bent.

"Did you see?" one shopkeeper yells. Nobody responds. "Are you seeing?" We peer into his store, where the television is blaring. This is the scene I will return to in fiction, in poetry: Arab men hunched over television screens, learning about their cities, their dictators, their young men, the catastrophes that have befallen them. The dream my brother and I would share for decades before speaking it aloud: the light across a face, the story of a crisis.

We keep walking. "Something's wrong," Karam says, but we don't respond. A woman is crying on the phone. We walk faster. I suddenly feel young, and my first thought is to call my father, my second is that he will want to know why I'm not on campus, why I'm wandering a strange town with two boys.

A crowd begins to gather on the street, mostly men, their voices laid atop one another's, gesturing toward the sky, toward the sea. They are arguing, they are explaining. Something is wrong. Karam gestures toward the nearest shop, and we step inside. The man is my grandfather's age, shaking his head at the screen. There is smoke, a fire, people gathering. The shot is aerial, then close up. The newscaster is speaking in formal Arabic, and neither of us can keep up.

"Uncle?" Karam begins. "What's happened?"

He turns to face us, his eyes heavy and red-rimmed. I am startled. I am always surprised to see men cry, especially older men, especially older men who then speak gruffly. "What do you think happened? They killed him. They burned him alive." He turns back to the television screen, the man's face on it: Hariri. The prime minister. He has been assassinated. His car blown up near the sea in Beirut, a site that will be honored for years with a counting clock marking the time since the explosion.

◆

Men gather on the street in Saida that afternoon. It is sunny. I am afraid, but excited too, my friends and I exchanging raised eyebrows, mouthing *What the fuck* as the voices gather, a fire starts, cars honk. They are burning tires, they are shouting. A man catches my eye as he jogs past and slows down. He grabs Karam's sleeve. *You should go*, he tells him simply, *before it gets bad*. We are in the prime minister's hometown, these men are his kin, they are furious. It takes us several tries to hail a cab. The smell of gasoline, already everywhere.

We take the cab north to Beirut, the sea blurring outside the window, the cab driver listening and cursing at the radio the whole time. The cab driver drops us off downtown, because Karam wants to see where the explosion had happened. We can't get close and so we wander through the empty streets, a ghost town, the stores closed, the eerie sense of children without supervision, a city without adults.

✦

Seventeen years later, it is October in Brooklyn. Seventeen years later, our block is transformed for Halloween. Windows alight with orange blinking fairy lights, child-drawn witches and ghosts, or for the more ambitious, a full murder scene, a towering Frankenstein, a cloaked woman that cackles when you walk by. I watch the mothers pushing their children past the decorations in strollers.

"A cat," they tell them. "Is that a cat? Do you see the cat? What color is the cat?"

I watch them point, their children's rapt, solemn gazes. I try to imagine doing the same, try to record myself describing the neighborhood to the baby. *There's a couple that lives two doors down, the woman's pregnant. They have this dog, he's kind of the worst? He's always jumping up on you, then running around himself in circles. And he almost knocked the pregnant woman down the other day, and she automatically put her hand on her stomach and laughed. I sort of hated both of them for a moment? I don't know. There's a witch hanging from their stoop.*

✦

When the port exploded in Beirut in 2020, many first thought it was an Israeli attack. Some thought it was a foreign entity. The betrayal, the true betrayal, was learning it was your own. Your own politicians. Your own government. It was a self, cannibalized. It was a match, lit, and then tossed back into the room you were standing in.

✦

All month, my friend texts me from Beirut. The port explosion caused billions of dollars in damages. Hospitals were destroyed. In the year since, the economy has fallen. The revolution has faltered. *People are starving, Hala,* my friend writes. There is a circulated video of a woman with a shawl half-wrapped around her face, storming a bank in Beirut at gunpoint. She is robbing the bank for her own money. *I just want my money!* she is heard shrieking. The manager looks wan. The banks have been limiting withdrawals. *It's mine!* she cries when the man tries to calm her. *Give me what is mine!*

Later, it is revealed the gun was fake. A plastic toy. The woman got her money. It was for her mother's treatment. I rewatch the video dozens of times. I am disturbed by her. I want to be like her. Taking what is mine. The shawl falling. My face visible throughout. Not bothering to hide.

✦

When I remember my drinking, I see it refracted through places. Beirut is a city without curfews or oversight, a place where things can be bought off, where things can be erased if you have *wasta*, know the right people, accent the correct vowels. It is a city where neighbors slaughtered each other for fifteen years, where entire areas are Shi'ite or Sunni or Maronite, where people rarely speak of the war. For years, it was the backdrop of my drinking, my mistakes, my unease, my attempts to recover, a place of music and trash and bougainvillea, traffic that ate up entire afternoons, stunning views from house party balconies. A few weeks before I graduated college, Hezbollah took brief control over several neighborhoods in west Beirut, including my own. More than gunshots or my mother's frantic voice checking in daily during that week, I remember ice clinking in glasses, my friend's rooftop, how every night we topped off each other's drinks and listened to the upcoming summer hits.

✦

There are dreams I have that are more like muscle memory: it is always night, the streets are always empty, I am walking through Centreville with its glowing mosque, I am in the backseat of a car driving up the mountains, to my grandmother, to Meimei where I weep on a couch while she strokes my hair.

I don't think you understand, I told her in Arabic, *how bad I can be. What I've done.*

She shushed me. *There's nothing you've done that the morning can't fix.* But it was already morning. Dawn had broken and I'd woken her, and I kept telling her things, whisper-crying things as she hushed me, things I'd forget by the time I woke up, things I could never bring myself to ask her to remind me.

If there is any night in my life I wish I could take back, it's this one.

✦

Another technique in narrative therapy: you ask the client to tell the story in second person.

✦

One summer in Beirut, your father takes you to the balcony one afternoon and tells you the drinking is a problem. Only he doesn't say *drinking.* He says *what you're doing.* He is unable to even name the damage. Unable to speak it into the air. He says your siblings and cousins look up to you, this can't continue. You say nothing. It will continue. It will continue for a long time. You'd come home the night before at four in the morning. You are twenty or nineteen, and your knees are still bleeding through the Band-Aids from where you skinned them jumping a fence the night before. You don't remember the fence. You don't remember the blood. You don't remember shouting into the empty street: *God, I'm so bored* right after, then starting to cry. Your father ashes his cigarettes and waits. You don't say *drinking* either. You just tell him okay.

✦

During my doctoral program, I moved into a shitty apartment with roommates across from Penn Station. It was chaos. Take-out containers and dirty laundry. The muggy endless summer. House parties on Saturdays, spilling onto the outdoor patio, the arguments, the crying.

Someone was always crying. I took to making recordings while drunk, little anthropological notes, heartbreaking moments caught on tape. I'd plead with myself on the recordings. Talk about how bad it was. How I needed to remember. There was a bar downstairs and it was ruining my life and when I said that to my mother, she said *I* was ruining my own life, but my mother was thousands of miles away, in Doha where it was sunny all year round, and the houses were in compounds with swimming pools and gyms and palm trees. Not here. Not on this piss-smelling corner in front of that terrible bar, smoking a cigarette, watching the Madison Square Garden clock. Every time I came outside to smoke, the clock had sped forward. It wasn't fair. It was a Tuesday. I had work the next day. I was supposed to be at school at nine a.m. and it was already two in the morning. I'd record my quavering voice, watching the lights of Penn Station. It was bleak magic.

◆

The next morning I'd hear the slurred, heart-punching messages: *Hala, please, please stop. Hala, please, please, please.*

◆

My friend who lives in Beirut texts: *The hospital has four more days of fuel.*

◆

There was a brothel in Beirut. There was a man who ran that brothel. I would go there just to drink sometimes. One night, the man asked me to leave. *A girl like you shouldn't be here.* I turned mean. What did he know about a girl like me, what was he saying about the other girls, I slurred, waving my arms at the working women, but they barely turned at my voice. He insisted, his voice turning low: *Please, this isn't right.* We argued until he capitulated, exhausted, pouring me another drink, my victory feeling heavy in my chest. I wanted to keep arguing. I wanted

99

to tell him I was no Midwestern apartment complex, no hardworking mother, no table manners, no prayers, nothing. I wanted him to understand just how bad I was, how much worse I could be. I wanted to tell him that about the latent thing in me. I wanted to tell him that, my God, it had woken up and I couldn't put it back to sleep. But I could hear him mutter to himself as he turned away, *But what's happened to her that's she's here?*

◆

There is no story of the drinking without the story of the Bad Boyfriend. There is no story of the Bad Boyfriend without the story of the lies.

◆

I can't tell you that story yet, I tell the avocado-sized baby during a walk.

◆

I put up a pumpkin-orange wreath in Brooklyn. The lines in front of gas stations in Lebanon are hours long. Someone gets shot over petrol. Then another. Then another. There aren't antibiotics in the pharmacies. The country defaults on its loans to the World Bank, and the economy collapses. Whenever I think of my grandfather, his grave next to Meimei's, the grief is so sharp it must be dodged. So I call upon my old trick: I pretend he is alive. Sometimes I can pull this off, the blessing of ghorbeh, the distance, that tentpole of diaspora. Death can be ignored, so long as the Atlantic stays where it is, the miles in the thousands. Like this my grandfather continues to live in a building overlooking the sea. Like this he breakfasts every morning on pita and za'atar, Sundays on ka'ak and knafeh. Like this he drowns it in syrup, like this he spends his afternoons reading articles on his computer, like this he tells the neighbors bint binti is a writer in another country, that I'll be coming home soon, maybe even this winter. The same logic works for the entire country: like this Lebanon can live in its former iterations. The gas shortage, the exploded hospitals, the gunfights in traffic jams, I don't need to grieve them be-cause they aren't happening. This is my shameful luck, my lucky shame.

♦

In Brooklyn, I google Halloween costumes. In Brooklyn, I read about what a womb does in one month, two, five. I wake one morning to a Johnny that won't speak. He moves from room to room, red-eyed. He is silent in the living room. He is silent in the kitchen.

Please, I say. Just tell me what it is. You're scaring me.

He turns to fill his glass with water. Something about the moment feels familiar: turning away, the clink of the ice machine, slow motion until I realize that his back is crumpling. His shoulders shake. The glass nearly drops, but my body has moved to his body without realizing it, two bodies that have known each other for years now. Two bodies now clutching each other. I walk him to the couch and for the first time in months—for the first time since the sesame seed turned into an orange, an avocado—he pulls me to him and sobs. He sobs into my hair, my neck, my shoulder. Outside the window, the trees are orange and red, blurring fiery in the wind. For a quick, disjointed second, I miss my mother, her smell of leather and flowers, the silver box of jewelry she had in Oklahoma, the inside blue velvet, soft as a cat's tongue. I used to want to sleep inside that box as a child, two inches tall, resting my head against the amber of her necklace.

"What kind of father," he begins. He talks. He tells a story I've heard before, but it's the first time I hear it on this couch, in this month, where somewhere, a baby with his eyebrows and my ears is turning in amniotic fluid. Even with all those letters, long as an afternoon, the story unfurls in front of me as though for the first time.

♦

What happens to a story when you hear it? The touching it makes it yours, changes its shape. But some stories aren't yours, no matter how long you live inside them, analyze them, remember them. I could write a thousand poems about this story, and it still wouldn't be mine.

✦

One night I go to Dave & Busters with my brother and cousin Omar and their girlfriends. We are bored and nobody can come up with a better idea. Children ping around the space like comets, the persistent lights and bells of the machines soothing. While everyone is getting drinks, my brother's then-girlfriend, Yara, and I try the claw machine. She wants to know about the surrogate and I tell her everything.

"She has daughters," I say. "She always texts me during the doctor's appointments."

For our birthdays that year, Yara and I had gotten tattoos: a small matchstick on the inside of my right forearm, a technicolor red heart on her shoulder. I'd had a whole thesis about the matchstick: it could mean destruction or warmth, a reminder that the same thing can do both things, depending on how you held it, how you used it. When I asked her about the heart, she shrugged. "I think it'll look pretty." It did.

"I've only told Johnny so far," I say impulsively. "But I did find out the gender."

She squeals. "Tell me, tell me, tell me!"

I tell her and she cries and laughs and jumps up and down. I snap a picture. The photograph is blurred, the absurd candy lights streaking her face, her expression animated with joy. It is the first real joy I feel in a long time, a response to hers: this moment, someone unabashed with their excitement. Unwilling to apologize for it.

✦

In this story, there is a boy who lives in Massachusetts. He has a father and mother and brother. He goes to a private school, lives in a three-story house, summers in Maine and ski trips in Aspen. There are no bombs in this story. There are no prime ministers being assassinated, no evacuation ships, no passports being hidden in the bottom of a suitcase. There are no food stamps, no immigration officers mispronouncing a name. There is a father who disappears into himself for days at a time. There is a mother who adores that father. There is a boy, the youngest, who is bright and talented and loved and punished for those things in equal measure. There is a boy who is given one medication, then another, then another. There is a boy who drinks for the first time at thirteen, and never stops. For years, he dreams of leaving that house, the snow, the people who love and punish him in equal measure. Then one day, he does. He gets on an airplane and goes to country after country, with a dusty backpack and worn-out sandals, places with names he beats his tongue against until he gets it right, until he says them perfectly, until he can ask for water and bathrooms and then explain his thoughts, the texture of his dreams, in another language. He goes from city to city, living on the beach, eating fruit from tree branches, spending hours under the sun. He decides not to die.

◆

My final year in Beirut, I meet a man named Daniel. He is Irish and Egyptian, and speaks in lilting, musical tones. He drinks as much as I do. His mother is dying in Dublin, and we spend nights closing down bars, then kissing in the street. I once forget a necklace at his house, and he carries it around for weeks before we see each other again.

◆

The boy travels for years. He goes to Seville and Costa Rica and Mexico and Chile. He gets a job doing it. He takes other boys and girls on trips, even though he is barely twenty, twenty-one, he takes teenagers to cities across a different continent, scolds them to listen to the local guides, laughs at their jokes, does head counts before excursions. One trip, in a new group of kids, the boy meets another boy, a few years younger. His name is Taylor. They play guitar together. The years between them feel like a chasm, but really they are both children. They both need protecting from what's to come.

♦

Every time Daniel offers me affection, I flinch. I cancel dates. I pretend I don't care when he dates a Lebanese bartender. One night, we spin on a dance floor and then he asks me to look at him, *just for one second, love,* without looking away. I can't do it. My eyes dart like fish. I leave Beirut. His mother dies. The worst nights in Manhattan, the ones that are the coldest, when the drink seeps into me like possession, when I can't stand for more than a minute, when I can't speak a full sentence, he's the name I whisper against dive bar bathroom sinks, as though I could invoke him.

♦

The boy takes the group of teenagers to a small town in Mexico, where there are trees and hills and a group of Mexican children. This is part of the trip, rich American teenagers playing with Mexican children, hide-and-seek and tag. Taylor is the first one to start a game, the children giggling around him. He tells them to chase him. He disappears between the trees.

♦

There are two ways to tell the story that is not my story. There is the story of the children, who chase after Taylor, this boy with parents and an older brother, this boy who lives a thousand miles from here, who plays guitar and piano, who will graduate in a year. It is a hot day in July. The children chase after him, they watch him run on his long legs, watch him turn back, give a broad smile, then jump behind a large tree.

♦

I was two years into Manhattan. We kept missing each other: when I was in Beirut, Daniel would've left the week earlier. Daniel was in

London, but I'd just flown back to New York. It was early August when we messaged each other. He was coming to New York later that month. He had a birthday party. He turned twenty-five in Dublin. It was a warm night. He was smoking. He sat on a windowsill. He leaned or he tipped. It was the first birthday he'd have without his mother. There is no other way to tell this story. He never came to New York. He fell. He fell and fell and fell.

✦

The other way to tell the story that is not my story: the boy. The boy who grew up with snow and money. The boy who left and decided not to die. The boy who is a few years older than Taylor, who has played guitar with him, talked about his future, the colleges he will go to, the music he loves. The boy hears screaming and then the children are running back, not being chased, they are running alone, crying out, *Se cayó! Se cayó!* and the boy is confused, shouting in English, then Spanish: Who fell? Who fell? But he already knows the answer, is already running to the tree, to the well that was hidden behind the tree, the impossible drop, the dark that will take days to mine, days to find the bottom, but before that there is the earth beneath the boy, his knees hitting it, his voice cracking as he begins to scream a name.

✦

Tell me what you fear and I will tell you what has happened to you, Winnicott wrote.

✦

It is October in Brooklyn. The avocado-sized daughter is four hundred miles away. The boy who fell to his knees in Pozos, Mexico, is panting against my neck.

"What kind of father," he says. The first thing he did after the falling was call Taylor's parents. He was twenty-two. He told a mother and father that their son had fallen. That they didn't know how far. They didn't know if he was still alive. For days, he spoke to police officers and journalists and medics. For days, he sat with a mother and father who waited for news, and when the news came, he was there. There was a father and he turned to the boy and asked, *Will we ever recover from this.*

Here is the crux, where two stories meet like rivers: two bodies in October, crying, two bodies that each fell in love with a person, with their history, the mirror they became. It took me years to realize we'd both loved boys who fell, then years to understand we'd learned different things from the fallings. About love, about grief, about the inevitability of one into the other. Here is the crux of our story: I wanted a child. He didn't. His reasons are as plentiful and vivid as mine. We came to each other with a wounding that wasn't ours, a wounding we gave each other nonetheless.

For the first time, pressed against his familiar salt and forest smell, I think: *She's going to be half me, and half him.*

✦

When people ask why I stopped drinking, I always say, *Because I knew I'd die otherwise.* I list the ways: I would fall out of a window while leaning to wave at someone. I would hitchhike with the wrong group of guys. I'd wake up not only to a strange man, but to him holding a knife to my throat. I talk about all the ways I had tried to die. This is the truth, but there is another one, one that I never talk about, which has just as much to do with love.

✦

My brother quit drinking in his twenties, too. Once, overhearing us talk about it, my father grumbled, *I don't know where you all get this from.* Nobody drank in his family, a lineage sprawling back to Gaza, to the villages that were dispossessed in 1948, generations upon generations living off the land, the sea, each other. All Muslim. Nobody drank, but there were stories of great-uncles, a wayward aunt, someone's grand-father who gambled everything away, a man who became so angry that he'd stopped another's heart. People who didn't know when to stop. People who wanted and paid for that wanting.

◆

What story can be built from a blacked-out memory? For years, I had fragments. Everything else would be a lie, conjecture, an attempt at guessing a life. Instead, I lived in montages: two days at the house of a stranger, who'd wake me just to give me more vodka, then watch me sleep. My finger tapping drunkenly against my own thigh. A gate I tried to scale. The meeting with the dean where I almost lost my scholarship. The mornings, always late, always guilty, always trying to remember: what had I said, to whom, where had I gone, why was my thigh bruised, to whom did I owe an apology. The night I showed up drunk at my friend Michael's house. What happened to you? he asked. I apparently replied, *Me*. I happened to me.

◆

I once went to a fortune-teller in Jordan. She was famous among the locals. I met with her for an hour and she told me I'd one day choose between two men. That's mostly what I remember. She said other things: that there would be planes and oceans I'd have to cross, lovers I'd have to choose between. She recorded the whole thing and gave me the tape; your guess is as good as mine as to where it is now. There was one other thing: she said I'd been a witch in a past life. She told me I'd died from either thirst or fire. That I'd burned myself up. She told me I was here now to make different choices. I was sixteen.

◆

The night of my twenty-second birthday, the last I'd celebrate in Bei-rut, I got so drunk I fell face-first on the pavement. My final months in

Beirut had a manic quality to them. I did not know how to leave, and so the leaving had to become necessary. I destroyed everything I could. I slept with the wrong people. I said terrible things. I fought. I saw the Bad Boyfriend again. I ripped clothing, I vomited inside cabs. I was making Beirut unreturnable for myself. For years, since the Bad Boyfriend, I spent most of my time with American boys. They were safe, disposable, always leaving, always drinking. The shifting tide of expats: the constant arrivals, how well it lent itself to longing, the constant going-away parties, the group shifting to make room. We drank ourselves incoherent on rooftops, balconies that overlooked bullet-riddled buildings. They didn't care about the messes they made, in bars, in taxis, on the street: it wasn't their city. I could hide under their cloak. In this way I was both inside and out, a local remade into an outsider.

That night, I turned twenty-two. My hair was dyed pink. I fell so hard against a friend's sink she heard it two rooms away. I ended the night cutting my friends' hair, and they cut mine. We did it like children at a sleepover, fondly, carefully. More, I kept telling them, more.

◆

Obsession is an illness of repetition. This was the task of drinking—an endless arithmetic. The hand outreached for a drink, once, twice, a thousand times, a loop.

◆

The next morning, I dragged myself to a friend's house for a miserable brunch. Halfway through I went to a bedroom alone. My face was scraped raw from where I'd fallen. My hair looked terrible. After ten minutes or so, the door opened. It was one of the expats, a few years older and from Massachusetts. His face was impossibly gentle.

"Can I sit?"

We sat at the edge of the bed in silence for a while. I knew it was over. My time in Beirut. The summer. My college years.

"You're lucky you have a pretty face," he said, and the tension broke. We both laughed, until mine caught in my throat. He put his hand on my shoulder, awkwardly, palm-first, and I knew he was trying to think of what to say. There were bad men, but there were other ones too. The other ones were always trying to think of what to say to me. They tried to cut me off, wrestled me into cabs, poured me water. He and our friend Michael had taken me to the ER once. They convinced the doctors not to call my parents. He'd forced me to go home the night before my GRE. I can see our reflection in the mirror, mostly out of view: my scraped face, the tufts of pink, his hand against my shoulder, his somber face. *I'll remember this*, I suddenly thought. That, among the violence, there was so much tenderness.

✦

A place teaches you how to love. How to grieve. How to destroy. I never got to live in Palestine. I got the Midwest, a year in Maine, the desert, a near-decade in Beirut. When I left Beirut, I didn't just leave a city. I left what it had done to me. What its men had taught me, what they'd taken. What I'd given.

✦

I left Beirut for New York a skittish, cigarette-prone girl with no radar for danger and nobody I knew around for miles. I found an apartment two blocks from the Columbia campus, lived with two other graduate students. The first month, I spend the darkening days going from bar to bar, drinking the way I'd done in Beirut, dye my hair a purplish red, wear the same men's gray hoodie everywhere. I am here to study psychology, but instead I skip classes, sleep until the afternoon, dream of Beirut every night. I miss the traffic, the unlocked doors, the chaos. I'd left the city like I was fleeing it, but I couldn't sleep without its noise.

A few weeks into Manhattan, I go out alone to a Columbia bar. I meet a woman, a sculptor or something. There are two men, tourists.

There is a couple. I keep flitting outside to devour cigarettes. I haven't washed my hair in days. *I might be depressed,* I text my friend Dalea, who lives in Florida and keeps telling me to move. When I finally visit, I can't believe we're in the same country: her enormous apartment, the unrelenting sun, the flip-flops and tank tops she wears to class. In Manhattan, the weeks blur into endless flights of stairs in subway stations, slushy crosswalks, missed 1 trains, psychology professors who speak about happiness unironically. I argue with one of the men in the bar about Palestine. The woman tells me I have interesting eyes, as though it's a fashion choice, but that I need to learn to put on eyeliner properly. I have one white wine, then another, then a third. I start feeling dizzy.

"I think I need to sit down," I tell the woman. Behind her, the couple are kissing. The bar is hot and the way the light is hitting the bar top is making me anxious. "Can I sit?"

That's the last thing I remember. It is a tampered tape, an erasure poem. I watch strangers kiss and then—shapes, blinking lights, my eyelids making sense of sun. There is a white ceiling. There is a scratchy blanket under my chin. I am alone in a bed. It takes me minutes to be able to sit up; I feel like I am upside down, moving through water. There are strange marks on my arms and thighs: rainbow-colored, dots in different colors, pen or paint. It will take weeks for them to fully disappear.

There is someone else in the apartment, a bathroom out of sight, the sound of water running. My instinct is to grab my phone, my hoodie, my shoes, dash down the long hallway, into a grimy stairwell. I walk down two, three flights of stairs, then a glass door, then pavement, then sunlight. I run down one block, then another, then cannot take another step. Something glitches in my brain, something shimmering and strangely colorful, and I realize that the line on the pavement is moving, or sparking. Two sanitation workers watch me.

"Late night?" one of them asks.

"Do you see this?" I mumble. It is the first thing I've said since waking and my tongue feels funny.

"What's that, sweetie?"

"She okay?"

"Just fucked up." He snaps his finger near me. "You need water or something?"

I shake my head. It takes a minute, but they eventually keep working. I call the first person I think of, my friend Andre. It is mid-morning, a weekday. He is in his apartment in D.C., his voice booming and familiar in my ear. I talk frantically about sidewalks and holes and shimmering lights.

"Hala," he says firmly. "I need you to look up. Look for the nearest street. What street are you on?"

I'm in the Bronx. I've never been in this neighborhood before. I realize my hands are shaking. I'm suddenly afraid I didn't run far enough, that someone is going to find me. But who? I remember the woman, the tourists, the couple. I hear him clicking on his laptop. He is finding directions. He's going to get me home. He promises.

"But the sidewalk. I don't think I can step on it."

"So maybe there's something wrong with the ground," he says amiably. "Or maybe there isn't. What we're going to do is assume that it's going to be like every other time you've taken a step, okay? The ground has been there. We're just going to remember that." He sounds conversational, casual. "So let's take a single step, okay? Can you do that for me?"

I take one step. The ground holds. I take another. He tells me what train to take and to call him when I get out. It is the 1 train. It is crowded, people headed to work, teenagers to school. There is a woman wearing a baby in a sling. She looks away when she sees me watching. The numbers blur by. I get out at 116th Street and call Andre back. He tells me where to turn, until I'm at the university health center.

There is a kind doctor, a litany of questions, and then she asks, "Is there anyone I can call?"

I open my mouth. I tell her about Andre in D.C. and Dalea in Florida.

She takes a breath. "Not your friends, honey. Is there a parent I can call? A family member?"

There is nobody nearby, I tell her. My parents are in the desert. My siblings too. My cousins, my aunt, my grandparents—Beirut. Everyone is thousands of miles away. It is the first time I really understand this and I start crying so hard she has to call in a nurse to help calm me down.

"Poor kid," I hear one of them say, and cry harder. I'm not a kid, I want to say, but I'm too busy wiping snot with my hoodie sleeve. There is a hushed conversation between them, another doctor who comes in and asks me a couple of questions, about sex, about if I'm feeling any pelvic pain, questions that make me cry harder. The three of them face me.

"We think someone put something in your drink," the first doctor says gently. "And we need you to go to the emergency room."

What is a story in hindsight? Conjecture, a guess. I don't remember how I got to the emergency room, just that there was a girl my age with me, a volunteer for a crisis center. I don't remember what tests they ran, just that the doctor said I could make a police report, but I'd have to get a rape test first. I don't remember the volunteer's name or the color of the doctor's hair or the color of the hospital gown, but I remember saying no to the rape test, even though they asked more than once. I said no each time. *I feel fine*, I said, and now, fifteen years later, I can't remember what the truth was. Only that, whatever the answer was, I didn't want to know.

✦

In the hospital lobby, the volunteer held my hand. We'd been together for hours. I never wanted to see her again.

"None of this is your fault," she says. "The thing is . . . it's not fair but . . . we have to watch out for ourselves. Girls, I mean. You can totally drink." She says this in a rush, so it sounds like one word. *Youcantotallydrink*. "But it just might mean that, like? Bad things are more likely to happen."

I smile at her. She is my age, maybe a year younger, but I feel decades older. She has shiny hair, a pretty coat. She wants to help. She is spending her free time doing this, meeting crying girls in hospitals, holding their hands, telling them it isn't their fault.

"Totally," I tell the volunteer. "Yeah. I'll stop maybe." She hugs me outside the hospital.

✦

I don't stop. The following year, I move to the shitty Penn Station apartment above a bar. It is named after a Shakespearean play. The bartender has long, sandy hair and reminds me of Dave Grohl, which reminds me of the Bad Boyfriend, but this one has kind eyes. I flirt with him and he wants nothing to do with me, except for one night when I black out and couldn't tell you what happened. This happens more and more, the blacking out.

One night, a homeless man blocks my building door. He tells me to look at him. *Something is going to happen to you*, he says when I finally do. He means bad. He means something bad. But something already has. For years, I waited for things to happen, and then they did, and now I couldn't stop the happening.

Every night. Every single night I tried not to drink. Every single night I failed.

✦

What kind of mother?

✦

And now? It is October in Brooklyn. Johnny's face buried in my neck. His own question: *What kind of father*. The grief between us cracks open and in that overture something in me revs to life. Here is the thrum I move easiest to: the excitement of misery, the somber hit of a crisis. I become obsessed with help. For two weeks I research therapists.

I calculate costs in a spreadsheet. I call ketamine clinics, rehab centers, addiction psychiatrists. I feel Johnny's unhappiness in my bones, as my own. I call between patients, on my way to errands, with the same rush of a first sip. I will fix it. I will fix everything. I imagine us in the waiting room of a swanky rehab, drinking orange juice in a beautiful courtyard in Arizona or Wyoming. We would talk about our lives. Our miscalculations. We would talk about our drinking. We'd spread our mistakes out between us like a picnic. We'd finally understand. The receptionists are confused when I call. There are long holds. Who is the patient? Who am I calling for again?

◆

One of the psychiatrists listens as I breathlessly speak for an hour. I've gone ahead and scheduled an appointment. I'm in his stuffy office, only I'm telling Johnny's story. I talk about his childhood. His father. The boy who died. I talk about the pills, the drinking, dropping thirty-eight years at the doctor's feet. Help him, I say at the end. Please.

The doctor grimaces. I can see something on his face. My stomach drops. It's worse than I thought.

"And you?" he asks.

"I'm . . ." I look around, confused. Had I misunderstood something. "I'm sorry?"

"Okay." He scoots his chair forward. "Has your husband said he wants to get help?"

I feel my shoulders tense. "Not yet, but I think—"

"Mm," he talks over me. "And do you think—I mean *really* think— that it's something he's ready to do right now?"

His question is a blade. I think of Johnny saying, "You're still trying to change me," think of everything he's told me. I feel myself shrink into the couch. My voice comes out small. "No."

He sighs. He says he's going to tell me something. I hate when people announce their announcements. I wait.

There is a kindness in how he looks at me. Solemnly. "If you're not careful, then *this*," he says slowly, waving vaguely at the room, the city, the man somewhere in that city, my own frenetic body, "is going to cost you *your* sobriety."

◆

The last night I was alone with Daniel, we went drinking at a bar in Gemmayzeh. Its sign was neon and red. A drunk British woman kept saying we looked in love. We laughed her off. My stomach flipped. She was outing me in a way that sex hadn't. But Daniel was drunk and so was I, and we kept drinking, and we looked at each other and for a second everything slowed down. We didn't say a word. His mouth softened and I knew he was about to speak, about to say everything. I looked away, ordered another drink. The moment broke. After he died, I thought of that night. How nobody on the planet would know about it. That lady. That rush of mezcal. How it was just me and my memory of it. Nobody could fact-check me. Just me and my memory, growing larger and un-rulier and more different every passing year.

◆

The night after the psychiatrist I go to bed spent. I have lists and nobody to give them to. I think about the doctor and the fortune-teller. I think about the meetings. The slogans. An avocado. The attempt to control is just an attempt to protect. But we hurt anyway. Trying to control the hurt only makes it hurt worse.

In the morning, I wake with a fever.

◆

There are doctors. An urgent-care visit. My urine is clean. The ultra-sound is clear. My lower back aches. The fever rages. My breath catches. The second doctor refers me to a third doctor and the third doctor tells me sternly to go to the ER. The IV bag reminds me of Beirut, alcohol poisoning, unimpressed doctors. *I have this sickness*, I once wrote in a journal. Everything reminds me of something else.

✦

A fever is its own kind of intoxication. I am fuzzy with heat. I cry from pain when I pee. I fall asleep nauseated, then wake craving my grandmother's lentil soup. I'm convinced she is in the other room. Johnny orders some for me, but it isn't what I want, and I weep as I eat it. The Styrofoam container, the plastic spoon clicking against my teeth. I watch a television show about a woman with a daughter, then half-dream that I'm talking to my own. The fever maddens me, wrecks me, ices my bones then sears them. I have spent myself like a bad check and there is nothing left but this tired fire.

✦

I have a cyst on my ovary. It has happened before. After the last miscarriage, I had grown one. I liked this language. My ovary grew the cyst like a rose, like I'd planted it there on purpose. It ached when I coughed or moved too quickly. My third trip to the emergency room, the new doctor takes inventory of my symptoms: back pain, breathlessness, urinary symptoms. Blood work clean. The fever is the outlier, she says. But she has a question.

"We'll check, of course. But. Are you sure you're not pregnant?"

I don't mean to laugh. I laugh so hard a nurse pokes her head in. I laugh so hard I start to cry a little. The orange. The avocado. The crying hardens. I think of the hours I've spent making the wrong lists. Not cribs or names, but doctors and rehabs. Wanting to fix someone that hadn't asked for it. Someone that had asked only for an afternoon, to be held while he cried. The pregnancy test they run is negative, of course. But later, I google the symptoms and she's right. I have all the symptoms of someone in their fourth month of pregnancy.

◆

They never find out the cause of the fever. *Fever of unknown origins*, the medical records read. *HCG negative.* The MRIs come back clean, the tests, the blood work. They can't find anything. The carved pumpkins rot slowly on the neighborhood stoops. I keep rewatching the same episodes of television. On the show, the daughter saves the mother. The mother saves the daughter.

◆

What got me sober wasn't the concept of my own death, but Daniel's. In his death, in the ensuing grief, I could see my own. The falling that happened for years. *Because I knew I'd die otherwise.* He was drunk. He leaned or he jumped and twelve hours later my friends Sarah and Dana called me and asked me to sit down. I was in Manhattan then, that shitty apartment near Penn Station.

My professors, the clients at the substance use clinic I interned at, my second year of the doctoral program. Nobody knew. Nobody knew, as I talked about breathalyzers and harm reduction and explained stages of change, that I was in the trenches with them. "It must be hard," I'd say, but mean *It is hard.* I know it feels like you might not be able to change. Am I going to be able to change? The sessions were marvelous, disorienting places to be: I spoke to two people at once. I listened attentively to the patients' insights: what worked for them, what didn't, what they wrote on Post-its to look at each morning, their reminders for the people they wanted to be.

◆

The fever breaks as suddenly as it came. A good fire purifies, licks things down to their bone. The fever cleans me out. On Halloween, I stand under the moon with a glass of water. I leave it outside, because that's what the spell books say, because I don't know what I believe anymore, because I'm thirsty right then and there, because I want what I'm already holding in my two good hands.

✦

In the movement to decolonize mental health, the goal is true cultural humility—in giving power away, in collaborating, in naming hierarchies to try to dismantle them. In meeting people where we are, too. But before I learned this language, I felt it in my body: how my suffering was no different than their suffering. How my graduate classes and DSM codes were useful, but how people needed to find their own language, their own system of meaning. I had patients that relapsed and never returned. I had patients that were forced to come in through ultimatums: a furious partner, an adult child. They didn't often last long. People needed to want the change, or at least needed to be curious about it. People needed to have hope, even if it was the slightest ember of it, for a different version of themselves. Future Them needed to flicker in form, the slightest glow. We built our future selves from our present selves, I started to understand. Every day I didn't drink was another day I learned I was capable of not drinking. Every day I didn't drink was another grace for my future self. I never told anyone I was getting sober that year. I administered drug tests. I read breathalyzers. I asked people how much they'd drunk the week before. I asked them what it would be like to have a different life. I asked them if they were willing to have a terrible hour, a terrible day, a terrible week, in service of that different life. I took notes for their files. I took notes for my life.

✦

It was my mother I called after my last blackout. In that same shitty Penn Station apartment. I'd gone a month without drinking after Daniel. I cried like a lunatic in Washington Square Park, on the 1 train, in the back of classrooms. I went to open mics and read bad poetry. I went to churches, a Buddhist temple. When I prayed, I prayed that his falling had felt, briefly, like flying. Then I went to a party and had one drink, then another. Then another. I went on a three-day bender. At the end of those ugly, telescoped days was me: waking naked and shivering in my own bed at noon. I was alone. I couldn't tell if someone else had been there. I didn't want to know. I shivered my way through the hangover, my one, simple task hovering above me like a moon: make it until the evening.

Evening came. I was in my bed, the Christmas lights I'd hung the only light. I dialed my mother's number from instinct; she was visiting my brother in San Francisco from Qatar. We spoke about her trip, about the weather, and I burned in shame at the last few days, the memory-fragments that flung at me like spears.

"Your voice sounds strange," my mother said. She sounded suspicious at first. We'd always had a difficult time of it, she and I. Long, terrible years. Arguments that would erupt from nowhere. Too much alike or too much different, never sure which.

"Does it?" I'd never noticed before, but some of the lights were flickering a little; it made them look like flames. I thought of all the things I'd tried: the phone reminders to stop after three drinks, the pacts with friends, my broken, recorded voice begging me to stop, stop now. I suddenly knew what to do. There was a moment of enormous, shattering defeat that fell over me, which felt suspiciously like relief.

"Actually," I said. "I think I need to stop drinking." I was twenty-four.

She didn't ask why. She didn't lecture me. Speaking the words aloud invoked them, like naming a jinn. My mother didn't gloat. She got quiet. My mother. My body had belonged to her before it had belonged to me. My pain had always been an unbearable thing, even when I wanted her to bear it. She spoke as though she was in the next room, as though she was in this room, as though her hand was in my hair, my hair in her lap as it had been in my grandmother's that night. My mother said yes, yes,

I should try, I could always change my mind, but who knew, it might make everything better.

✦

A decade later, I walk across the East River after the last pregnancy scan, the one where the doctor tells me there is no longer a heartbeat. It is February, months before I meet the surrogate, before the poppy seed that turns into an almond that turns into an orange. It is February, and cold, and the water dances under the sun. I call my mother first. My mother, from whom I had learned the lists, the frantic urge to fix.

"I have to tell you something," I say.

My mother. From whom I learned to fix men, to leave cities, to have a temper, to have faith. I hear her take a deep breath, like an engine revving, with advice, with instructions to pray better, to keep hoping, with offerings of prayers and advice, then the breath hisses out. Not this time.

"I'm sorry," she says instead, her voice breaking. "Hala, Hala. I'm so sorry."

It is everything I need. She lets my pain land in her hand like a bird. She catches it. She holds it. It stays as long as it needs.

Month Five

In the fifth month, your baby is the size of a banana! Your baby is starting to turn from side to side, or even head over heels.

In the fifth month of pregnancy, the baby begins to sleep and wake. Noises in the world wake the baby. Dee and I text every day. We talk about our dogs. We talk about her daughters. She doesn't want to know the gender and so we say *Bud*. Bud is kicking. Bud is sleeping. There is a strange worry I'm starting to have, a desire for the baby to be a good houseguest. "Is Bud kicking too much?" I ask, as though I'll have a word with her. All I've known of pregnancy is misery, so I keep awaiting disaster. Instead, eyelashes grow when they're supposed to. Heartbeats get stronger. She turns and turns, like a ballerina in the dark.

◆

We go to California. We rent a beautiful house in Topanga, overlooking the mountains, and when I can't sleep, I watch the sunrise from the enormous windows. Our friends have come along, and I am grateful for their buffer, their endless uncorked bottles, their insistence on giving me a makeover. Johnny is warmer; there is drink after drink. He is laughing more, but I can feel my chatter like an extra limb. There is something glassy about my tone, easy to break.

✦

This country is always reminding me of itself. The highways remind me of other highways, the side streets, the flat-roofed houses of states thousands of miles from each other. There is something distinctly American about the neon 7 of a convenience store, the gray sign of a strip mall, the manicured lawns of a wealthy neighborhood. In California, I dream of the gymnastics school in Oklahoma, the cloud of chalk against palms, a woman telling me to try the balance beam, again and again and again, even though I keep falling.

✦

A question in narrative therapy: How would your younger self tell a story?

✦

Not the first America: that was before memory, before language. The one that came after: Oklahoma, Texas. Vine Street, where your parents buy their first house. The small bright kitchen, the cold garage. Your mother plants a rose bush in the front yard. She buys an actual picket fence from Home Depot and paints it herself: white as a funnel cloud. It's the nineties, the decade of bleached highlights and presidential blow jobs. But to you, it will be the decade of America. The first America. An America that feels more American than anywhere else. To you, America *is* this house. The longing of your mother turned manifest, turned brick and mortar. The half-decade of America that led to it. Stitched pillowcases on the sofa, the Palestinian flag atop the television. But the terrible wind finds you even in this house. What kind of land survives such wind? This land. The house doesn't have a basement and you're always nervously pointing that out to your parents. Your mother points out the tree in the front yard when they buy it, saying, *Look, a tree you can climb*, and you look around to see what other kid she must be speaking to. You are not the kind of kid who climbs trees. You once dislocated your shoulder reaching for a cereal box. You are the kind of kid that gives adults advice after they fight with each other. But you know what your mother wants: to belong to Vine Street, to belong to this house. To have an American child. To have done this one thing right. To build a new life. To infuse her English with a southern twang, even if it makes you wince. So you pretend to love the tree. You hop a little up its trunk, then pretend you sprained your ankle.

✦

I am in the bath when I get Dee's email. I'm making a point of doing this: the hottest baths possible. Weed. Sushi. It's the anatomy scan, the clearest photos I've seen yet. The nose, the heart. I can see the baby's organs. I see her spine and for some reason it moves me to tears. I had forgotten about spines.

✦

I look at the photos over and over. I look at the white parts, but also the black, the shaded part around the body: the fluid, the womb. Her first house. A house I don't share with her. A house I will never share with her.

✦

Our first houses in the Midwest were not houses at all. They were small apartments in ugly complexes. We received assistance from the government. The tufted blue couches, secondhand. My father watching the television in Texas, then Oklahoma, with other men, other Arabs they met there. This is the image I return to: men watching the invasion, then the burning oil fields, then the war, from thousands of miles away.

Their faces blued by that light. Decades later my brother and I talked about working on a screenplay together.

"In one of the scenes," he said of a character, "he'll be watching the news, his body outlined by its blueish light."

Something in me sharpened into focus. It felt unbearably intimate. As though we'd both been dreaming the same dream for decades, and never thought to share it.

✦

In California I go rogue. The bougainvillea, the clear sky. The Santa Monica mountains. The outrageous stars. On a trip to the vineyard, I take a sip of Yara's wine. I think of that doctor. It tastes like Beirut. I tell a shopkeeper I'm divorced. I tell a bartender I'm visiting from Spain. California feels like a bruise, like it always does. In my mid-twenties, I'd had a long, vivid dream about California. It was nighttime, I was in a laundromat, the gleaming white tiles making me terribly mournful. There was a neon sign above the laundromat, and I was outside again, I was walking through the streets, I was under hundreds of palm trees. It was too late for me. I'd missed California. I'd never live there; I woke up unspeakably sad, aching with all the lives I'd never have.

✦

In the Oklahoma airport in 1990, my aunt Reem took me to the bathroom. In the stall, she kicked my leg gently, smiling with anticipation. I remember this perfectly. I remember not knowing what she was doing. More than anything, I remember somatically: that visceral awareness of knowing someone wants something from you that you cannot give them. Her face fell, its plain hurt.

My aunt had left for Oklahoma the year before the invasion. She'd been my favorite. My memories of her in Kuwait are always blurry, her white skirt mid-flare while she danced with me, her curls framing my vision. There had been a game between us. She would kick my shin gently, I would giggle and kick hers back. She'd left for America for her husband's PhD. She'd birthed Layal the day of the invasion, spent the first few days of her newborn's life not knowing if her family was alive, watching the news in a haze in the hospital.

She'd watched the invasion on the television, tracked our family's journey through infrequent phone calls in Jordan, Syria, Kuwait. I was wearing a striped T-shirt. I looked wary and nervous. *Like a little adult*, she tells me much later. *Your eyes. You kept looking for something.* She was certain I'd remember the game. She was devastated when I didn't.

I felt her disappointment in my bones. It was unbearable. What could I have understood about what was lost, at four years old? About war, and what was gone for good? What I knew in that moment was that adults needed things from children, too. And I would learn how to give it to them.

I would encounter that feeling of others' wanting hundreds, thousands of times in the coming decades. But I would never again freeze. I learned, quickly, fluently, how to give people what they needed. How to read them. This must be when I started to lie.

♦

I almost see a fortune-teller in Los Angeles. Instead I get a tattoo: three dots interrupted by two short lines on my middle finger. I'm scared of what a fortune-teller might say. I'm scared I might get a bad fortune, scared I might believe it. Besides, I don't want a white girl and crystals. I want my grandmother's living room: nice sofas covered in plastic, ugly fluffy blankets with brown rose patterns for the winter, Persian rugs, crystal lamps. I wanted the woman I'd met in Palestine, who'd read dregs for me, a fortune I forgot within days. I wanted the woman in Amman. Where are the tapes? Vanished. My life, its predictions read to me at sixteen: gone. You'll cross water, she'd said. I did. Don't we all?

♦

A question in narrative therapy: What is a story you never tell?

♦

Everywhere you went, adults told you secrets. There were some you told. There were others you kept. They sat in your mouth like animals that won't be coaxed out. They remind you of embroidery coming loose, a run in a pair of panty hose—stayed by your quiet mouth. One pull and everything comes undone. These are the secrets you forget over the years. You forget them because remembering is too hard—the singe of someone else's pain—and sometimes you are on the R train or someone says a name you haven't heard in years, and you are eight or twelve or fifteen again, your hands going slack with remembering. You didn't ask for these secrets, but they are yours now. Some of their owners are dead. Some have forgotten them themselves, truly forgotten, which strikes you as deeply unfair. It's always like this with you. Once, you asked someone if they still dreamt of diving and they looked at you like you were insane, like there had never been a dream-cove or dream-death or their husband sleeping with another woman waiting for them when they woke, like they'd never cried to you in a drive-through, while you waited for paper bags of greasy food. The dream is yours now, like an abandoned cat, yours to remember.

♦

The first time I was caught in a lie: it was first grade and my mother was picking me up from school in Oklahoma. There were a few lingering children in the classroom. Everything before and after the moment is gone. Then: the shame of the moment burning a hole in my consciousness, three decades deep. One of the boys sitting on a desk, his legs dangling. He asks my mother, "So she does have scorpions?"

My mother's blank face, looking between the boy and me.

"She has pet scorpions? At home?"

I remember my mother's expression. I remember how quickly she understood. I remember how she muttered in Arabic to me, *This is what you've been telling them?* before turning to the boy.

"Well," she says. "Yes."

I remember the flush of my relief, the gratitude at her loyalty. I'm sure she yelled at me afterward. I'm sure I paid for it. But in that moment, she saw my face and she let me save it.

◆

In California, the bougainvillea is like shaken hair. When Johnny drinks, he speaks. It is warm and we sit at wrought-iron tables on sidewalks, in beer gardens, the deck of the rental house. I long for the tilted bottle, for someone's open mouth to catch it. I long for the spill of his laughter.

◆

What is a story without truth? I can always tell when someone is lying. For years I counted my lies like seeds: they grew into sprawling things in other people's yards, things I had to keep an eye on. That level of shamelessness, that *commitment* to the bit, is preternatural. My lies had lies. They wandered off, they outsmarted me. In college, a guy I knew gathered our group to tell us of a horrible car accident, his brother's injury. I felt nauseous, a tingle in my teeth. *Bullshit,* I thought. But I stayed silent. To reveal it would be to reveal something about myself. *How do you know?* people would've asked.

The truth came out later. The brother visited. Someone mentioned the accident. What accident, he said. My friend's panicked face, rushing to change the subject, the way it flushed red, someone caught. It made me shudder.

◆

In college I sat in an auditorium. The Bad Boyfriend played a guitar solo. His fingers flew across the strings under the stage light. Afterward, his eyes scanned the audience. He never found me. He spoke into the microphone: *That was called "Succubus."*

This was after the breakup. Before the phone calls began.

Afterward, the Bad Boyfriend asked if I liked his song. He was smirking. I couldn't say no. I nodded, as though it was his fingers guiding my skull up and down.

◆

When Meimei died, we were told to lie. She died on a Monday and my aunt's wedding was that Friday. My parents, my grandfather, uncles were in Lebanon and called my siblings and cousins and me. *She doesn't need to know yet*, they said. *Meimei will be dead for a long time.* When I protested, my father said, *Let her have some joy. Let her dance. The truth isn't going anywhere.*

◆

This can be the truth: soft as unbaked dough, pliable and tame. My great-aunt, ailing with Alzheimer's in Syria: her husband has been dead for over a decade. Every time she asks, they tell her, *He just called. I'm sure he'll call again later.* The lie is a good soldier, the first line of defense. Held in this light, it is a gift. Are we entitled to the truth if that same truth will maim us? Stop our heart? My aunt never danced at her wedding. There never was a wedding. We told her and she spent that Friday cloaked in black on her mother's balcony in Lebanon.

◆

Each story is flint for the next one. You can't tell the story of Johnny without the story of the Bad Boyfriend. You can't tell the story of the Bad Boyfriend without telling the truth.

◆

I've been forbidden to tell this story.

◆

We'll call him Saif. Saif because it means sword, Saif because none of the letters are in his actual name. Because, decades later, I'm still protecting him. The boyfriend with the clouds. The boyfriend with two names. One I called him and one that was his. Saif because it's neither of them.

◆

Eight years after I graduated college, well after I'd moved to New York, I went to a house party during a summer visit to Beirut. I had stopped drinking by then, and had the nervous habit of chain-smoking around drunk people, to keep myself busy. I met a man—handsome in that curated, self-satisfied manner of some Lebanese men—who'd gone to college in Canada. We flirted and complained about Beirut, its smallness, the way it could feel simultaneously irrelevant and all-consuming. He asked about my history, my travels, when suddenly his face changed.

Wait, he said. *Did you know someone named Saif?*

I felt the animal in me go alert, ears pricked at the sound of his name.

Yes, I said reluctantly. I did.

He let out a sound, the love child of a whistle and sigh. He looked at me again, but this time differently.

I know you, he said. *You're that girl he dated.* He could've been talking about a sitcom character. He wasn't in the conversation anymore; I knew that look. He was amassing a story, cross-referencing what he'd heard with the person in front of him.

I don't need to ask what he knows. I don't wonder how even eight years and the Atlantic Ocean haven't erased a bad reputation. I shrink back into myself, lifting my hand as though protecting my solar plexus.

Meanwhile, he has recalculated me. There is a new conclusion. He leans in hungrily, his shoulder brushing mine. *You want to go back to my place?*

♦

In college, I called Saif a different name, after a famous drummer, because he had similar eyes and a band. Our friends started calling him
that as well. We met at freshman orientation or, no, I first saw him then.
We met later. I liked his skateboarder's slouch and floppy hair. He spoke
with a perfect American accent; he played guitar; he loved poetry. I'd
had a deeply sheltered adolescence and was newly unfettered for the first
time in my life. The freedom was dizzying. There were no curfews, no
rules, no eyes on me. Having never learned moderation, I spun to ex-
cess. Saif and I didn't meet; we consumed each other, a spectacle that
broke apart our friend group, leaving a trail of emotional casualties. We
exhausted everyone. But there was the normal magic of first love, too:
we'd eat burgers with a ridiculously good green sauce from a restaurant
on Bliss Street, wander through campus telling secrets. We were both
clumsy and new and romantic, with bad idols. The relationship lasted
for half a year, maybe a little more. It took nearly seven years to recover
from the fallout, and by then I had met Johnny.

♦

I lied to him about not being a virgin. I've never forgiven myself for
this small theft. Why lie? He was a virgin too. Why would I rob myself
of a first, the vulnerability of meeting Saif in *his* vulnerability? Beirut
then isn't Beirut today. The girls who had sex were known by name.
The boys talked. The girls talked even more. But mostly I wonder if
he'd have felt a responsibility for what was to come. If the same cultural
laws that would destroy me could have protected me. If he'd known,
would he have felt the need to keep me out of the mouths of others, as
the aunties say. Would it have kept everything that was to come from
happening?

♦

I hurt him too. I feel it important to say this. I don't know why—perhaps as a way of reasserting authorship, of controlling the narrative: he hurt me, I hurt him, ergo equivalence? Or maybe it's something quieter. That he had been my first love, and I'd been certain he'd be the last. That in moments I can feel a very real tenderness toward him, a tenderness I hate and love in equal parts, because it represents my own capacity for taking perspective.

I lied to him about everything, or nearly everything: about past relationships, my whereabouts, the music I liked. I stayed up all night doing drugs with a friend of ours, a man I knew was in love with me. Meanwhile Saif stayed across the street in my apartment, watching the light in the balcony. Our breakup was nasty and inconsistent. We'd have public arguments. He once tried to set my miniskirt on fire because I'd been dancing with another man.

I started dating a white guy soon after we were through. I'd walk hand in hand across campus with the white boyfriend. I kissed him when Saif was watching. He had broken my heart and I wanted him to think I didn't care. I wore pastel dresses and kept my eyeliner heavy. The phone calls started soon after.

✦

Halfway through my sophomore year, my mother called me at eight in the morning. She was visiting from Qatar, staying with my grandparents. She sounded frantic.

"Where are you?"

I hesitated. "Home," I lied. My white boyfriend was curled beside me. He pawed at my waist. "It's really early, Mama."

"You think I don't know that?" Her voice was like a tack. I woke up.

Shoo fee? I whispered in Arabic, scooting to the foot of the bed.

"You know what's wrong! I need you to tell me right now. *Everything*. If you've been doing something bad, I need you to tell me."

I mentally reviewed my catalog: blackout nights, a slacker's approach to classes. The white boyfriend burrowed under the blanket and I added him to the list.

Hala!

"Mama, nothing!" I could hear the guilt creep into my voice. "Just tell me, what is it?"

"I got a call this morning," she said. "Then your grandfather got one too."

I breathed out my relief. It must've been the phone company. I wasn't great at paying bills. "I'll call Alfa."

Do you know what people are saying about you?

I opened my mouth, then closed it.

"I need to know right now, who you've been dating? How far have you gone with them? Do you have any idea"—here she shuddered, her voice breaking—"what you've done to us?"

She had gotten a call from an unfamiliar number. It was a woman's voice, middle-aged. The woman asked if she was my mother, and when Mama said yes, the woman made a spitting sound. She called me name after name. She said I was sleeping with half the men in Beirut. My white boyfriend peeked an eye open, blew me a kiss. He was my second. He kissed my temple as we fell asleep and told me he loved me. The woman told my mother that everyone who knew my name wanted to spit it out. *Your daughter's reputation is dead.*

"Mama, wait—"

There was more. The woman had hung up on my mother. Ten minutes later, a man had called my grandfather and told him I was a whore. My grandfather—a man who'd been a political prisoner for months, who'd lived through three wars and three displacements, who adored his first granddaughter, who'd carried her on his shoulders for knafeh, who knew her as his darling, his first daughter's first daughter—had nearly fainted where he stood.

✦

A story is like a match. It matters how you carry it. How you angle it to the wind.

♦

The phone calls shook my parents. Their life in Qatar meant I had rare privileges for an Arab girl: an apartment of my own, late nights out. I was able to take day-long trips to the beach with my white boyfriend, and had already learned how to lie well and frequently. I often snuck into the boys' dorms, drinking rum and watching bad movies until dawn.

My life changes within days. I am moved into my aunt's house for the rest of the semester. My parents obtain a copy of my class schedule and call me several times a day. The white boyfriend moves back to America and tells me to join him. I don't. He says my parents can't do this. I reply less and less to his emails. I stay in Beirut. My phone is monitored. There is talk of pulling me out of university, transferring me to a college in Doha. There is a lot of talk in those weeks, long conversations where my mother cries and yells, where I am referred to in the third person and she asks rhetorical questions about her mistakes as a mother.

"She's ruined our lives," my mother tells my aunt one night. I am sitting next to her. "She's dragged our name through the mud."

It takes me a very long time to realize the damage of these months. To understand that the response to my being threatened was my being punished. I was responsible, the implication went, *because* the peril was so high. The very horror of the threats was evidence of my fault, a circular sort of logic that left me squarely in the center of my own persecution.

This doesn't happen to other girls, my mother would hiss.

♦

I asked Saif if it was him. It was a late autumn night, and I begged him to meet me at our favorite bench on campus. He showed up late, an unlit cigarette behind his ear. He used to fiddle with guitar picks all the time, and the sight of the slender plastic between his fingers made me want to cry. I missed him. I missed something.

"There have been these calls," I begin.

He looks at me curiously. "Okay."

I stop and scan his face. He seems relaxed. His expression is open and unassuming. I find myself exhaling in relief. Of course **it wasn't him.** In that same split second, a sensation crept along the back of **my neck.** Of course I was relieved it wasn't Saif. He had held my head, carved lyrics into a bathroom stall, pinned a dead butterfly for me. He was often the last thing I thought of before I fell asleep and, I couldn't know this at the time, but for the next decade and a half, when I would be at a loss for a word or someone's name, his would be the one that would rise unbidden to my lips, like a curse or compulsion.

But if it wasn't him, the voice whispered, then it was someone else. Which meant somebody in the world hated me that much. To ruin my relationship with my parents. To wish death upon me.

"What calls?" he says

"Someone's calling my family," I say, feeling stupid. I don't want to continue. He already hates me, and I don't want him to know that somebody else does too. "Telling them. Well, telling them shitty things about me." I look him in the eye. "*Untrue* things," I say pleadingly.

He tilts his head. "That sucks. I'm sorry."

There is something true and kind in the *sorry*, and I nod. I want to ask him to get a drink, but we've rebounded before, sweeping each other up like crumbs. I'd promised my friends no more; a freshly broken heart is a tiresome thing to be around.

"Thanks," I say. "I'll see you around."

"Your parents must be so pissed," he says lightly, and there's the ghost of a smile on his face. The air crackles for an instant, but the smile is gone before I'm certain it's there. I turn to leave; some instinct pulls me back.

"Please," I say, hearing the desperation in my own voice. "If it's you. If it's one of your friends. Please make it stop."

♦

Johnny never lies. He tells the truth, and when he doesn't, he excises it, carefully and coolly. He is a collagist in that way, an instinct for editing born of avoidance and kindness; at worst, he trims the truth. In our first apartment, I made Johnny turn the lights off one night and I told him about the lies. Every single one. It took a long time. I shook with shame as I spoke, burning like a candle in the dark. But when the lights came back on, he was still there.

♦

The rumor started slowly. It bobbed from room to room across campus, then spread throughout Beirut like sludge. The rumor had his voice. It said that I had cheated on him. That I had slept with his friend. That I had brainwashed Saif, creating a rift between him and his parents, causing him to fail his freshman year. I heard it from a lab partner. From my friend's neighbor. Nobody seemed to know where it started, just that they knew it, as though it had arrived fully grown. One afternoon, a professor stopped me in the hallway and asked if I was okay.

"I just heard some things," he said when I asked why. He glanced around him. "But you're a nice girl, right."

It wasn't a question. *But you're a nice girl.* The phone calls continued. Saif stopped talking to me, unexpectedly and abruptly, like a faucet turning off. I would text him, accost him in front of bars. I'd started drinking more; it didn't seem to matter. Nothing I did seemed to matter. No matter what, the calls would continue. I would hurry through campus after sundown. I would examine the faces of strangers buying cigarettes in front of the main gate. Everyone was a threat. When I did see Saif, I'd ask if he'd heard anything about phone calls. He swore he hadn't, then went back to ignoring me. My mother hired a private detective. Other suspects emerged. An old friend of Saif's. A campus security guard. The seasons passed.

✦

There was no sex tape. There was no cheating. But it didn't matter. The intimation was worse than evidence.

✦

Saif calls me one night, months after the breakup. He is drunk and loud. I can't make out what he is saying at first.

"Tell me," he slurs. "Tell me I did."

Did what, I ask. Is he drunk, I ask.

"Tell me I made you come," he demands, his voice turning sharp. There is a muffled sound on his end. He makes a shushing sound. "Tell me how I made you come a thousand times."

There is the sound of male laughter. An explosion of voices. I catch a stray word. *Sharmouta.*

I hang up.

✦

My mother forbids me from telling this story. This is how she protects me. She knows what happens if you keep telling a story. She wants me done with it. Purged.

✦

The phone calls continued for a year. They would stop for months at a time and resume, like a phantom. I would think it was behind me, then get texts from my father quoting the callers. The callers said I was asking for it. They said they were sending a dozen men after me. They said watch your girl, we're going to get her. We're going to rape her. We're going to kill her. One of the callers said before hanging up, *You're not going to recognize her body when we're done with it.*

✦

In *Girlhood*, Melissa Febos writes, "What is a reputation but a story most often told about a person."

I told the story of Saif over and over after I moved to America. I became addicted to it. I couldn't believe we'd never found the culprit. I told my new white boyfriends. I'd stopped dating Arab men. The white ones felt safer. Sex didn't *mean* anything to them. They weren't trying to pin you to it. Your identity didn't revolve around having it. I told the story in bars and teahouses, outside nightclubs. The reaction was always the same.

"I don't understand," they'd say, shaking their heads. "It was him. Of course, it was him. How could you believe him?"

This was my cue. I'd sigh like they were cute. They *were* cute. I'd explain I had asked him several times. The bravest one was more direct. He interrupted my monologue. "You're still defending him," he said. That was all he ever said.

I thought about the songs we'd make up. The guitar-pick necklace he gave me. The way we mended each other too. I didn't know how to say all of it.

"He sounds worse than he was," I finally say.

✦

Saif braiding my hair. Saif pretending my body was a guitar. Saif planning a scavenger hunt for my baby sister. Saif telling me to shut the fuck up from the front seat of his friend's car, everyone falling silent. Saif kissing me on the beach the next dawn, apologizing. Saif pushing me against a closet. Saif's voice breaking on the phone as I told him I'd met someone else, the white boyfriend, hours after we'd last seen each other.

137

"We're broken up," I say and don't believe my own words, "you said you didn't want to get back together." He is crying and I know I've made a terrible mistake, though at the time I don't accurately guess which one. Saif kissing my knuckles. Saif smirking in the dark as his friend Qassem tells me not to speak. It is after midnight and I have run into them; Qassem is drunk. He hates me. I know he hates me because everyone knows. He is older than us by several years, and I have broken his little brother's heart. This isn't actually what's happened, but I can't tell Qassem that. I just nod and stop talking when he tells me to. His eyes are glassy and menacing, and Saif shrugs when I turn to him. Afterward he says, don't fuck with Qassem, he'll hurt you. Saif in my bed, fumbling in the dark. I no longer remember when this is, before what, after what, just that it is hot and airless and he is crying, he won't stop touching me, even when I beg him to stop, he won't stop holding me down, and I start crying too, and finally push him off, tumbling myself to the floor. That's it. Nothing else happens. I lie awake most of the night, my heart pounding, listening to him sleep. I never tell anyone. I still haven't.

◆

There was a bar in Beirut. It's named one thing but everyone calls it another. In the bathroom, my scrawled handwriting is still there, Saif's in response. In the most dishonest era of my life, I'd written, *The truth will set you free*. I liked how it sounded.

◆

The lies got worse with drinking. I can remember the electricity of certain lies, how I planned them like school outfits, or else their spontaneous tumbling out of my mouth, that split second of realizing I'd committed to something I'd have to keep alive for years. I found myself telling stories I'd later have to deduce, then face the terrible choice of outing myself or reaffirming the dishonesty. I had lies that outlived friendships. But the lies always had one thing in common: they pulled people in. A conjured grief, so that others would care for me. A wild fact, so that others would be magnetized to me. Something that refashioned me as different, outlier, tragic. A thousand tiny hooks, sent off in every direction. In recovery, they say you're as sick as your secrets. You're probably sicker than your pretend secrets.

◆

In some ways, the phone calls were the smartest thing a person could've done. They pitted me against my parents. The caller was a true scholar of the culture. The calls exposed me in a way I'd never recover from, no matter how hard I tried. And I tried. I tried and tried before I stopped trying, before I started to sink myself like a stone. The caller also hit the raw, inflamed nerve of misogynist cultures (which is to say, most): the honor of the girl. The daughter. The wife. The sister. In attacking me, he attacked all of us.

While the calls were happening, everyone involved was concerned about their reputation. My relatives. My mother. Fifteen years later, she still is. *What will my friends think, reading about it?* she wants to know now. I have no answers. My roommate at the time came home one day, saying she had run into Saif. She'd scolded him for talking so much shit about me. My heart rose. *I told him,* she continued blithely, *it's reflecting badly on me, and he needs to stop.* My heart dropped.

◆

My mother once asked, if I ever had a child, a daughter, how I would explain those years. She wanted to know how I'd explain myself. But this was before Dee, before the image of the spine. For years what I saw when I closed my eyes was a photograph of myself from my first year of college. My hair spilling over a notebook, fishnets torn, lace-up boots, so untough. So obvious. So certain nothing about her was worth loving and so she called upon those lies, her little army, her golden birds. I want to tell her to stop apologizing. I want to tell her that when the hurt comes—that it will come for both of you, you and the boy you love; that you'll be damaged by it, but you'll get hurt far, far worse; that I'm sorry; that I didn't make the rules—not to pick up the bottle. I want to tell her that my wish at nineteen—the one I'd make in hiccupping sobs—came true: he never did have daughters.

◆

The last call we receive comes on the heels of a series of texts. They are awful, sickening texts. *We have a videotape of your daughter. We're going to share it. We're going to send it to every house in Beirut.* My father calls me from Qatar and makes me go to a Lebanese police station. The officers grin and make me read the texts aloud to them, over and over. *What'd you do to this poor guy,* one of them jokes. He asks me out afterward.

I go home and throw up.

The following morning, I wake to my mother's frantic voice again. There was another call. This time I hang up before my mother finishes telling me. This time I reply to the number. I've been forbidden from doing this. All year, my parents, the detective, have said the same thing: *Never, ever reply.* I text scathing things to the number. You coward, I say. You pathetic coward. You asshole. Do you feel important, do you feel strong, doing what you're doing? How do you look at yourself in the mirror?

It'll take me a long time to understand that my only currency as a young woman in Beirut had been destroyed, systematically and deliberately. That without that currency, I was wrecked, but I was also liberated. But at the time, standing in that bedroom, alone, furiously typing, I only knew I owed myself this. I already knew my mother would be screaming when she called back minutes later, I already knew they would've told her I'd written them. I apologize to my mother. I apologize over and over to her breaking, angry voice.

I'm not sorry. Not even a little bit. I wasn't then and I'm not now.

✦

I'd tell a daughter that he shattered something between me and my mother—each, in a moment of crisis, failing the other—and that he shattered something in my relationship to my body. He took my trust in Arab men. He left me hungering for whiteness, for escape. I'd tell my daughter how nobody objected on my behalf. That it took me longer to put myself back together than to fall apart. I would tell her the worst part is I went back for more. That's how much I couldn't stand to have him hate me. That's how badly I wanted to fix everything. In research studies on abuse, the mistreated woman is more likely to apologize. I never could bear a bad ending.

✦

What kind of child lies about pet scorpions? What kind of girl steals everything she can get her hands on? In *Raising a Secure Child*, the authors write, "Behavior problems are not a demand for attention. They are a sign that the child finds the cost of revealing their true need higher than living with the painful consequences of their misbehavior."

✦

For years, I judged my younger self by the metric of an adult. My lies, the stink of them, their murk, haunted me. I was secretly convinced that I was a sociopath, or whatever my understanding of that term was. I swam in shame. If anybody knew, I was convinced, there would come something worse than rejection, worse than arrest. As a teenager, I'd been caught shoplifting in a mall in Lebanon, and it wasn't the security guard, my parents' fury, the mirrored room in the basement of the mall, that scared me most. It was metal detectors, which I suddenly noticed were everywhere, metal detectors that for years after I'd be certain I'd set off, long after I'd kicked the habit. My dread of being found out for lying was nameless and unending. The closest thing to the great nothing of abandonment I knew. I was certain the rejection would be celestial. I would be kicked out of humanity in its entirety.

This was how it always felt: my badness was formless, vast, an enormous and panoptic thing.

◆

In *The Annotated Arabian Nights*, Paulo Lemos Horta writes, "[T]hese tales are constructed around an imminent threat of violence, but they also showcase the power of stories to avert this threat." I couldn't control the story of Saif, but I could tell it. The phone calls couldn't follow me to America—a different place with different currencies—but I didn't know that then, and the not knowing meant they did.

◆

It only occurred to me much later. I once lied about a boy. I once lied about loving a boy. I once lied about death. Six years later, there would be a boy and an open window, and the boy would die. I lied about violence and later it found me. I lied about men's heavy bodies, their strong wrists, and they found me. I lied about love and spent years running from invisible men.

◆

I tell the pirouetting baby the story on a hike in Topanga. She is in Canada, I'm in California, Saif is in a desert thousands of miles away. I am alone, walking among the shrubs and birds, and I start recording: *I have other stories. I don't know if you'll want any of them. This is your history too*, I say, *these fallen boys, these bottles, these cities made in the image of our fathers. These stories are yours in a way too, have made you, because they've happened to those that made you.*

◆

I believed in my mouth. I believed in my ability to talk men out of their anger. I'd keep returning to Saif to disarm him. In Beirut, a cab driver once drove me south instead of north and then wouldn't turn around. What can you do now, he asked. It was after midnight. He already knew the answer. The question was rhetorical. There was nothing I could do at sixty miles an hour, on a highway, in the middle of the night. Instead, I asked him questions about his wife, his village, his sons. He named politicians and asked me what I thought of them. He turned the car around and drove me home. In Istanbul, I told a man in a hammam that I'd be right back. In college, a man locked a door and I pretended to look at his bookshelf, his photographs, the view from his balcony. Wait, wait, I'd say. Tell me more. I want to hear about his journalistic assignment, his travels, all the things he has to say.

✦

The last time I saw Saif, we sat on his couch afterward. Watched Gaza on his television screen. They will never stop doing this, he said. I don't know what I said back. I don't know, twenty years later, what I would want to say: in that room with my quiet mouth, my mussed hair, that room of men and violence, all that hurt, all the ways we were right and wrong about everything.

✦

The last time I saw Saif, there was an invasion in Gaza. There was white phosphorous misted on buildings like plants. It was my first trip back to Beirut after moving. I was three years into my drinking problem, and tried to act like I didn't care about anything. *I've been trying out celibacy*, he said afterward, and I saw he was as defeated as I was. Within a year or two, I'd hear he'd found God. Stopped shaking women's hands. He'd get married, have boys, become a school principal in the Gulf. I never see him again.

♦

When I ask my mother about my childhood lying, there is a long pause. She asks do you know something. I say I don't. *You didn't lie before.* Before what, I ask. But I know what she's going to say. Before the invasion. Before those weeks leaving my father behind. Before America.

♦

The lies scare me. Telling about them scares me. Will they undermine the other stories? Will they slowly siphon belief? Will I be forgiven if I forgive myself for my lies? Or is it the sort of thing you must repent for forever? Tell me. I can do either. I can do whichever one will make you love me more.

♦

I remember what month it was when my friend called me. December. I remember I was wearing a peacoat from Zara. She said she'd seen an old friend. They talked about the war, who had evacuated, who had stayed, who had never returned, about the old pubs we used to go to. Unlikely couples that had long broken up. My friend had mentioned me and Saif, the phone calls, the trip to the police station. The guy had tilted his head, remembering. He said Saif had gotten drunk once, during college. That he'd told him everything. How Saif's parents had helped with the calls. His friends. His neighbors.

My friend said, *After all this time.*

My friend said, *I thought you should know.*

♦

For eleven years, I believed what Saif had told me about the calls. For eleven years, I didn't know. That's longer than I have known.

What happens to a story when a crucial fact appears? Suddenly it changes, like weather. There is furious editing, a scribbling in, a revisiting of all the old sites. Now the worst part wasn't that I had gone back for more. It wasn't the years I lost to a mystery villain. It was that I believed him. I really did.

✦

In California, I tell the story again quickly, recklessly, in the Santa Monica mountains. It singes my voice. There was a boy. The boy made phone calls. It ruined me. Then I drank. It set me loose upon myself, upon a city. I never saw the boy again. I didn't forgive him. Then I did forgive him. It was worse not to.

✦

I look him up from time to time. There's a fishing line, tenuous and corroded, that still yanks me to him absently. I dream about him every few months. In the dreams I'm not angry, though my dream self knows I should be. I don't want a fight. I want an explanation. More than anything, I want to tell him. Say, I know it was you. Say, I know, I know.

✦

Mama, there's a spine now. I saw the photograph of it. I saw the outline of lungs developing so they can someday take a breath, a mouth to call for milk, giggle at a pigeon. Mama, I'll tell her that you have to be careful what stories you listen to. That if you're told you're something enough times, you become it. That if you tell a story enough times, you become it. I'd tell her that this was Saif's true legacy: he told a story about me and people believed it. He told a story about me and my parents believed it. He told a story about me and I believed it. I'll tell her about the theory of arson: that it isn't usually a single fire that burns the building down. It's one fire that lights another, then another, then the merging.

I'd say if you're going to regret telling something, let it be the truth.

Month Six

In the sixth month of pregnancy, your baby has hair and is the length of a ruler. Your baby's eyes are slowly beginning to open!

In the sixth month of pregnancy, babies can get hiccups. They have fingerprints. The same fingerprints they'll have for the rest of their lives. They have eyebrows. Eyelashes. Taste buds. This is the month that morning sickness stops for Dee. But her hands start going numb unless she constantly flexes them. I read along in the book about what to expect. I'm the audience here, I realize.

◆

There had been a winter where I had dreamt of the desert almost nightly. I was twenty-nine and something happened to me in late autumn: my mind started looping, my hands shook anytime I left the house. *You have a lot of trauma*, the therapist I saw told me. I didn't go back. Another: *Have you heard of complex trauma?* I hated those afternoons, the train I took to see the doctors, the cure I so desperately wanted and that eluded me. At night I dreamt in violent colors. I dreamt of a different kind of desert: purplish skies and black sand and lanterns. I dreamt of the house in Kuwait where we had left my father. We would wave at each other. I'd wake up crying. That winter, I wept everywhere: on subways, in Italian restaurants, crouching in line at the drugstore. I couldn't shake loose the image of saying goodbye to my father. Did I cry, I wanted to know. Did I seem scared. Stop asking these questions, my father finally said, softly.

✦

For years I didn't ask my parents for the story of our leaving. I didn't ask because I thought I knew the story. I lived it, after all. It felt strange to ask for what is already mine. But what is a story that you can't remember, that colors everything? It's only when I come to tell it that I realize I've never heard it. My mother doesn't want to tell the story. *I don't want to be in your book*, she snaps. *Pretend you don't know my name!*

✦

I dream of my stomach. I dream of my hands. I dream I am split open, my water breaks, I feel it so acutely it must be true. It is true.

✦

Within some Islamic traditions, a dream shouldn't be repeated aloud. Sometimes, the dream you dream could be meant for another person.

✦

I dream of a mouth at my breast.

✦

I dream of a daughter being born to me. I dream of a daughter born to another woman.

✦

If there is a house in a dream, you are the house. You are its broken windows, its chandeliers or strange carpet, you are the banquet, the doorbell that won't stop ringing, the music coming from—*where is that music coming from.* Carl Jung spoke of empty houses in dreams as the representation of the mind that needs to be explored.

◆

During the fever-filled nights, I've started dreaming again of desert, a bird that speaks my grandmother's name, "Seham, Seham," a book I open to find the baby's name. A name I forget upon waking. I dream of the squeak of packing tape, a room full of moving boxes, the muscle memory of my girl body. I dream of Oklahoma. I dream of a passport with my discarded name, my borrowed name—Holly—and a long drive up a Lebanese mountain to meet a woman who says she can change it. I dream of Alaska. I dream of Saudi Arabia. Places I've never been. I dream of Kyoto, my friend telling me the baby is here, I need to hurry. I dream of writing a poem, and I can only remember one line: *Reinvention requires departure, an absence to then fill with return.* I spend the hours-long dream chanting the line, determined to remember it, because the part of me that is awake, that is aware, knows I will want it later.

The fever breaks. I book a flight to Arizona.

◆

I sleep for most of the flight and wake right before landing. The landscape is unfamiliar, flat, ranch-style houses, stretches of red earth. In the taxi, the landscape blurs by: enormous saguaros, flat-roofed buildings, the sky settling into a winter sunset, pale red and magenta. The hotel is sprawling and too expensive, a ranch that was once an all-girls' prep school, with saguaros standing guard outside the rooms. My balcony overlooks desert. There is a discreet sign in the room warning of snakes. When I take a shower, I try to slow my breathing, calm myself. Even here, even among the rust-colored tiles, the orange blossom shampoo, the steam. It won't stop. I remember the spine. I say names aloud, her names, against the hot water. I wish I could take my self off like a coat. Just for an hour. Just for an afternoon. I'll come back, I want to promise.

◆

I ask for the story before I travel to Arizona. I am visiting my parents in Connecticut, where they live now. Where they live again. After twenty years—years in Abu Dhabi, in Doha, in Beirut—they returned to America during the pandemic. It is my father who begins talking. He starts with the night before—what they'd eaten, how we'd gone to bed early. We'd all slept in the same bed, even though I'd had my own room, with frilly bedsheets and toys. It was before dawn when the first sound rumbled outside. A thunder that was out of place. A thunder that was not thunder. We all awoke at the same time.

My mother interrupts my father, who quips, *I thought you didn't want to talk*. She falls into sullen silence, then interrupts again a few minutes later with corrections: It was two days before they went to my grandfather's house. The invasion was announced on the television, no the radio. The story is derailed by their arguing. They bicker. After her interludes, my father turns back to me and says, grinning, *Okay, now back to Scheherazade's turn*.

◆

I order a beer my first night in Arizona. It tastes different than the two sips of ruby-red cabernet in California. There is something dangerous about this beer: nobody will know if I drink it or don't. Nobody cares more than I should care, and I don't care. The not caring has come upon me suddenly. I am only as accountable as I will myself to be, and I will myself on the balcony of a desert resort, lifting a frosted glass of beer foam to my lips, washing down chipotle shrimp tacos and guacamole.

◆

My first night at the resort, I sweat through the sheets, then shiver when I turn the heat down. I dream of my own life, of Johnny: the wine bottle we used as a rolling pin in our first apartment, the bouquet of flowers he bought me in City Hall. The lace of water rolling around our legs in southern France. There had been a time we'd go to bed at the same hour. I couldn't remember when that had stopped. I dream of our first sheets, maroon red, the canopy net above our first bed. In that first apartment, we kept a jar of sequins on a windowsill. I can't remember where it came from. Johnny stitched the curtains himself. He'd surprise me with trails of rose petals from the long hallway, red velvet cupcakes and posters of Beirut. I had no idea what I was doing back then, with him, with love, was just a skittish girl with an ugly story. *You have a video game heart*, my friend Olivia once tells me. *You have a heart that keeps regenerating*. It's true. It is the only part of me that is patient and I'd brought it with me: my pulpy, eager heart. All one thousand lives of it.

✦

It was just after four thirty in the morning. My father knew this because the first thing he did after the noise, after the non-thunder, was look at the clock. The sound was whooshing, like air being gathered backward. It was the sound of fighter jets. They turned all the lights on. There was nothing on the television yet, no news report. Only an eerie silence outside the windows. He was young when they'd left Palestine; he didn't know how to place this silence yet, the held breath after a loud sound. He told his daughter to return to sleep, and settled in front of the television. It took thirty minutes, thirty minutes for the monotonous, official tone of the Ministry of Defense to crackle on. (Who is the voice of the Ministry of Defense? he wonders. Is it decided ahead of time? The voice that will clear itself in case of disaster, deep and sturdy enough to hold a nation steady, to contain its panic.) The voice repeated the same line, over and over again: *Iraq has invaded the borders in the north. Iraq has invaded the borders in the north. Iraq has invaded the borders in the north*. My mother was five months pregnant with my brother, Talal. I had turned four exactly one week earlier.

It was a Thursday, my mother reminded Baba. What does that mean, I ask, but she is looking at him, she is looking past him, she is remembering. Thursday means she didn't work at the bank that day. It means she was at home with me, and so my father had showered and dressed and left the house alone. He had driven toward the bank where he worked. There was something skittering about the way the cars moved. The Ministry of Defense released another message: the invasion is only in the north. The borders are defended. There is no cause for alarm. He drives through Salmiyeh neighborhood only to find a roadblock, a tank and some soldiers redirecting traffic. The military, he thinks. Of course. Tightened security. A soldier gestures for him to roll his window down and he does. *Allah ysa'adak*, the man greets him. All men in uniform look the same. But the greeting gave it away. Iraqi.

♦

In the Arizona desert I awake afraid. The fear is something unnameable and bodily. Alone but more alone than alone. Scared but more scared than that. It is the first thrust of a plane in the air, the suspension right before something crashes to the ground. No, it was another dream I'd been having: bodies that lean into windows. The spark of their cigarettes. The falling that lasts a long time.

♦

Were you scared, I want to know. My father waves these questions away. I couldn't believe it, he answers instead. The Iraqis were already here. They were in the city center. They had taken over its streets. They were directing traffic. What my father hadn't known, what most people hadn't known, was that the small Kuwaiti army had been given their own instructions earlier in the morning: put your weapons down. Dress in civilian clothing. Surrender. Only it wasn't a surrender as much as a complete reshuffling. The Iraqis were conducting the city by daybreak. It was like the city had already fallen. Like there had never been a time it wasn't theirs.

✦

The cold is different here in Arizona, bracing, sudden. I need a coat after sunset, the same one I wear in Brooklyn. Even during the day, in the warmth and sun, there is something I cannot escape, an internal winter. It doesn't matter how much I resist it. It doesn't matter that I buy hot tea and drink it as I walk through the Tucson campus. It doesn't matter that I hike through saguaros and pretend it's the middle of summer. My body knows what it knows.

I spend the days bopping around like that nineties battery bunny—turquoise jewelry shops, an Indigenous museum, vegan bakeries—and my evenings lying in the hotel room watching terrible television. But at night, the fear returns. The desert outside the window is infinite.

✦

I love the desert. Or maybe I love the memory of the desert, the romance of it. It moves me like a good poem. You cannot cling to anything in the desert. Everything prickles. The sand rewrites itself after every rain, every wind. I write the names of desert plants in my notes, even though I know I wouldn't call a daughter *Aster* or *Reza*. *What about Sabr*, I text in the family text group. *It means patience* and *cactus*. *What about Chill*, my brother writes back. *It means cold* and *laid back*. It takes me a minute to find the middle finger emoji.

✦

My father used to sing me a song. It was about praying for a baby with my name. Let the baby be nice, he'd say. Let the baby be nice. Evenings in the hotel, I flip through the images of her heart, lungs, kidneys. She has kidneys. *Bring us a baby named Hala*, my father would sing, and my chest would soar, because he'd asked and now I was here, the thing he'd asked for. I sing the song into the recorder, but stop short of the name. There is a silence. I listen to the whirr of the HVAC, which means she, through placenta and womb and skin, listens to the whirr of the HVAC. *I don't know what songs your father will sing you,* I finally say. I am surprised to find that I've started crying. *He'll sing you something. I promise. But I'll sing this one for you. I'll sing it to you in the right language.* I'm speaking to her in Arabic. This is what I've started to do in the recordings: everything in Arabic, until I forget a word, then the English dashes in, always eager, always ready.

✦

I don't know if I love the desert or my father loves the desert or what, if anything, is the difference.

✦

This was all underwater once. Of course it was. The scraggly plants. The moony rocks. In the artsy stores, I introduce myself by the names I've been rehearsing for her: *I'm Aya. My name is Zeyn.* They're all correct; none of them is. I want to name her after the night, or more precisely, the dusk. The dusk in the Gulf, vaguely mirrored here in the Sonoran Desert, my favorite time of day. My favorite kind of light: crisp and unambiguous. I walk and walk the land and my eyes drink.

✦

Kuwait fell the way most small nations fall: quickly, soundlessly. The Kuwaiti dinar plummeted. Iraqis filled the city, not just soldiers, but civilians, tourists, people who had come to shop the broken, cheap currency. For ten days, my parents split their time between my father's family house and Jiddo's house. One of the first things the Iraqi army had done was knock out the telephone lines. There was no way to contact each other, and so they stayed together. Back and forth they went, between two neighborhoods—Salmiya and Fahaheel, night after night. The men spent the evenings smoking, the women talking. They watched the news. They played cards. My mother let me sleep on her lap, in the living room, surrounded by adults. There are theories: the Americans are coming. There are opinions: the Iraqis won't be here for long. They plotted and theorized, talked about which borders are easiest, which cities are most livable. Leaving still seemed impossible, though more and more people were leaving. Professors and doctors and politicians and engineers. Their neighbors.

Don't forget about my doctor, my mother interrupted.

My father had forgotten, so my mother reminded him. She had been five months pregnant. She was a high-risk pregnancy, since my birth had been a C-section. But several days after the invasion, my mother's doctor had fled too. Then the hospitals were looted. They took the incubators from the maternity wards. My mother heard the news and pressed the heels of her hands against her stomach, as though to plug my brother's ears. She imagined a newborn the size of a kitten. She imagined his translucent skin. She imagined him shivering in the palm of her hand. He'd need doctors. He'd need warmth, fluids, light.

✦

You only know a disaster has happened afterward. In the middle of it, you are still warming your coffee in the morning. You are still singing your daughter to sleep. You are afraid, but you don't have a point of reference for the fear, not really. You have to have lived through something for it to become a point of reference. The elders have a point of reference and they know what is happening. They have felt this fear before. But you haven't. So you don't leave yet. Because you can't yet articulate that leaving. Because you have spent your entire life in Kuwait, minus a semester in England. Because you know this country like your own body. Because this is where you wed, where you went to school, where you buried your youngest aunt. This is where everyone you love lives.

This is where you will raise your daughter, your son. They will go to the same school you did, the one run by nuns, the one that teaches French on Thursdays. Because other people chose this country for you a long time ago, and so it became yours. Your parents, your grandparents, your aunts: they chose it for a reason. They chose it because they couldn't stay where they were, because the wolf had come to their door, because they had no other choice. Or they had a choice, and this was the one they made. You don't leave yet, though the baby kicks restlessly inside you, and your daughter is starting to whimper in her sleep, and you don't know what to tell her, so you tell her not to be scared and then you burst into tears. You don't leave yet, because where would you go. Because nobody wants to believe their life is changing, not like this, not in the middle of the night.

✦

What made me leave, my mother finally said, *was the human shields thing.* She was no longer pretending not to tell the story. The story had infected the room. The story had drawn the three of us in. We were at its knee like children. We were drunk off of it, laughing nervously at the worst parts, speaking over each other. It occurred to me that this is the first time the three of us had ever discussed this, the three of us alone, the three of us who had endured it. Now that the story has started, we can't stop it, we don't want to, it feels like medicine.

✦

After the invasion, Saddam started gathering American and British children and families to use as human shields. Passengers were taken from a British Airways flight and placed in strategic parts of the city: five-star hotels, next to army bases. *Bomb Iraq,* my father says wryly of the strategy, *and you bomb your people.* My grandfather's neighbors were Iraqi. They'd lived next to each other for twenty-five years. Two weeks into the invasion, my parents and I arrived for our night at his house. My grandfather met us at the door shaking. *You need to leave*, he told my mother in a strange voice.

What are you saying, she asked. *What do you mean.*

The soldiers came this afternoon, he said.

There had been two of them. They'd been polite, nonchalant. *We know you have an American granddaughter.* Jiddo's mouth had gone dry. But he was steady, a journalist for many decades, quick on his feet.

Yes, sir, he said. *That's right. I do. But she's gone. They already left. They left days ago.*

My mother had to sit to stop the shaking in her knees. Her father was speaking to her loudly, urgently, like she was a little girl again. *Are you listening*, he asked. *You need to leave. You need to take her and leave.* She looked at him. She looked down at her daughter. Her American daughter. At her. At me. She had a question, but her father was already answering it, as he walked them back down to their car, looking over his shoulder.

It had been the neighbors. They'd informed on him. On me. On my passport, the one my mother had nearly died to get me. The one that now meant danger. This is when my mother decides to leave.

◆

The fever comes back for a single night in Arizona. Only this time I receive it alone. I've eaten something bad. Or I've taken too much sun. There's no way to know; I shiver under the stiff hotel sheets. Outside the window, the night pulses with life: there is a howl, there is the distant roar of cars, there is the sound of an animal. The night becomes an excuse: I talk aloud to nobody. I find an old video of my grandmother, her cackling laughter, the way she'd throw her head back, the way my mother laughs, the way I laugh. I half-dream of a daughter, her dark curls in my lap, which becomes Meimei's lap, which becomes a swell of sand, a dune spilling against white marble. I wake up certain I'm in Beirut, in the old bedroom I shared with my baby sister, the metal slats we'd lower every night to keep the sun out. It takes me a second to adjust to the dark, to remember I'm not in that room, to remember nobody is.

◆

Did I hear him say that? I ask.

Who?

Jiddo. About the neighbors. About the soldiers. Did he say it in front of me? That something was coming for me.

My mother shakes her head at my questions. *Everything is a novel with you,* she says. *Who knows what you heard. Who cares.*

She knows me well. I imagine my mother's fear, how it must've enveloped her. Their story, hers and my father's, is disorienting, like watching a film quickly, half-listening, but upon rewatching you see another character in the corner. A little girl. I am still thinking of my mother's fear, but a different fear, decades later. The phone calls, my university years: the second time in a lifetime, something coming for your daughter, a threat that came from everywhere. A woman's voice through the phone. An untraceable text. Your daughter's own choices, your anger at her, rational or irrational, who cares, didn't she understand by then what the world could do, what men could do, didn't she understand, this dumb precious daughter, that the threat was as big as a country itself, as ubiquitous as years. You didn't know where it started and where it ended.

◆

This was what Saif had understood. Or his parents. Or his neighbors. It was what my mother understood, the terror underneath her fury in those years. You want to come for a family? You come for its eldest daughter.

◆

My mother and I went to Baghdad with my father's brother and his wife. She was trying to find another way: another visa, another passport.

"That's how it was then," she says of driving into Iraq. "To escape them was to go to them." I think about the American Dream, the trope of gratitude, the foreign policies and wars and meddling that brings immigrants to shores, borders, airports. In Iraq, she'd gone to the Lebanese embassy. "It was a *wasta*," she says and I understand. Some cousin, some official's friend. A favor, either returned or borrowed. Someone had called in a fake passport. She hid the American one with my uncle, who would eventually return it to my father in Kuwait. By the time we left the building, I'd become Lebanese.

◆

The drive to Amman takes a day and a half from Iraq. It is the thirteenth day of August, the day Iraqi authorities issue a new law: if you leave their borders, you won't be let back in. That same day, Jordan closes its borders. In between the two borders, my mother sits in the backseat of a car, with a Jordanian driver hired by her cousin, hurtling toward a no-man's-land of Bedouin desert. The car won't reach Jordan in time. We will spend the better part of a day in that desert. There is no water, no money, no food. Just the heat. Just the heat and a daughter and a stranger. My mother speaks with the man. She speaks to keep him awake once night falls. There is a vendor selling melting ice on the side of the road. She takes small sips of the ice, gives some to her daughter, who starts clutching her stomach. The ice is dirty, streaked with sand.

◆

There's a reason the unsettled go to the desert. The spiritually famished. The heartsick. The heat wears on your soul. There is no room for adornment, for vanity. *Do I reek?* I overhear a woman cheerfully ask her boyfriend in a diner. He leans in, sniffs. Yes. Yes, she does. The desert carries tricks, remarkably vivid mirages. If miles of sand can birth visions of water, if mysterious objects can whisk their green lights across the night sky, what else is out there?

✦

After hours in the desert, the driver says he's made a promise. They've been idling among the other cars, countless cars, other families, other women trying to flee. The soldiers have bisected the highway, which bisects the desert. They have made an imaginary border. Nobody is to cross. The driver tells Mama about the promise he made to her cousin. *He entrusted me with you*, the driver says. *If we stay here, we'll die.*

Later, she'd learn that people did die in that seventy-kilometer stretch: died of thirst, died of heat.

There is a long silence. Then the man speaks again in a low tone. He tells my mother to hug her daughter to her chest. He tells her to get low onto the floor of the car, keep her head down. Hold her and not let go.

The floor smells musty. There are scuff marks from other shoes. She holds me against her chest. The driver tells her, *Say Allah.* She says Allah. She says Allah. Then she feels the rev of the car engine, the rush of motion, her heart leaping with it, as the car flies past the others, past the barricade, the sounds of startled men first curious, then shouting, the rain of noise against the car, batons and sticks, then the sound of gunfire. The sound is loud, filling the air, like another body in the car with them, something that is catching up. Then it gets farther and farther away, until it is a distant purring, a blip, something already in her past. A noise she can already remember, only because it is over.

Then: more night. More kilometers. More desert. Another hour until the Jordanian border.

✦

The first sentence from the *New York Times* article "Refugees Flooding into Iraq–Jordan No Man's Land": "Tens of thousands of people were caught today in a vast stretch of scorching desert no man's land between Iraq and Jordan as this country struggled to cope with a tidal wave of refugees fleeing the threat of war in Iraq and Kuwait."

◆

Once, when I was in a dark, dark place, a friend told me *I won't let this happen to you forever. I won't let this keep happening to you. I promise that.* I clutched the words like a rosary bead over the months. It was shocking how powerfully the sentence allayed grief. It was a toothless promise, outlandish even. A check that would've bounced. But it was a kindness that carried me from morning to morning, like an invocation that you believed, and so the invocation worked. Every time I felt the suffering would never end, I'd remember and the suffering would lessen. This became the antidote to the suffering. In the end, what broke the spell of misery was being told it would end.

◆

Later, you'll hear yourself using that line on others. After someone's parent died. During a terrible breakup. I promise I will not let you suffer forever. I use the line and it works. They calm down. They believe me. They believe I will not let their suffering continue forever, because the only thing we want to believe when we are suffering is that it will end, because some part of us knows that it will end. One way or another, it will end.

◆

The night of the fever in Arizona, I dream of another fall. I dream of waking, but it is in another room, years earlier. The Midtown apartment, the one with the canopy and the red couch, the one where we wrote vows and tried out nicknames for each other. The one where I found out I was pregnant for the first time. The one where we had arguments about free will, children, furniture. It was a January night in that terrible winter. I was twenty-nine. We'd just returned from Abu Dhabi. I was jet-lagged and sad and cried myself to sleep. I missed the sun, my parents, my sister Miriam. It was returning to America that always made it feel like a pit stop, my new American husband, the life that felt on loan. I didn't see Meimei that winter; I'd skipped Lebanon. I'd see her the next year, or the one after. I made a vague plan to return in the summer. I never saw her alive again.

✦

That January night in Midtown, I take a sleeping pill. I pull on my eye mask, my earplugs. Sleep is tugging my jet-lagged body when there is a sound. The sound isn't one I know how to describe. It is the sound of falling or, more precisely, the sound of falling ending. There is a heavy thwack. Something being slapped. We sit upright in bed, then mumble ourselves back. There is a different sound. It is a moaning. An animal calling out to itself. Pain, refracted through space, through the winter air. A signature on the night. This time, we scramble to the window, but it is the wrong one. There is nothing in the street below, just a lone garbage truck. The moaning grows.

"The kitchen," Johnny says.

There is a small window above the tiny sink and we crowd above it, on tiptoes, to crane below. It is too dark to see the courtyard, the square the building is built around. He wedges the window open. The cries waft in like street music.

"There's someone down there," I say in a strangled voice. I remember the sleeping pill, but for the first time all winter—months of panic, sobbing in subways, of dreaming of everyone I love dying, of war tanks and sirens, a brain I could not ease—I feel awake. Sturdy. I am putting on my shoes, my coat, at the elevator before I know it, Johnny rushing behind me. In the lobby, the doorman has a frazzled expression. He is dashing around, calling someone.

"It's the courtyard," Johnny says to him, a response to an unasked question, and in that moment, I love him immensely—how resolutely he moves.

"Where is it?" I ask, and though we have no authority, though there is no reason for him to show us, the doorman leads us, through a hall-way, out into the cold night. I've never been here before. It is a plain, ugly concrete space, imprisoned by the building. There is a heap in the middle. A body. A body making that sound.

"The ambulance is coming," the doorman says. "We're going to need to go through one of the apartments. We'll have to clear a pathway."

"I'll help you," Johnny says. I hear them speak, their voices getting lower, but they haven't started moving yet. I am walking away from them. I am walking toward the heap. It isn't until later that I think of our respective instincts. My moving toward the body, the men leaving. I don't realize I'm alone with her for minutes, not until I realize it's a *her*, a woman I've never seen before, a woman who is shaking in shock, whose hand I slip into my own before I say a word, whose hand I am squeezing as she continues making that low, horrible noise.

"You need to breathe," I say to her, and in this moment I understand how alone we are—that I've been left with this woman, this woman who blinks at me in panic, whose teeth are chattering, who is mum-bling, then closing her eyes. "Please. You need to breathe." It occurs to me she might die here, and I try to think of what I'd want someone to say to me. "You're going to be fine. I promise, there's help coming. A lot of help. They're going to make this better. You're not going to be in pain forever."

Her moaning slows. She opens her eyes. I tell her not to move. I tell her I'm right here. I tell her morning will be here soon, though it is barely midnight, though there are still so many dark, winter hours left. I tell her it will end. This pain, this pain, it will end.

◆

It feels like hours, but we are alone for minutes. The EMTs arrive. The police arrive a minute later. They ask her if someone pushed her. They ask me if I saw someone push her. They ask the doorman if she lives with a man. These are the first questions. "Please," I hear myself say to nobody. "She's in pain." I do not take my eyes off her. I watch them bundle her on the stretcher. I watch them wheel her away. There is a smattering of people left in the courtyard, a few onlookers from the building, police officers, the doorman. Even then, I keep looking at the concrete where she'd lain, where I'd knelt just minutes earlier, where I'd been the first to touch her.

◆

The boyfriend was innocent. She'd propped herself against the window to smoke, leaned a little. The frame didn't hold. She'd fallen through the screen, into the night air.

◆

Twenty-five years earlier, we are near the Jordanian border when another checkpoint appears in the night. Here my mother stops the story. We are alone now. She is walking me to the train station in Connecticut. She moved here during the pandemic, five thousand miles from Beirut to New England. She points at a train ticket booth. She says, They were that far away from us. She means the soldiers. I tell her I still can't picture it. My mother thinks. She says, Okay. Okay, imagine that's a little outpost. I follow the line of her arm, her pointed finger, watch the Old Greenwich train station transform into a drab building. I watch as the asphalt turns into sand. As day turns into night. As Mama turns back decades. Here is my small hand in hers, as we walk through the dark. I watch us creep into an empty, dirty bathroom, then emerge minutes later. I watch my mother step silently past the soldiers' outpost, peering into the window, then letting out a gasp. My young, beautiful, pregnant mother. Her wide smile. The smell of her skin. My mother, who still believed her old life would be returned to her, any minute now, like a borrowed book someone had kept too long. My mother sees our names on the wall, a square, official-looking paper, *Hala* and *Hanine* in black ink, sees our names through the window, and makes a noise. *Our names,* she calls out into the night, to me, to nobody. *Our names!* She thinks of her childhood neighbors, of the soldiers with their new greetings, of hotel rooms filled with American children, and grabs my hand. *Run*, she rasps out. *Hala, run.* We run.

We run. We run for as long as a pregnant woman and a small child can run in the dark. We run as soldiers, who heard her voice, rush after us, yelling at her to stop. We run for two minutes. We run for the rest of the night. We run, my mama and I, for a week, then a month, then years. Two years, ten years, twenty. We run because the threat is coming. We run because the war is coming. We run because there is always another war, there is always a border closing somewhere, because you have to be on the right side of it. We run because the men won't stop loving us, or they won't start. We never stop running. We never let go of each other's hand. We run from city to city, toward love, from love, we run into our futures. Against the clock. We never stop. We never leave the dark. We run and run and run.

⁘

I became obsessed with the fallen woman. I dreamt about her, the two of us gathering feathers in a forest. Every day I'd ask about her. The doorman knew some: her boyfriend slept in the apartment every night. She'd had one surgery, then another. Her mother had flown in. She'd broken an unspeakable number of bones. She'd walk again. She'd live. She was coming home in a week, then two days, then tomorrow. I bought a bouquet of roses, white and red, with baby's breath. The doorman gave me her apartment number. I took the flowers to her door. An older Latina woman answered. It was her mother. I suddenly felt foolish. Who was I to her. Nobody. But the mother was already ushering me in. The woman was in physical therapy. They'd be back in an hour. I should wait. She'd walk again. Could I believe that. The mother had yelled at her about the cigarettes. Imagine, she said, her eyes shining. She could've died. Just like that. She snapped her fingers and the snap shook the air like a gunshot.

The mother's relief was still raw, a little frenetic. I held the flowers awkwardly, the cellophane crinkling against my thighs. The mother remembered, filled a large jug and took the flowers from me. She told me about her daughter, things I immediately forgot, because I was buzzing with anxiety, distracted that she might come home any minute. I felt like a stalker, a bad date. I realized whatever I was looking for, I wouldn't find it there. There was the smell of cooking on the stove. The woman wasn't a footnote in my recovery. She was a whole story. I was the ancillary part, flowers that would wilt by Thursday. I would leave in a few minutes. I'd never come back, though the mother would urge me to come back later, so you can meet her, what was your name again, what apartment number? I told her. "I found her," I told the mother sheepishly at the door. I sat with her for a minute. Maybe four minutes? I talked with her, right after she fell. The mother smiled tightly. She didn't want to hear this. She wanted to talk about the doctor, the surgery where they placed the small, metallic plates in her daughter's spine, she wanted to talk about the miracle.

◆

The soldiers' voices boom. They tell my mother to stop. And we stop. She is panting in the dark, bent over at the waist.

What is your name? a voice demands.

She almost lies. But then she remembers the forged passport in the car, the paperwork, the driver. She says her name aloud. Then mine. There is a brief silence, then a cackle of something. Laughter.

Good God, sister, where have you been? We've been waiting for you since the morning.

The *wasta*. Her cousins in Amman. They'd put in word. The soldiers laugh her all the way back to the outpost, where they pour her and the driver coffee, and stamp her documents.

◆

From the border it is two hours to Amman. The sun is rising as we drive. The night has ended and my mother has survived its ending. It is night that cloaked us. It is night that delivered us to safety.

◆

We arrive in Amman at dawn. The driver goes directly to the house where my mother's cousin and friends are waiting. They'd all slept there the night before, have been waiting for hours. There are no phones, no letters. One of the aunties makes a pot of tea. She lifts the teapot to pour and it slips from her hand. The glass shatters into pieces on the tile.

Khair, she tells the others. *Hanine's coming. She's safe.*

The car pulls into the street minutes later.

◆

I never did see that neighbor again. But for our last few months there, I'd scan the windows across the courtyard for her figure, a flash of hair. I didn't know which one was hers, so I pretended any window that was lit was hers. Spring came. We left the apartment.

◆

My mother and I are waiting for the train in Connecticut. The train will be here in a few minutes. We are nowhere near a border. Nowhere near a desert. I am crying. The train finally arrives. I wave through the window at my mother, who waves on the platform. The air conditioning is a blessing. There are no soldiers. There are no rifles. Nobody will stop us. Only a uniformed man who asks to see a ticket. I show him the barcode on my phone and I am waved through, allowed to cross back into my life.

Halfway back to New York, I get a voice note from my mother: *You are everything to me.*

My love. I text my mother back. For the first time I say: *Thank you for saving my life.*

✦

My last day in Arizona, I go for one final walk near the hotel. I wander farther and farther from it, that old schoolhouse for girls. I walk until the hotel is in the distance, then not visible, then nothing, until the trail ends, until I'm stepping through brambles. The sun is starting to set, but I don't want to turn back. To turn back is to return to my life. I am a little dizzy. My hands are shaking. I've forgotten to drink enough water. Suddenly, I get the eeriest feeling, a prickle on the back of my neck. An animal, I think. A man. There is a sudden buzzing in my ears, like a static from several feet away.

But when I turn, there is nobody. There is just a clearing to the right of me, in the brambles, a space the size of a wolf. The buzzing gets louder. My mouth is dry and I shove my hands into my pockets to still them. There is nothing in the clearing. I am certain of it. I say it aloud. Nothing. But for a second, for a split, unreal second, I blink and I see her, a little girl, a girl I instantly recognize, a girl with short dark hair, wan-looking, her big sea-colored eyes unblinking and scared. I remember that shirt, from my passport photo when I arrived in America. It's the fever, I think. It's a dream. It's a trick of the light. A dehydrated brain, an overwrought nervous system. But there she is. I know what I see. I cannot lie to myself in the desert.

I crouch by the brambles. I close my eyes because I know that when I open them, she will be gone. I close my eyes and sink into the familiar night of my eyelids. I extend my arm, touch the air, touch her hair, touch the brambles, touch the soft of her arm. I crouch by the child. This child that was loved. This child that lay on the floor of a car. This child that was summoned in song before she took her first breath. My father's voice: *Bring us a baby named Hala.* I keep my eyes closed. I whisper for her. I feel her come closer. This child walking through the desert. This child kissing her father's cheek. This child in one country, then another, then another. I feel her against me, one step away. She loses a language.

167

She develops tics. She prays like her life depends on it. It depends on it. She lies about everything. She tells stories. They get uglier and uglier, because they're not the right ones. She loves whoever appears. She attaches wildly, recklessly. She makes people her higher power. They don't ask for it, but she gives them her heart anyway. This alert girl. This girl who loves like her life depended on it. It depends on it. It depends on it.

✦

When I open my eyes, there is air and dusk. A distant bark. The clomp of my own sneakers as I walk back toward the lights.

✦

In the end, there is the same story: you entered a desert and you emerged from it. Does it matter when this happens? Does it matter if it was the past or now or the future? You walked into the desert. It swallowed you. Then you escaped. This is the story. The rest? It vanishes with the light.

Month Seven

Your baby is the size of a coconut. Her organs are maturing and
her skin is smoothing out. Your baby has taste buds now!

She will be born in the year of the tiger. The same as me, thirty-five years after *my* tiger year, the year my mother spent two weeks cramped in a rental in Carbondale, Illinois, learning how to breast-feed, how to distinguish hunger cries, recovering from her C-section, before flying me back to Kuwait. I celebrate the New Year with my lips pressed against Johnny's, a tangle of lights in the distance from a friend's rooftop. We count it down ourselves, incorrectly, and I make two wishes against his collar. One will come true, one won't.

◆

Now that there is a spine, I write in a poem, *there must be a name.* I flip through novels, holy books, plant glossaries, for names. I make a list of flowers, cities, writers. I suggest Scheherazade at a family gathering and everyone groans. I suggest Bayan. Luz. Mimi. Am I naming a nightclub?

my brother wants to know. Am I naming a new strain of virus? Am I naming a cat?

I drive them crazy. What about Zaytoun, I say. What about Birdie?

What about you shut up, my mother finally says.

◆

One day, my brother tells me to close my eyes. He says we need to settle the matter of the naming. This is how it always is between us: a kinship bordering on telepathy. We both drank in the same way, got sober in the same way. We feared the same things, loved the same music and shows and comedy. He was always ahead of me in taste, teaching his older sister in high school about grunge music. We are ruthless at charades, everyone's least favorite pairing, sometimes guessing the word from a raised arm or smile. I've always known what my brother is feeling before I know what I'm feeling.

Close your eyes, he says.

A better way to say it: He *is* how I know what I'm feeling. A few years into my time in New York, he would visit from college at Syracuse. He got a respite from drinking and I got a respite from my solitude—I was avoiding friends, avoiding bars. We'd get pancakes from Kellogg's Diner in Williamsburg, go to movies or comedy shows or take walks along the river. We'd have an argument nearly every visit. We were too similar, sensitive and abrasive at the same time, too easily hurt by each other. Still, Sunday would come and we'd hug tightly and send each other texts saying I love you and I'm sorry. Once, after a long apology text from me, he replied, *I'd still rather spend my weekend arguing with you.* Our proclamations of love and apology were vestigial, holdovers from long separations, living in different countries. I'll see you again in two weeks, we'd say. A month. There was a thrill in speaking those words, that short time, how it would arrive in no time at all.

Close your eyes, he says. I want you to imagine her. She's right here, she's in the other room.

I find the recording months later. His voice, telling me to imagine a toddler in the next room. He tells me not to think. He tells me she has my curly hair and her father's coloring. He tells me I need to call her to me. Quick, quick, without thinking, say her name.

✦

In the video, I say a name automatically, without thought, with a little lilt in my voice, as though I'm already calling someone from the next room.

✦

Johnny and I go on a babymoon, though we don't call it this. Escaping winter, is what we tell people. Several weeks in Mexico: Puerto Vallarta, San Miguel de Allende. I am teaching remotely, workshopping stories about affairs and lost girls and ruined friendships. Every day I see a couple of therapy clients. He is returning to the place the boy fell. "I think you are both doing something brave," our therapist says.

✦

The days in Mexico feel hyperpigmented, alive. We spend hours on rooftops, walking the cities. We talk about baby names: Dala, Samira, Kaia. I talk about Daniel. I remember a secret he'd once told me. I tell Johnny. Lara, Aza, Yasmeen. He tells me about going to the police station decades earlier, miles from here. He'd answered the same questions over and over again with his new Spanish: the boy had not been pushed. Nobody pushed the boy. There was no pushing. The boy had fallen. Mira, Abeer, Fairuz. The boy had jumped and met air instead of earth.

✦

Fatima, Nadia, Seham. I cannot bring myself to invoke the dead, cannot bring myself to dilute their name, to superimpose it onto another creature's voice, pair of eyes, future.

✦

There was a story I'd remember during the miscarriages—whenever a nurse would blow out another vein, when the bleeding came. The story was the white of a cloud, the center of a flame. In Meimei's first years in Kuwait, before she was Meimei, before she had daughters or granddaughters, she was Fatima and Fatima was pregnant. Fatima gave birth to a screaming girl. She named her Yaffa, after the Palestinian city, which she later said was the most beautiful name she could imagine. She bought her daughter clothes and shampoo and a rattle. She brushed her wispy hair. She put her in a bed. Then, a little over a month later, Fatima woke and the baby wasn't breathing anymore. This was before the other children. This was her whole world and it shattered like ice. Half a century passed. I sat in a kitchen in Lebanon and watched her bob a teabag into a mug, and asked: *Do you think about her?* We both cried in that kitchen, listening to the traffic in the street below, and as she spoke of her first child, the one she'd loved and borne, the one she'd named for Palestine, her hand had risen automatically to rest on her belly.

✦

One day, I'm sunning myself on the rooftop of our rental in Mexico, watching birds move across the sky in indecipherable swoops, when my phone dings. It is Dee. "I'm bleeding. Something is wrong."

✦

I run down three flights of stairs. Johnny is on a call, the sunlight dappling his back, the beautiful weaving in the colors of a sunrise. *Who cares about sunrise*, I think. Who cares about anything. Dee said there was pain. Dee said there was snow. Dee said she would drive carefully.

"Where is she now?" His face is urgent.

"She's going to the hospital." There is nothing to do but wait. There are flights and trains and cabs, but none that will get us there in time. In time for what. I don't want to answer myself.

✦

There is a coding term Johnny once told me about. It allows other signifiers to collapse into it, like a closet or a suitcase. The coding term means both itself and these other things. A woman can mean both a woman and a country. A spectator can mean both a spectator and a mother.

✦

When we arrive in Oklahoma, I am neither an immigrant, with my passport, nor a real American. I am lost in between, a decimal point, a halfway landmark between immigrant and first generation. I don't remember missing things, but I must have. I'd been just as dislocated as the adults—I had lost my home, the giraffe exhibit at the zoo, the sea, the toy store, all those familiar streets.

✦

Dee tells me about the butterfly needle. She tells me about the blood. The sonogram, the flickering white, the held breath. The doctor's exhale, the heartbeat. The heartbeat. The heartbeat.

✦

The coding term meant container. It meant metaphor. It meant you could call for one thing and be calling for others.

✦

For the first four years of my life, I spent nearly every day with Meimei. I sat with her while she cooked, I walked around her garden. In home videos, I speak in her lilting Syrian accent. Every weekend, we gathered at my grandparents' house with dozens of relatives and neighbors. When Kuwait was lost, everything that had lived within it was lost too. It was my loss as much as the adults'—I just had no language for it. And even if I were to try, that language was being eroded. It was being replaced. I lost my Syrian accent. My English was nasal, Midwestern.

♦

Dee is back home by lunch. "False alarm," she says on the phone and I can hear her fumbling with keys in the background. I sit on the rooftop tiles under the Mexican sun and weep. I have glimpsed the terror that accompanies love like a bodyguard. My pregnancies have taught me caution, a moratorium on daydreams. I've watched my wanting, measured it carefully, a teaspoon here and there. But now there is a spine. Now there is an army of names. She sends me a recording of the heartbeat, the one she'd taken at the doctor's. There are all sorts of wild plants on the rooftop, flowers the color of candy. There is the muffled, insistent thumping against my ear. It takes a minute to realize, as I listen to her heart, my hand is pressed, protectively, against my stomach.

♦

There's a scene I've tried to write in short stories before. It never works. In it, a character, often a woman, is in an apartment. Something is coming. Someone is waiting for her, downstairs, in a car. There is a fire. Or a wave. Or a flight she has to catch. She faces the objects of her life, tick tock, tick tock, she has minutes to decide: what to leave, what to take. What to take. What to leave.

♦

As a child in the Midwest, I wait for tornadoes, for lightning, for the next emergency that will sweep everything away again. I see what is safe and what isn't. My world shrinks with loss, becomes the pale walls of three rooms, filled with my mother's cooking, my father's laughter, the mumble of the television. I see my world. I see all the things that can upend it. I see what the adults cannot see: the hairline fractures in their own sense of safety, the liability that was their fragility. It could be our undoing. And so I begin my long watchings. In the middle of the night, I watch my parents' bodies, count their breaths. I whisper my labyrinths of prayer, the suras, the names of my family, in one order, then another, my four greetings of Allah, a salutation of my own invention. The adults will not catch every threat, and so I watch the sky from February through August, learning the difference between funnel clouds and cumulonimbus clouds, a watch and a warning, a sky that is clearing and a sky that is assembling. I will catch whatever comes next.

◆

Children locate loss by becoming mirrors to those around them. The loss from the war was reflected back to me. I saw it through their seeing.

◆

We both love the name Luna. I keep scribbling *Inez* in my journal. I write our hyphenated last names. My own last name alone, an island. A name. Her name. A name that will pin her to herself. Even if she changes it, even if she hates it, it will be her starting point, the beginning. The thing that future things will be in response to. I used to name my Barbies with the solemnness of communion. I had renamed myself, for years thinking my parents had done it for me, to ease American tongues, until my father corrected my memory: it had been my doing, my insistence. I'd stage-directed my family to change my name. They were allowed to call me Hala only in our home. Everywhere else I was rechristened—had orchestrated my own rechristening—as Holly. Now, the name sparks only the faintest alertness when I hear it in a stranger's mouth: someone at a party, a woman giving her order to a barista. Holly, a long-ago dream, my fingers remembering the twitch of the *y*'s tail, the trick of the broad *o*, a tunnel I could walk through and emerge into the ordinary.

◆

The story of an American childhood that wasn't intended for you. Not white, not Black, not Mexican. The story of endless recesses in the bathroom, in the corner of the playground, faking stomachaches, faking sore throats, pretending not to speak English, praying for a snow day. I loved learning, and hated every other thing about school: my breath fogging the air on winter PE runs, the other kids with their flawless language and enthusiastic parents, group projects.

◆

In recovery programs, steps eight and nine are connected. In step eight, you make a list of all the people you've harmed. In step nine, you make your amends. You make them wherever you can, to whoever you can. There is no further instruction. There is no elaboration on the meaning of *harm*. No explanation of what making an amend must look like. Every grievance has its own unique corollary, its own repair.

◆

Once, after a miscarriage, I hurled at Johnny, "I bet you're relieved, huh." He said something terrible back. But when I find him to tell him Dee's news, he is sitting at the edge of the bed, looking at nothing. I watch him hear his name.

"Johnny," I say. He turns. "She's okay. She's going to be okay."

I watch something slacken in his mouth, the relief dart across his face, a reluctant bird, something flying in spite of itself.

◆

In the myth of Scheherazade, the king never makes amends. He marries her because she has succeeded; there is no mention of the other murdered wives. We are left with the uneasy sense that she is to be forever accountable to his attention span. Scheherazade is the architect of her liberation and the corollary of this is that if she'd failed, the failure would've been hers alone.

✦

Amending is not possible without the truth. Otherwise it is merely equivocation. In Layli Long Soldier's poetry collection *Whereas*, she plays with the doublespeak of the U.S. government through the congressional Resolution of Apology to Native Peoples of the United States in 2009. It is a dense, verbose document, signed by Obama and witnessed by nobody: not a single tribal leader was invited to the signing. What is an apology in the absence of its intended audience? The resolution contains a series of statements beginning with the preamble "Whereas," which Long Soldier reclaims throughout her collection. The qualifier is deadly and precise. It precedes language about—as Long Soldier puts it—the "new chapter in the history of Native Peoples," a "chapter" that the colonizers began. The word sanitizes. The word absolves itself of whatever comes after.

✦

When the photographs from Abu Ghraib surfaced, they showed naked prisoners in stress positions, prisoners cuffed to bunk beds, prisoners hooded, prisoners face down on concrete. A snarling dog lunging at a prisoner. A man smeared with dirt or feces, his arms stretched out like Jesus. A picture of a young woman giving the thumbs-up gesture next to a man with taped-over eyes and ice on his chest. The woman is Sabrina Harman and I find a long feature on her, a bizarrely sympathetic portrayal in which she is described as smiling over a blackened corpse with a "forced but lovely smile." I screenshot the image of her face, glance at it periodically over a few days. I try to catch what is forced about it. What is lovely about it. She looks like a valley girl, a volleyball player, someone I've met but can't remember where.

✦

While the feature names the abuse at Abu Ghraib as "de facto United States policy," the authors are relentless in their desire to absolve Harman, quoting her as "picking up" the thumbs-up gesture from children in al-Hillah, a bizarre and sly reattributing of blame, as though if it hadn't been for those Iraqi children she might've stood somberly next to corpses, might've looked appropriately remorseful. "I know it looks bad," she'd later say, which is not any apology I've ever heard of. The essay mentions, "Harman brought her Iraqi friends clothes and food and toys," quoting her sergeant and other unit members, transcribing lines from a letter she sent home. Not a single Iraqi is quoted in the article. There's a lot of energy put into describing Iraqi violence, the "fever heat," how "[f]rustration gave way to hostility, hostility gave way to violence, and by summer's end the violence against Americans was increasingly organized. It was demoralizing. Every Iraqi might be the enemy." Later, a soldier is quoted as saying, "I always used to say, 'God, if I go out, if I have to die, don't take me in my sleep. I want to feel it.'" We are not told what the Iraqi prayers might've been.

◆

From one of her letters back home, Harman notes, "Until Redcross came we had prisoners the MI put in womens panties trying to get them to talk. Pretty funny but they say it was 'cruel.' I don't think so. No physical harm was done." Later, she writes, "But pictures were taken, you have to see them! A sandbag was put over their heads while it was soaked in hot sauce. Okay, that's bad but these guys have info, we are trying to get them to talk, that's all, we don't do this to all prisoners." That night, she sends another letter saying, "Okay, I don't like that anymore. At first it was funny but these people are going too far." *Too far* is a prisoner being sexually assaulted. *Too far* is a man whimpering that he is just a taxi driver.

◆

It is unclear what we are meant to feel about Harman's *too far*. Be grateful that it came? Recognize it as a mark of her humanity? The article mentions that Harman has a "Gilligan tattoo . . . a private souvenir," referencing the image of the hooded prisoner that circulated for years afterward. In the end, she was sentenced to six months of prison and a bad-conduct discharge. Not a single higher-ranking official was convicted of anything. Not a single charge was ever made for an abuse that wasn't photographed. At her sentencing, she said she had "let down the people in Iraq," then went on to name her failures to protect soldiers and Americans everywhere, saying her actions "potentially caused an increased hatred and insurgency toward the United States."

◆

Harman is not alone in this preoccupation with potential retaliation, as though an act merits apology only for its potential response. Across American foreign policy, this is standard: when Americans do egregious things, those things are egregious because they put Americans at risk. Even the badness is outsourced, a thing to be invoked in others. The apology is to protect the perpetrator.

◆

I was in Lebanon, in the mountainside high school I'd graduate from, when the photographs came out. I'd written a paper the year before about the invasion of Iraq. I remember what I felt when I saw those stripped men, what it did to my throat, the rage I couldn't give to my hands. I wouldn't use the word "shock." Nobody spoke of it with shock. This is what America does, a teacher said. Then, clearing her throat: Not all Americans.

◆

An amend doesn't guarantee redemption. It is un-sly, artless. It sustains itself, does what it does not for outcome or gold star, but for the doing itself.

◆

How to explain America? How to explain being Arab and American? To be both the indictment and the courtroom. Both the fire and the rescue. But which is the fire, which is the rescue?

◆

We returned to the Arab world when I was twelve. I stayed until my twenty-second birthday. In Lebanon my memory bursts into color. Lebanon was traffic and beach and broken air conditioners and electricity that cut twice a day and the sweetest figs I'd ever tasted. It was also my grandmother. My grandparents had moved to Lebanon after the Kuwait invasion. We called the apartment *Meimei's house*, as though she lived in it alone, as though she'd built it with her two hands, the white marble tiled floors, the rooms that received random, indelible monikers—*Mehiar's room, the middle room*—and there was always a meal about to be served, always someone being yelled at to wash their hands or turn the television down. Always some gossip rippling through the house like weather, my mother and aunt and Meimei. The lowered voice, the delicious intonation: *You have to swear not to say anything.* I am borderless, unallegianced, the eldest of the children, the youngest of the adults. They tell me about their marriages. They tell me about each other. *Swear*, they'd screech. *Swear on Allah. Swear on your mother.* Sometimes they make each other swear on a child, and this alone is momentous: swearing on your child is the highest form of pledging, and the child you choose to swear on is revealing.

Years later, while Israeli bombs fell in southern Lebanon, we watched the Lebanese president weep on that same television. He begged. I felt fury watching him, shame for his tears. The bombs were miles away and we only heard their thunder, the claps that shook our balcony doors and windows.

In the house in the mountains, in the house that was my grandmother, we watched the United States destroy Baghdad. We watched

180

a president in front of a microphone, a flag behind him. The same flag I'd stood to as a child. The same flag my parents pledged to when they received their passports. We watched Baghdad light up like a carnival at night.

✦

How to explain that flag? How to explain I loved its blue, the rows of stars until I heard different stories.

✦

The construction of any place begins with an idea of that place. The Levant came to mean a place to leave, a port, a harbor, a place to return briefly to. It came to mean that perpetual departure, a border that always changed, belonging as a tenuous thing. It would be a place you could leave, but not really. A place you could return to, but not really. The Levant became a husband who would never fully return, because he never fully left. A better truth: the Levant, a wife that never stops leaving, so never stops returning.

✦

I once tried to write a story about a woman who could only say one word: a single name. It became the answer to every question. It became every question.

✦

In America, Meimei would come every year or so for a few months, sometimes sharing my bedroom. She seemed so tiny when we went to department stores or the supermarket, negotiating the world with her broken English, her quick smile. I wept for days when it was time for her to leave. "Please," I'd tell her. "Please. Just stay." *I have to go back*, she once laughed, *to make your poor Jiddo a proper dinner*. I hated Jiddo then. I hated that she belonged to other people.

"He could make his own dinner," I told her. She laughed and laughed. *You're right*, she said. But she still left.

During one of Meimei's visits in America, I woke to a sound I'd never heard before. I was eight or nine. It was a devastating sound, like an animal in a trap. Meimei was huddled on the couch in the living room, surrounded by my parents and aunt. The adults didn't notice me at first. Her brother had died in Syria. She was wild with grief. She howled and howled, she grabbed at the arm of the sofa, at my mother's knee, at nothing. It reminded me of my baby cousin, how he flailed for something to hold on to when he cried. It took hours for her to calm down and the next day she looked like a different person: old, ashen. I felt an enormous, terrible guilt. When she was here, she was leaving a life behind. I wanted to apologize for not understanding before, for all the times I'd begged her to stay. I understood that morning: how a leaving in one place is always a returning somewhere else. There was never enough to go around. My grandmother appeared in my life as a function of her disappearance in another's life. She took me and my brother grocery shopping at Shawn's, bought the brightest Florida oranges and missed her brother's last breath.

◆

The day Meimei has a stroke, there is no war. The war has been over for years. It is summer and we are visiting, our lives back in America now. Nobody knows she has a stroke. The blood clot, her brain glowing white in a scan days later. That day, the only thing that changed was her face. She sat in the midst of a gathering, looking confused. She blinked and smiled politely and we all continued our clamor, the music video channel in the background, someone always yelling to turn it down. When she spoke, her voice was polite: *I'm late. I have to get going.* She wants to know who will take her. She doesn't want to keep her father waiting. Her brain falters and she is in Syria, there is a bus she cannot miss, there is a father she must see this afternoon.

✦

Only once was I part of Meimei's journey to America. I was sixteen and we flew from Beirut to Texas to visit my uncle. This time I watched the ocean below with her. This time I ate a bad sandwich in the Frankfurt airport, spent those long impossible hours talking with her. I waited in the longer line once we got to America. My blue passport couldn't help her here. Her visa had lapsed and the Border Control agent looked at her paperwork, then at her.

"Ma'am? This is expired."

I'll do it when I get back home, she replied in Arabic. She spoke some English, but right then she stared innocently, unknowingly, at the man. The man sighed. He told us to follow him and we went to a small room, where we waited for an hour. When another man entered, Meimei kept interrupting my explanation, pointing out things in Arabic. Their visa system was silly. That lamp was broken. Why had they kept us waiting so long.

Meimei, let me handle it, I finally said through a gritted smile, but she kept going. Did Americans understand that people didn't even want to come to their country? She was just here to see her son, her grandson. He was a baby! Did this man want to stop her from seeing her grandson? Finally, she tilted her head at the agent.

"Oh no," she said in broken English. He was Asian and tall, his skin pockmarked with pimples. "Your poor skin!" she exclaimed. "Not good. You are *maybe* handsome," she ventured, squinting at him as though trying to envision it. "But you need to . . ." Here she mimed vigorously scrubbing her cheeks.

"Oh my God," I said.

But the man was already laughing, and Meimei was laughing with him. He'd let her in, he said. Just this once. But she had to do her paperwork. Yes, yes, she said. As he led us out, she patted his arm like a reward. After we found our baggage and my uncle, and stepped out of the airport, into America, into the muggy Dallas heat, I kept waiting for someone to stop us, certain we'd gotten away with something.

◆

The grief when my grandmother died bordered insanity, my mouth sickly sweet whenever I thought of her, no tears, no keening, only a strange, frozen knot in my stomach, so that I always felt full, always felt like I'd just eaten too much bread. I told anybody who would listen, "There's nothing left for me in Beirut." Of course I went back. I didn't want to see her grave. I wanted to see her house and so I did. How to explain the empty rooms, the cigarette butts in her flower beds, the single, decomposing chair in the kitchen. The chair was where we'd sat for gossip and birthday cake and lectures. The chair was the most violent part of all.

◆

I once tried to write about a grandmother and the story became a list. Her Dior perfume. Her lentil soup. Her nickname. Her handbag filled with tissues and honey lozenges and lipstick the color of sunset. Her handbag filled with her smell. Her smell. Her—

◆

Our second to last night in Puerto Vallarta, Johnny and I go to a restaurant. It's like so many of the restaurants that we've visited: beautiful and on the water. The absurdly gorgeous sunset. The fire-throwers wander from restaurant to restaurant. I feel something stir inside me watching the fire. But tonight we are laughing, tonight he has ordered a bottle of white wine, has poured an inch of it for himself. Tonight the rage is absent. Tonight he is smiling boyishly at me, not a ghost but a man, a man with sand between his toes. A toast, he says. He has never seen me actually drink. He watched me taste those mimosas, sip that wine at the vineyard. My sobriety wasn't through programs or chips and so it was a vaguer thing. He has heard friends tell stories about it, the emergency rooms, the way I'd disappear from parties for hours. To-night I laugh. Tonight I keep my hands to myself until I don't, eat the mediocre tilapia, see the man I love clear as that first day in Brooklyn Bowl. I see our story like a newsreel, one frame leading to the next, to the next, to the next, until we've arrived here: this beautiful beach, this music, this chatter, all that we've survived. Our resolution. The ending I want more than anything in the world. The ending I'd kill for. I imag-ine the fruit-sized baby and for the first time, I can think of them both at once: Johnny and her, can imagine the three of us, cobwebbed, our stories, our histories, not stuck but bound. I am thinking of the moon, of the water, of Johnny's lips, and suddenly I am lifting my glass and holding it out to him. His surprised, slightly excited eyes. Suddenly, there is wine being poured into my glass. Suddenly, I am lifting it to my mouth.

◆

The summer of 2006, before my junior year of college, I slept through the airport bombing in Beirut. I woke up in Hamra with a sour mouth and trembling hands. I'd had an unimaginable amount to drink the night before at a bar with expats and journalists, one who seemed partic-ularly somber. Hezbollah forces had kidnapped two Israeli soldiers and taken them into southern Lebanon. People were making jokes about the end of days, drinking shots capped with fire. The somber journalist said, "They don't understand what's about to happen." Another one, drunk and Lebanese, shot back: "We understand, you fucker. We just can't do anything about it."

I woke and there were dozens of missed calls, texts from my mother, grandfather, friends.

◆

Recovery talk loves aphorisms, metaphors: Hang out at the barber shop long enough and you'll end up with a haircut. Stop going to the hardware store for milk. Your addiction is always doing push-ups in the corner. It is wily. The villain. It is always waiting to pounce. But when I think of my addiction, I think of murmuring, a delicious itch, the feel of silk against my cheek. I think of beautiful women in robes, spellwork. Promises of one more time. Promises of better. Promises of change.

✦

I hated Didion's famous quote when I first heard it. "I think we are well advised to keep on nodding terms with the people we used to be." It seemed disingenuous. I thought the future self was the powerful one, the one who had more control. It would take years to understand the past self could hijack the future far more than the reverse.

✦

Before the invasion of Iraq, we'd watched the towers fall. My mother's voice low and breaking: *Oh no, oh no, oh no.*

✦

How to explain watching a country get hammered to pieces? How to explain being inside that country, but also not. To be within and outside at the same time. My mother and aunt, my siblings, my grandparents, my cousins, we all stayed in that house in the mountains of Lebanon that summer of war. We watched television and we listened to the bombs.

When the bombings happened during the day, my cousin Omar and I would stand on the balcony and blow bubbles in their direction. He was eleven. Toward the sea. Toward the shoreline. The smoke. I said I was doing it for him, but I loved the glisten of soapskin in the sun, the way the bubbles seemed to drift, like a spell or plea, toward the terrible noise.

What is to be in a war, a friend once asked. *We were there and we weren't there.*

✦

I relapse like I do so many things: impulsively, half-heartedly, in complete opposition to what I actually want. There is a beach in Mexico and there is wine and I drink it. Johnny gets a phone call and wanders for ten minutes. I order another glass, drink half of it while we are getting the check and he keeps glancing at me, trying to gauge my own reaction. I keep my voice steady, cheerful. As we are walking along the beach, he suddenly doubles over. We return to the restaurant for him to use the bathroom and when he comes out, he looks pale. He thinks he's eaten something bad. Food poisoning. We should go back to the Airbnb. I keep my voice measured: He should go back alone. I'll just wander for a bit. He eyes me for a second. *Okay*, he says finally. *You deserve this. A night out. I don't want to ruin it.* Watching him walk away, feeling that old delicious feeling, of getting away with something, the glee of a mistake that has been years in the making.

✦

I go to a bar and lie to the couple I meet. They are two men in their sixties. Each one is named after a different month. "That's wild," I keep saying. I say I'm divorced. I tell them I grew up in Paris. The lies are as exciting as the wine. Both fill my mouth like pop rock candy.

"My name is Fairuz," I say when they ask. "You can call me Fey."

When the couple turn to get their check, I leave. My cell battery has died. I slip through the street filled with loud music and neon-signed bars, feeling dangerously free. I go inside another bar and order another white wine. I hate white wine. This is why I'm drinking it. Even as the night starts to blur, there is some co-pilot in there, one that keeps a few fingers on the steering wheel. Find a phone charger, she whispers. Text your husband. Drink some water. *Please, Hala, please.*

✦

An evacuation ship came and took Americans out of Lebanon. We stayed. My mother tried to convince her parents to leave, but they refused. *I'm not leaving again*, Jiddo kept saying, and nobody asked what he meant.

In Arabic, these weeks are called *harb tamouz*. The July war.

♦

There is a bachelor party at the next bar, a group of thirtysomething men from Mexico City. They are rowdy and handsome and the groom is sober. "So was I," I squeal, lifting my wine glass. He looks pained. "Maybe you stop?" he whispers to me at some point. Maybe you can still stop, he meant. Maybe, I grin back. It is shocking how familiar it all feels, not like revisiting so much as pressing the unpause button, as though *this* is the real timeline, the only one that matters, and I'm back.

♦

We take the next evacuation ship. Our blue passports. The rows of stars on the flag. The day before the ship, my mother drives me to Beirut.

"This is a mistake," she keeps saying, and I keep begging her not to stop.

"Just a few things," I say. "I don't know if I'll ever come back." I am nineteen.

The city is hushed, nearly empty. It looks like a city in a dream: familiar, but subtly, irrevocably altered. The people are gone. The cabs are gone. The billboards look eerie above the empty highway. Keep going, keep going, I think silently. My stuff, my books, my journals. I'd left my apartment thinking I'd be back later that night.

"What if we never come back? What if the war never ends?" I ask my mother questions like I'm the only one asking them. I don't think about how selfish I must sound. I don't think about my mother's fear, irritating to me and my brother, overdone and high-pitched, her endless phone calls to my father in Qatar, her voice rising with argument. I don't think about the fear behind that fear, what these weeks must remind her of, how she spends her days glued to the television, talking to my aunt about borders, mileage, ships. What she must've thought when the airport was bombed. I don't think about her alone again, alone again with her children, alone again with her children in a country on fire.

✦

I'm making rules again. Only white wine, I decide. I'll only drink half of whatever glass I'm poured. I will stop when I feel the edges of a blackout. At some point, I go to the bathroom and have a thought, which isn't a thought but something I'm saying aloud, a woman at the nearby sink looking over.

"Wow," I say. "This really wasn't worth it."

The woman smiles at me. Perhaps she doesn't speak English. Perhaps I look wasted. She leaves and I start to laugh like a maniac. I'm delighted by my discovery. I'm safe, I realize. Maybe not tonight, because it's too late, the wheels have spun off the tracks, I know I won't stop, I know I won't go home. But I'll be safe after this. When you get sober, even for good reason, there is no way to fully rub the gleam off. The nostalgia. The wondering. The what-if. The feeling that what you've exiled isn't an act, but a self, a part of your very being. Now I've peered into it, pressed my nose against it. There's nothing I want here.

It is a lovely epiphany. Then I go back to the bar and order another glass.

✦

Once, in an airport as a child, I asked my mother how you knew if you were carrying something dangerous. She looked at me strangely. *There's a list of things*, she said finally, *that you're not supposed to have.*

✦

Once, in an airport, Johnny said the word "bomb," jokingly, over and over until I snapped at him to stop. I was near tears.

189

◆

Once, in an airport, an Israeli security guard ran her hands through my hair. *Who knows what you might be hiding in there?*

◆

One of the groomsmen is playing a game. The game is his hand on my knee, then on my shoulder, then on my cheek, pretending to pick an eyelash. I am playing a game too. My game is that I am Cinderella and there is a clock somewhere. Tick tock. My game is the clock is running out. I have one night. Even as I'm getting drunk I know that.

"You're divorced," the groomsman says. It's not a question.

I hold up my ring.

"You're going to be divorced," he says. It sounds like a premonition.

One more order of white wine. One more half left untouched.

"My girlfriend wants to get married," the groomsman says. What do I think? Should he? Or are there still more mistakes to make in the world?

Another lifted hand. Another uncorked bottle. Another sliver of pale light.

◆

My mother parks the car under my apartment building. It's where I've fallen in love, been touched, smoked weed, crammed for finals. It's where I've played at being an adult. Hosted a dinner party. Stayed up with my roommate. Called Saif and begged him to stop. Believed him when he said he had no idea. My mother doesn't cut the engine. You have five minutes, she says. I'm not an adult. I'm her daughter. I'll get in the car. I'll get on the ship. Five minutes, she repeats. The key feels clunky and foreign in my hand. It's only been a few weeks and already I've forgotten which key opens the building door. I move quickly, shakily. There is no one in the apartment. There is a lone honk, my mother in the car. My mother telling me to hurry. I face my room: the heap of dirty clothes in the corner, the flower-shaped candles, my books, the posters on the wall, Kurt Cobain, an abstract painting of a naked woman, all the things that told me who I was. My mother honks. I have four minutes. I have three minutes. I am frozen in the face of my life, in the face of the choice of what I'll take. I have two minutes. I have no minutes at all.

✦

I agree to join the men at a nightclub. We walk along the beach and I keep lagging, watching the water in the moonlight. There had been a night and I'd forgotten it. I'd gone skinny-dipping in the Mediterranean, all of us drunk and laughing. I remembered it now that I was drunk again, how the moon had looked, how my friend joked about finding me in the water: *I followed the trail of white men.* The water was freezing that night, but I don't remember that at all. I'd been drunk and what I remember is how beautiful it all was, how safe I felt, whether I was or not. I decided to tell the story that I was safe, and so I was.

✦

The groomsman: "Why are you crying?"

"I'm not."

"You are. Look at your cheeks."

"I just miss something. I miss it right here." My hand, a fist, my fist a stone I push against my stomach.

✦

A relapse is the betrayal of a tidy resolution. It disrupts the plot, the ease of the third act. Postscript, surprise, *shit.* The nightclub is thumpingly loud, streaks of bright strobe lights, women in glittery dresses, tables overlooking the dance floor. The bachelors have a private table. They order recklessly: bottles of Grey Goose, bourbon. The groomsman slips his hand around my waist. Do I want something else, he asks. Even this

I remember: the Pavlovian leaning back into danger. The itch. The fire when you moved your nails across skin. Mezcal, I say. Then I say it again, in case he hasn't heard me. He nods, then shouts it above the music to the waiter. It feels like slipping a dress off, balm and moonlight, like reaching for a tree branch, one millimeter too short, the split second when you realize, the split second before you start to fall.

✦

Before the mezcal arrives, I go to the bathroom. It's sleek and strategically lit, with little trays on the sinks: napkins and tampons and condoms. Gum. Peppermints. Hair ties. My reflection is fifteen years younger. My eyeliner is smeared. There is something tousled about my dress, my wild hair. Here she is, Didion's old girl. It is the strangest thing: remembering the self. Remembering the self you've evicted. *I want, I want.* There was something that screamed and there was something that could muffle it. I'd not kept on nodding terms with this girl; I'd buried her, or thought I had. And here she was, twelve years later, in all her messy glory, hurling her laugh across the room like an arrow. She was awake after a hundred years of slumber. She was hungry. She was taking the whole city down with her. I look into the mirror, blurred from drink. I blow a kiss. She blows one back. There it was. I'd wanted to do it and now I'd done it.

✦

It is the white that catches my eye. Later, I'll know the story where I don't see it, where I walk back into the music, hold a shot glass in my hand. Where I tilt my head back. Where I follow a stranger onto the dance floor, into the night. But I see the white. Not the makeup-remover pads. Not the floss. A phone charger. Three, actually. Plugged into the walls, waiting, their silver tips eager as tongues.

My phone into the silver. My hand waiting for light.

By the time the white apple blooms on my screen, he has texted twenty-eight times. They come in one after the other, rushed, a river of metallic chirps. There are eight missed calls.

✦

In a city of a quarter million people, he found me. He'd returned to the Airbnb, his stomach settling, and fallen asleep. Twenty, thirty minutes passed, when he woke up in terror. For a few seconds he didn't know what was wrong. Then, he remembered the beach, the white wine, my strange calm smile. He remembered the stories. The ones I'd told him. The ones my friends had told him. What if I had changed, but not enough? What if I had changed, but the drink hadn't? He'd leapt through the streets, going from bar to bar. It was a city of bars, a city of nightlife, of music and wine, a city of dark-haired women, curly-haired women, drunk women. Maybe he followed the wrong girl? He is sorry. He is so sorry. Please, Hala, please. Call him back.

✦

The moments that show us we've changed are rarely dramatic. There is a sliver of a moment, a white apple, the chirp of texts. I read the texts. I know that I can turn my phone back off, that I have plausible deniability, that I can be the victim, that I'm an alcoholic and I shouldn't have drunk, that there shouldn't have been any wine to begin with, that I can't be held accountable for what I do next. But here is the truth. I see the white of that apple and I see the white of her spine. And just like that, the plot rearranges, the names flood back to me, the baby, the girl.

✦

The night before the evacuation ship from Beirut, I dream of my grandmother. She is standing next to a window. It is the same house it's always been. Her couch has seeped onto the Oriental rug. There is a single name that lives in her mouth like a bird. By the time I hear it, I'm already awake.

✦

There are two timelines and in both of them, I am my future self, I am my past self. In both of them, I walk through the club, across the dance floor, avoiding the private tables. I leave without saying a word, without a goodbye. I disappear from the lives of those strangers. I walk outside to the warm, salty air, I look at that water that could be any water, and, with the sliver of life I'd just been given, the battery, I call him.

✦

The water is nearly green when we gather at the port. The ship cuts through it for ten hours straight. At some point overnight, some woman thinks she has lost her teenager. There is panic. They find the girl with an American soldier. I am hungover again, had spent the night before evacuating drinking from the tiny Bacardi bottles I kept hidden in the dresser. I slept through most of the drive to the port. I can barely remember anything about the ship, only emerging at night onto the deck, the way the sky looked, how it felt like I wasn't even there. I felt like I'd blinked and woken in someone's dream, about teenage girls and ocean and war. We docked in Cyprus in the morning. The water blue as anything.

✦

The next morning in Mexico, I wake to find I've time-traveled. The messy room. The cabinets flung open from where I'd looked for more alcohol when we returned the previous night. I remember the doctor I'd spoken to months earlier. *If you're not careful, it's going to cost you.* Here was the cost. It was as awful as I remembered it.

✦

For years, I'd wake and think I was in Beirut. Back in that house, still living within its walls, haunting it from thousands of miles away. I'd hear the traffic from the road below, the faint chatter of my grandmother's Turkish soap operas in the living room. It would sometimes take full minutes to remember, for my brain to understand the window and chair and pillow, to place them in their right place. This happened for years. I don't know when it stopped.

✦

We go on a hike. "You'll feel better," Johnny says softly. My head is throbbing. The bus is bumpy and the ride takes over an hour. When we arrive, the guide reminds me of my cousin Omar, beaming and muscular and oblivious to my misery.

"Are you ready for beauty?"

I am ready for beauty. The dewy vines, the glittering water visible in clearings. There is a photograph of me, sweating, my shirt wrapped around my head, Johnny looking at me like he's about to ask a question. We walk and walk and walk. My head is spinning. I keep remembering shards from the previous night, hot colorful bursts of arguing, crying, dancing, kissing Johnny in the Airbnb, trying to run out for more cigarettes. We climb and stumble over rocks. Once we reach the shore, there is a boat that takes us to a seafood restaurant. I barely make it to the bathroom before I vomit. I hear someone running lightly behind me, then feel Johnny's hand in my hair, pulling it back, the other rubbing circles against my back. "I'm sorry, I'm sorry." "I'm sorry too," I hear myself saying, but I'm not sure to whom. My stomach heaves again. *Remember this*, I tell myself. I wash my mouth, my hair, in the tiny sink. He waits for me outside. His arms open like a door and I walk into them.

✦

After the restaurant, we take a boat ride back with the other hikers. Johnny and I sit entangled in each other, the water spraying on us. The story changes depending on where you hold it to the light. The tape is different depending on where you start it. Sitting on that boat, I imagine all the other versions of ourselves on boats nearby. Dozens of Halas and Johnnys, past and present and future, bobbing in their own boats. A man that packs a suitcase and leaves. Rewind a few years: a woman who gives an ultimatum. Fast forward: a promise made, an interrupted pregnancy, relief and heartache in equal measure. I close my eyes shut against the bright sun. The water sprays on our faces. Each pair plays a different story, an orchestra of grievances. Behind each story is the annihilation of another, something that had to die. I'm sorry, he says. I'm sorry. I say it back. We are apologizing for nothing, for everything, for our fathers, our mothers, for the griefs they carried, the ones they named, the ones they didn't, for the names they gave us, for the things they would not sit with, and so now we sat with, our cheeks wet with seawater and tears. You know a body can fall to the ground, you know a body can fall from a window, into the earth, through a night. What happens the next time a body appears to you, a face lit by street lamps, a voice that tugs at something in you, what happens the next time love clears its throat? What lesson have you learned? What will you protect, by what measure, at what cost?

◆

An amend asks nothing of the other. It is an offering. It is an offering that ends at its presence.

◆

In the class I teach on addiction, I ask people to think of something they clasp onto. Something they turn to because the alternative—the now, the feeling nestled in the now—is unbearable. What is a feeling you're not willing to feel? I've asked patients before. Then: and what are you willing to do not to feel it? Everything can be an addiction: therapy, love, thinking. The desire to time-travel. The desire to rewrite the past. The story we tell, the one we can't let go of.

✦

There was an original pain and a house had been its antidote: being left, leaving behind. Leaving behind, being left. It was the feeling of a clock, the feeling of fire, a boat somewhere casting off without you. The thud of girl feet running. Tick tock. What will you take. What will you leave behind. The whirr of a plane engine. Tick tock. The feel of a hand in your hair, perhaps for the last time. Every time might be the last time. Tick tock. You never know when it's coming. The blare of a news report. The static of a call, the news of what is gone is gone is gone. The thing about the coding term is it doesn't know what it's carrying. It just carries it. A man becomes a jailer, a king, an invasion. You marry a man and you think you're marrying a house. You marry a woman and think you're marrying an escape route. I'd married what couldn't stay, the dropped shoe, the blanched headline, the border overrun with cars. I'd married a clock, tick tock, and what of yourself will you salvage before the time is up?

✦

We leave for San Miguel the next day. We arrive late and starving, wander around the town square looking for food. We find a beautiful courtyard with live music, the musicians earnest, their foreheads shiny with sweat. We sit and the weather is windy, cooler than Puerto Vallarta, this place that we've made it to despite everything, this place that took courage to arrive at. He hasn't been back here since the boy fell. And I felt it, that old rising, like a tide or stray strand of music, inside me. I feel it—my hope, my one rechargeable heart, only I feel it toward myself now, my mistake, my poured wine. That same forgiving heart, rivering back in my own direction.

Month Eight

Your baby's movements are becoming more and more noticeable. Your baby's skull remains soft and malleable, but her bones are hardening.

In San Miguel de Allende, my friend moves us into her mother's gorgeous, palatial house. We are two thousand miles from Brooklyn, spending these weeks in sunlight, working remotely. There are eyes in every room of the house. My friend's mother is an artist, and her photographs remind me of dreams: smoky, blurred, intense. Her subjects are women, lithe, long-haired, dark-eyed, unclothed, sinewy, their bodies mid-motion in most photographs.

The house is named after an army general and the place feels deliciously haunted, filled with damp shadowy corners, towering trees, a courtyard twice the size of our Brooklyn apartment, and a rooftop that reminds you—suddenly, thrustingly—of sunlight. It is the kind of beauty that cannot be replicated or repaid, and I get used to its splendor disconcertingly quickly.

✦

My friend Alexis is pregnant. She sends a voice note: *Don't you think you should use this time to, like, nest?* But there is no bed rest. There are no birthing classes, no Lamaze exercises. I don't have to prepare my perineum for anything. I don't have to buy cocoa oil for my nipples. I am absent from the baby registry, having copied the items from another friend's, and removed the maternity products. Instead, I walk through the beautiful cobblestone streets of San Miguel and look at art, listen to Arabic music, avoid making eye contact with liquor bottles. I tell my friend Michael about the relapse in the storefront of a gallery, bronze sculptures and cerulean paintings. It feels hard to connect with the act, those jewel-toned bottles. The altitude is high here. I'm always drinking water. I'm always looking for a bathroom.

"But you're okay now?" he asks in a worried tone.

"Yeah, it's hard to explain," I say. I don't say: I feel like I'm describing a friend, someone who isn't here anymore.

✦

I'm a simulacrum of waiting. I'm no Penelope, no Eurydice. Dee texts me updates: her cravings, the burning sensation around her belly, the baby's frequent kicking. I've ordered a monitor, a crib, a yellow painting. My tasks feel like a child's—what you'd give someone to make them feel useful, a child chopping fake tomatoes at their mother's hip. The real adults have to do the real work now.

✦

Almost immediately after moving into the house in San Miguel, I dream of tidal waves, earthquakes, cities disappearing under claps of unspeakable light. I dream of blood pooling in teacups, knives clutched in my hand, guns that won't fire until I kiss their holsters. I dream of my grandmother, the baby, bulldozers, people trapped on balconies, fires. They scream words in Arabic I can't understand. You forgot, they finally say in English, their faces dismayed and tear-stained. You forgot.

✦

"Exile is strangely compelling to think about," Edward Said wrote, "but terrible to experience. It is the unhealable rift forced between a human being and a native place." How to explain being a Palestinian child nowhere near Palestine? You become a magpie. You wait for the adults to slip: to tell you stories, to miss signs of danger. You are trained from childhood on nostalgia, on history, on witnessing. You, after all, are the proof: That others have endured. That something once existed.

✦

In the Plaza Allende, with my matcha latte, I walk from bench to bench recording for the coconut-sized baby. *I got you an olive branch*, I say. I tell her that I framed it. I tell her I always think of the Yasser Arafat UN speech when I think of olive branches. *Do not let the olive branch fall from my hand.* I tell her who Yasser Arafat is. I nearly trip over a tiny dog. There's a piece of tatreez that my friend has ordered me, I tell her. I mean you. She's ordered it for you. I can't wait for you to see it.

✦

My first month in New York, I got into an argument with someone at a bar. There was a girl who'd just returned from a Birthright trip. She was arguing about the term "Palestinian."

"It just feels unnecessarily . . . controversial. Like you can say 'Arab.' You can say 'Middle Eastern.'"

I was drunk and sputtering. The tips of my fingers felt like they were on fire, my ears, the edge of my jaw. I wanted to say something about Balfour or Herzl or any of the thousand things I'd half-learned in my political science classes, to parrot my father, my professors, but the words wouldn't come. I couldn't say what was fair. I was suddenly aware of the slight edge in the girl's tone, how the bartender kept glancing at us, her tall, silent boyfriend with a biceps tattoo. *I'm not among friends*, I remember thinking. She kept talking about her trip, how Israelis she'd met had told her about terror attacks, about how Palestinians would never want peace. I drank so I wouldn't speak. Then I spent fifteen years learning to steady my voice.

◆

There is no such thing as an assault on people and land that doesn't first begin with an assault on language, on truth. The Levant was not the name we gave ourselves. People told us a story about ourselves and the story endured.

How to explain being Palestinian and American? You must disavow the former to prove the latter.

You exist in both identities like a ghost, belonging to neither. You watch white phosphorus burn the flesh of middle-schoolers. You watch politicians equivocate about the meaning of a civilian. You watch press conferences, infographics, maps. You watch a bulldozer rip a house apart like teeth into flesh. Perhaps this is your only utility: your witnessing. Your not looking away.

◆

We meet a Mexican couple, a painter and sculptor. Their work is surreal: his sculptures marvelous conversations between stone and rusted metal, limbs, clocks, while her paintings take up entire walls of buildings, portraits of people squinting in the sun, lifting their hair. One evening, we walk with them and their enormous dog through the streets of San Miguel, Johnny speaking easily in Spanish, the woman and I picking through English like a rack of dresses. We are talking about the baby; it takes me five minutes to explain surrogacy, the other womb, the woman I haven't met in person yet, but who knows my daughter more intimately than anyone, to explain that the baby is ours in the biological sense, and not in any other sense, not yet at least, that she will be the second she takes her first breath, that she is my grandmother's first great-granddaughter, she will be Syrian, she will be Palestinian, she will be white. I talk about the other heartbeats, the ones that stopped, the years at the clinic. She listens, her kind face pained.

"It is good bad luck, no?" she finally says. She explains how she lost a job years earlier, which meant she had to move to San Miguel, which meant that she met her partner. Bad luck, but through the lens of enough time, it was transmuted good again. "So now," she continues. "Your daughter. She will change the bad luck." Yes, I tell her. Good bad luck. Exactly.

We eat tacos in a narrow restaurant: cactus and edible flowers, avocado halved and filled with tuna tartare. The conversation turns to politics, borders, the Mexican hometowns they left for this one. They ask about Beirut, Palestine, Syria. "Will you take her home?" the man asks, and I don't ask what he means. I don't flinch. I ask myself the question constantly. I ask it in my sleep, my fretting, my dreams. But my appetite wanes just the same. I look down at the beautiful food on the beautiful plate. It is the forever question: what am I doing here instead of there? The *here*, the *there*. The man is already asking another question. "Have you been there?" He says the name. Palestine. "How was it? How was it to return?"

✦

How to explain the airport line in Amman? The weeks of preparation for passport control, the deleted Facebook account, the burner phone. How to explain the plane circling green and blue and mountain, breath fogging the moon-faced window, the insistent thought: *Look, look, look.* And its silent corollary: Feel, feel, feel. They kept me in the airport for hours and hours. They made me write down everything, unlock my phone, list the men in my family. One name after the other. *Every man you can remember. As far back as you can go.*

I went to Palestine alone. Each city was surreal, a place I'd read and heard and spoken about, each a celebrity sighting. Suddenly I was there: Jerusalem and I wore black skirts. Ramallah and the sun was unbearably bright. I filled two notebooks during the trip. The lines felt useless later, unplaceable anywhere: *It's like a house inside a house. It's like wearing two coats.* In my feverish pages was the clear wish not to forget: *A bird outside the hostel window, red, like an omen. The applause after the reading. The university student holding out her hand when I tripped.* Everywhere I went, I saw the place twice: as it was, soldiers and settlers and walls, and as it had been. The latter lived inside the former, it still pulsed with life.

◆

San Miguel was the first Spanish settlement in the state of Guanajuato, named for a Franciscan monk. The house is in Centro, in the heart of the town, a short walk from the Parroquia, a massive gothic church the color of pale flamingos. Everywhere we go, people speak to me in Spanish, but it is Johnny who replies, in his perfect accent, a fluency that surprises everyone. Everywhere we go, people guess where I'm from: Granada? Greece? Turkey? Am I from the north? From Chile? They speak to me in Spanish and I smile at them with my dumb mouth. "No sé," I say.

◆

In Jerusalem, in the Old City, a shopkeeper showed me jewelry boxes and asked where I was from. He wouldn't stop asking. I said, "I live in New York." He said, "But before that." I said, "I've lived in New York for years." "But where are your parents from?" His lips flattened. "Where is your father from?" "Here." His eyes turned to knives. "From here? What here? What here?" "My father was born here." "Where? You show me where, right now," as though I could take him by the hand and lead him to the very house. His voice rose. "You show me where, right now, you show me where." "Gaza." The word, a silence. He let out a bark of laughter. His eyes flashed over me. "Go, go to Gaza. Go. I'd like to see what they do to you there."

✦

In the house, I dream of drowning. I dream of saying her name in the water but it is the wrong name. Then I'm next to the water, a baby in my arms. There is a boat and it will leave without us. I dream I take her to the water. I hear myself say, This is yours, baby. This is all yours.

✦

"It would be the simplest thing to say, my homeland is where I was born," Darwish writes. "But when you returned, you found nothing." The diaspora canon is littered with stories of disappointing return. It is the same story, over and over, with different protagonists, different longings—sea, mountains, a grandparent's lemon tree, the sound of a street—years away, then finally a return where nothing is as the diasporic remembers. Or, even worse: where nothing is as *others* remember. There was an archway next to the mosque, the aunties and grandparents and fathers will tell him. Don't forget to walk the marina. The fishermen line up at dawn. But when he gets there, the diasporic is confused. There are no fishermen. The archway is a new building, or there are no buildings, or there are only buildings and the marina is gone. The street he was told about sounds different: no vendors hawking melons, just car horns and neighbors' voices and the same pesky bird. Everywhere the air tastes of exhaust. Pesky place, pesky memory. The diasporic leaves disappointed. He returns to his adopted city. He returns to the skyscrapers or the Southwestern landscape or the European city. He returns to his new name, his perfect accent. But something funny happens in the coming days: His memory starts to vibrate, like asphalt under heat. It starts to stretch, its edges overlapping like paint on paint, until there are new colors, until the disappointment feels fuzzier and fuzzier, farther away, a voice in another room, then another house, then the first dream comes, the one of that street, only this is the correct street, the way it was always supposed to be, the way in fact it *was*, wasn't it, with the bruised fruit and the vendor and the sound of hudhuds. The diasporic is comforted. His story of home is renewed. It is returned to him. He tells the story of his visit to his family, his date, the coworker who always talks about the new Palestinian restaurant in Bushwick. He tells the story the way it was always meant to be, the way he willed it, the way he remembers it now. And if the other memory ever returns, that uneasy feeling of being an intruder, the way the cab driver had stared at him as he fumbled with the foreign coins, the way he kept forgetting words for utensils and plants, he is certain the mistake was his memory, not the way things were. He'd almost touched the homeland, he is certain of it, that original thing, he nearly had, he will get there. Maybe next time.

✦

The Levantine was carved from absence. To be Levantine was to want. It is easy to forget, but: the Levantine was *created*. The Levantine as a concept was based on the idea of endings: borders, historical eras, the ushering in of modernity. It required nostalgia: to create an idea of a place that was connected but also, forever, being undone.

✦

What is a story that is constantly being erased? How can you pass along what you know only in fragments?

✦

Let me start at the beginning. Let me start at *a* beginning: my father was born in Gaza. What, then, is my claim to Gaza? A good witness should be wary of how the *I* rearranges the air in the room. Nonetheless: my claim is my father. My oak tree of a father, born without a passport, now an American. He was born on a Wednesday in a house, the third son. He spent every summer of his childhood in Gaza. He played with chicks in a courtyard. He learned soccer there. He was bathed by his grandmother. He ate her hot bread. He was born in Gaza because the other villages—Iraq Sweidan, al-Majdal, places of farming, of almond trees and grape crops—were eradicated.

✦

I can only find one book about Iraq Sweidan, out of print. Meanwhile, a university is bombed in Gaza. Meanwhile, the archives are wiped out. Set on fire. The poets are targeted. The journalists sniped.

✦

In July 1948, David Ben-Gurion wrote in his diary: "We must do everything to insure they never do return."

✦

The diasporic can't win: you are discredited for your proximity to the land or disputed for your severance from it. "Why don't you go back to Gaza." Or: "Keep writing from your warm house." Compared to those *there*, the diasporic is ridiculously buffered: by our passports, our time to create musings, our code-switching. But in the end, we are Palestinian mouths, are Palestinian eyes: those wayward thresholds, they are to be doubted. Our allegiance will always be questioned. Our truths will always come with an asterisk.

✦

In Gaza, my grandmother's family lives in a rented house. She bakes bread on an oven shaped like half a globe. A year after my father is born, she moves to Kuwait, where my father's father will teach science to schoolchildren. Every June until the mid-sixties, she and her sons return to Gaza. They sleep in that rented house, in the neighborhood named after stairs, a house with an open, roofless space in the middle. A house with a large bedroom and little mattresses for the children and grand-children to sleep. A room filled with mattresses. A room filled with sleep.

✦

My first year in Manhattan. A woman at another bar: *They don't exist.* I look down at my ghost hands. Clear my ghost throat.

✦

In San Miguel, I'm ravenous for color. I do tatreez with fuchsia thread, fill a sketchbook with yellow and green drawings. I want to do a series called "You Can Have Your Life Back." I want to do a series called "Ask Me About Beirut." I want to do a series called "Are You My Daughter?" The sunsets are the color of backyard fires. There are sculptures in the hotel lobbies, copper and stone and wire. Everywhere we go, we point out colors to each other: the clementine in the salad, the dusty-pink houses, teal scarves in storefront windows. I want to do a series called "We Can Heal If We Let Ourselves."

✦

After the Six-Day War, Israel banned the Palestinian flag from the Gaza Strip and West Bank. A little over a decade later, a law was passed ban-ning artwork composed of the flag's four colors: white, black, red, green.

✦

In Oklahoma, my father had a small Palestinian flag. My brother would hold it in his tiny hand and chant *Falasteen arabiya* while the adults clapped. Where had my father gotten the flag? I cannot bring myself to ask. Online, I find distributors everywhere: Iowa, India, Madrid.

✦

During the Intifada, people sliced watermelons and held them above their heads: black, red, green. A makeshift flag.

✦

Here is the most shameful thing I could confess: I forget about the land all the time. I forget about the sea. I forget about the stones stacked into houses, forget my grandparents and great-grandparents lived next to water. I forget about their sage, their za'atar, their olive trees. I forget about their sunsets. This is connected to a larger grief: I forget about land in general. I've spent my life in cities and am besotted with their chaos, but I come from a long line of farmers and peasants and custodians of earth, as recently as two generations ago, and this forgetting feels like treachery. When I finally do dream of Gaza, my dream-self drives down a road, finds a rooftop, kneels to touch water, with the same thought echoing: *This is a place and I'm here.*

✦

When I was sixteen, we visited my father's mother in Syria. Seham. She was dying, it was understood. We spent the days in her hospital room, the insistent beeps of machines, tubes running through her nose. She winced every time she moved. I asked her stories about Palestine, then felt greedy. Her breathing was heavy. The water is filling her lungs, my doctor uncle said matter-of-factly, then took a deep puff from his cigarette.

✦

Once, when I look up the difference between diaspora and migrant, a question auto-populates in the search bar: *What is the difference between diaspora and nostalgia?*

✦

When it was time to leave the hospital, my grandmother, my Teta, said: Nobody give Hala a hard time. She said: Forgive me. She said: Forgive me, forgive me.

✦

My father, my oak tree. His face crumpled as his mother wept. This is the only time I've seen him cry: he ran to the bathroom, came out red-faced. She was dead within a month.

✦

My father, my oak tree. The texts come in the middle of the day. Johnny and I are in a vineyard in San Miguel and a teenage girl is telling us the history of the soil. The chirp of my phone interrupts her. My hands go cold as I reach for my phone. Every ding makes me think *Dee*: every rainbow, every stroller, every pregnant woman. I keep dreaming the baby comes out speaking in full sentences. I keep dreaming the baby is lost. I keep dreaming my grandmother is telling me the baby is on the way.

✦

But these texts aren't from Dee. They are from my brother. He is with my father at a hospital in Manhattan. It takes me a minute to remember. He was meeting with a specialist today. His numb legs. His slow gait. For months, there's been a numbness and now my brother is texting rapid-fire, dozens in a row, broken words, a column of alarm: *doctors ordering more tests, something wrong, neurologist, neurologist. Wait*, I type back. Wait. Neurology means nerves. It means spine.

✦

The hospital admits him. Talal's voice in my ear, while I sit at the base of a tree. His voice is shaking. They found a fistula, he says. Neither of us knows the word. It connects something, he says. There is the sound of rushed voices in the background. He hangs up. I blink up at the blue sky. The ground is cold, seeping through my pants. I cannot clutch the ribbon of a single thought, my mind a jumble: I'd spent so much time. I'd spent so much time. On the wrong things. My brother calls back. He explains to me what the doctors explain to him. A fistula, a faulty connection of spinal arteries. "Where is he now?" I ask. I want to talk with him. My brother sounds far away and next to me at the same time. They are doing the procedure on him now. The surgeon had taken one look at the MRI images and told the nurse to prep him for surgery.

✦

When my mother and I left Kuwait during the war, my father stayed behind. He stayed for a few weeks and when I ask him why, he says, *We didn't know what was going to happen.* I think this is his answer, but later he says, as though mid-conversation, *I thought it would end soon.* Maybe this would all stop, maybe they could resume their old lives, as though their lives were huddled animals waiting for them to return. Maybe he thought that if he left, it would make it real.

✦

My father wakes from his procedure and can't move his legs. My brother describes the surgeon as quiet. He quietly examines my father's toes. He quietly asks him to move, shake, flex. He quietly says he's not sure what will happen next.

✦

My father is an oak tree: six foot three, wide-shouldered, too large for most chairs, airplanes, long-legged, booming voice.

✦

That afternoon, I pack. There are no flights until the next day. We have to spend a final night in the house and suddenly I feel the eyes on me in every room. When I finally speak with my father, his voice is hoarse, like he has been shouting or singing. He keeps saying inshallah. There is another surgery tomorrow, inshallah. They will slice into his spine while I'm in the sky, inshallah. "The doctor says it will work," I tell him. "That they'll find it." I imagine the fistula, new word, new nemesis, a tiny glittery clot. My brother takes the phone. My brother says he'll see me in the hospital tomorrow. My brother says I should try to sleep. My brother says I shouldn't be told any stories because I'll give them all away.

✦

In 1990, my father stays in Kuwait for three weeks. His parents will not leave. His mother says, I'm not leaving. If I'm going to die let me die here. She has left al-Majdal, left Gaza, will not leave this place. The civil services stop. Trash piles knee high on street corners, there is no mail. My father is thirty years old. His daughter and wife are in the backseat of a car for two days. We didn't want anyone to see your passport, he tells me. So he'd kept it. My mother took me and my forged Lebanese passport, and my father kept the American passport. You see, he asks me, smiling like he's still tricking an army. I had the passport, but didn't have the girl. Your mother had the girl, but didn't have the passport.

✦

Here is my part of that story, the one I was in but didn't construct. I have one memory of Syria during the weeks we waited for my father. It is at night, in a room with a white coverlet blanket on a bed. My mother and I are kneeling on the floor and her hair is covered. We are praying, she tells me. We're praying for your father to get here safely.

✦

The next morning, our plane cuts through blue and my father wakes up from anesthesia. He wakes up and he can feel his legs. He can feel the muscles. He can move his toes. The surgeon smiles quietly.

✦

Just like that: a miracle. Just like that: legs, dancing, returned.

✦

In Gaza, my father is born. It is 1958. He is born in a small house by the sea. He is born a boy without a passport. By his first birthday, his family moves to Kuwait. But for twelve years, they return in late spring. For twelve summers, he plays on the beach in Gaza. He plays in his grandmother's garden. He plays with chicks in a courtyard, kicks around a ball with his brothers, a new brother every couple of years. For twelve years, he loves a grandmother, a sea, a house. Then he never sees any of it again.

✦

There is an art print my father has had for decades. It is black and white, a photocopy of a cartoon black duckling. The black duckling watches the other ducklings play and splash in the water. The duckling is alone. The duckling looks sad. He'd taped it on the inside of a binder where he kept important papers. There is a tenderness in this fact that I cannot look directly at, the thought of my father finding tape, cutting the paper out carefully. Smoothing it down. Why do you like it, I asked him when I was younger. I don't know, he said, and I believe that answer.

✦

We take a taxi straight to the hospital from the airport. I was afraid he'd look small in the hospital bed, but he is tall as always, the gown too short on him. We'd spent hours the day before wandering San Miguel looking for a shirt large enough, one the color of pale tulips, early morning sky, and when I hand him the bag, I feel dumb, the festive color in this room, a relic from another world.

✦

"Have you thought of a name?" he asks me that afternoon. He is eating a sandwich. The nurse comes and he says, "This is my eldest daughter, she flew home today." I can barely say hello without my voice breaking. "I can't stop thinking of one," I tell him, then say it aloud.

✦

What is a name but something that cannot be taken from you? A name is what my father gives me. A name is what his father gives him. A name is what I will give my daughter. Every bookstore my father goes to, he looks for his last name, the one he gave me, the one I will give her.

✦

After the second novel I wrote, another one about families and Arab cities and secrets, he told me, Maybe you can write something different now. He says if I only write about Arabs, they'll think I can only write about Arabs.

What else should I write about, I ask.

He thinks for a while, the line quiet. I don't know, he finally says. Cowboys?

✦

When I ask my father if I cried when we were reunited in Syria, he says, Of course not. He says, Why would you cry. He says, It was wonderful, we were all so happy. My oak tree father, who tapes sad ducklings on the inside of folders, who never speaks of his own sadness. My father, who was once a boy, a boy with stories I'll never repeat, and stories I'll never hear. My father says we reunited in Syria, two months after the army invaded Kuwait, and we were happy, and so we were, we were happy, nobody cried, why would we, why would you even ask that.

✦

I don't remember saying goodbye to my father. I don't remember our reunion. But I know there is a single feeling I've done everything I can not to feel. I know every fear telescopes from another fear, one after the other, until you get to the original one: leaving behind, being left behind.

I had the passport, but didn't have the girl. Your mother had the girl, but didn't have the passport.

✦

Mama and Baba took the passport and the girl on a plane from Damascus. They flew toward America. The layover was in Frankfurt, the day of the unification of East and West Germany. Imagine. They wandered through the airport, blinking, nodding at the foreign language. The world felt like an aquarium. Imagine. Around them, everywhere, the present was becoming history. What was there to be nostalgic for? In the Frankfurt airport, raw with loss and hope. Everything.

✦

This is a place and I'm here. This is a place and I'm not there. There is a place and I have never once genuinely imagined myself there. It is this failure of imagination that feels like the deepest, truest defeat. No: that I've imagined myself everywhere but there.

✦

I wrote not of cowboys but the streets I'd spent decades trying to leave, streets my father grew up in, streets I'd never see. I wrote of something dead and alive, pulsing and buried. It didn't matter what I did to forget, it didn't matter that I married this country, a son of this country, learned to pass. Some leavings are not consensual and therefore do not abide by grief's normal timeline. You leave places but the leaving becomes its own story. You become defined by it. In this way, you stay and stay and stay.

✦

The night my father is discharged, we enter the cold February night together. We all fill our lungs. It is his first time outside in over a week. We'd all wished for this: the fresh air, his legs returned. After his cab drives off, I walk down First Avenue, the same walk I used to do during the infertility years, down to Fourteenth Street, passing the familiar bodegas and smoke shop and Greek seafood restaurant. I reach the train station and read the Fatiha at its entrance, like a sermon, among the barflies and traffic. The cold air hits me with a memory I haven't had in decades. It is Oklahoma, Halloween, an itchy costume. There is a hayride. There are pumpkins and trees decorated with spiderwebs. There were blankets on the hayride, and music, and my parents pointing things out to us. My parents who had come to a new country and dressed their children up and took them to look at pumpkins. How had they found the hayride? What had they thought of it all? I'd fallen asleep in the car afterward, and I remember the lift of my father carrying me inside, tucking me in the bed. I remember the impossibility of that safety, a premonition, how even as a child I understood something melancholy about this moment, half-awake, him kissing my forehead, that it was fleeting, that I wouldn't be carried inside houses by my father forever, that it would all need to be mourned, and so I was already mourning it.

✦

Diasporic identity is a matter of engagement: how coupled you feel to your roots, to your homeland, to language, to your kin across the world. The most effective displacement is that which becomes metaphysical. Ben-Gurion wasn't just talking about physical return, a horde of Arabs brandishing keys, but something more embedded. The fantasy he had was the diasporic not returning even in imagination.

✦

My father worked at a gas station in Oklahoma. Sooner Superette. He was a cashier. They showed him where the gun was. He left Kuwait a bank manager and arrived in America a refugee twice over, a seeker of asylum in a place he'd never thought he'd live. He worked, took night classes, raised children. He drove two hours for an adjunct position. He tried on a drawl. He called his children Timmy and Holly, kept a small Palestinian flag and a picture of a lost duckling.

In America, my father wore sneakers and baseball caps with a football team's name stitched on them. In America, my father ordered Diet Coke without ice. In America, my father sang me a song about a baby he wanted, a baby called Hala. *He spoke me into a name, he spoke me into being.*

✦

The exile is a character of reinvention. A performer. The exile is a teenage girl who wears a sequined dress of red and gold and walks onto a stage and lies. The exile is a teenage girl pretending to be Scheherazade pretending to be a woman telling her own story. The exile is both the performance and the audience. So what am I performing when I tell you of Hezbollah tents in Centreville, when I tell you of my friend's neck in the arm of a soldier, my Arabic saving us all. When I tell you I can hardly think of my father's ducklings without weeping. When I tell you Nadia died in Syria after all, and I tried to storyboard her death into an essay on the industry of flying diasporic bodies home for rest. What am I performing, what am I witnessing, when I tell you Nadia died in Syria and they buried her in Syria, but her sisters are in Russia, Amman, Beirut. When I tell you my Syrian grandmother is in Lebanese dirt. The Palestinian one in Syria. The uncle in Kansas. It is nearly time for the curtain. One last story: There are sisters and they have similar dress sizes. They borrow land. Just for an evening. Just for a jaunt. Just for eternity.

Birth

*Your preborn baby is preparing for birth. She is moving
closer to the pelvis and starting to position herself for
labor. Your baby already knows how to breathe!*

Canada feels like the rehearsal before opening night. I am nervous about
meeting her. Her. Her. It reminds me of the first part of a new move,
Oklahoma, Al-Ain, Brummana, how before each new school I'd spent
weeks deciding who I was going to be. I'd practice new handwriting, study
the vocal fry of Topanga from *Boy Meets World*, listen to growly voiced
rockstars. Punk girl. British transplant. Bookish mystery. I'd try skipping
meals. I'd pretend I could play guitar. My body carried me from one performance to the next. It was train tracks, passageway, an instrument.

✦

We arrive in Toronto on the second day of March. Dee lives a few hours
away; we rent the surrogacy agency's allotted apartment, a threadbare du-
plex filled with diapers and baby cots and three separate car seats. The bed

is hard and the walls thin, and the apartment is in the financial district: all high-rises and banks and Equinox gyms. The first few days are slow and surreal. We go to a smoke shop. We wander a massive Whole Foods. At night, I kick the sheets into a tangle around my body, fall asleep to the sound of my heartbeat through my earplugs. I get a runny nose. My neck cricks. I can't get comfortable. The days are slow, but my body is on edge, an engine running at all hours. It reminds me of the days after the last miscarriage, how I'd walk from Manhattan to Brooklyn without realizing I'd done it, moving from borough to borough like I was being chased.

◆

In her second month of pregnancy, Dee craved pasta with butter and egg yolk. Two months later, she sent a photo of five different orange sodas, from Orange Crush to Sparkling Ice, captioning it, *Wants orange pop but won't tell me which one.* The cravings changed: horseradish, vanilla ice cream. Cookies and milk.

◆

My new selves never lasted. My handwriting would always wilt back to the floppy r's. I couldn't pull off the broad vowels of a British accent for long. Once I got excited, I'd revert to myself: barking laugh, overeager pitch of voice, unable to resist a good lie. Once, in second grade, I dislocated my shoulder trying to hoist myself on a kitchen counter. I told everyone I'd fallen out of a tree. I've never climbed a tree in my life. I never could hide my appetite, outeating my father at dinner. I hummed with desire for a revolving door of crushes. But there was nothing I wanted without feeling ashamed I wanted it.

◆

When I quit drinking, I started dreaming of food: banquet halls filled with velvet sofas and slices of cake, a plate as long as an avenue, brimming with salty cheeses and olives.

✦

In Canada, I find an article about a woman who used a surrogate. She writes about all the suggestions people offered her: "You just need to relax. Did you try acupuncture? Soy milk makes you infertile. You're in front of your computer too much. What's the problem with all you career girls? Did this cycle work? Are you pregnant this time? How many shots? Where? A low whistle: Boy, you must really want a child."

She writes, "You must really want a child. As if that were a bad thing."

✦

This furnished apartment in Toronto is the culmination of all that wanting. Johnny and I watch episodes of *Parks and Recreation* and laugh and sometimes he turns to me with a bewildered gaze. I see him a decade earlier, tousle-haired, the night in December we met, the first New Year's a few weeks later, where we kissed and tossed tinsel into the air at a house party. I feel younger than I felt then. I feel like no time has passed at all, as though the previous decade was a blip, an overslept dream, a mistake we both didn't make. His sea-green eyes. It's happening, he says without saying anything. My God, I say back wordlessly. I know.

✦

When you tell the story of a body, you tell the story of other bodies too. The story of Dee's pregnant body is nominally mine, if at all. The story of my body was my mother's more than mine for years. The story of my body, my cousin's body, my aunt's body: it was the story of the countries we lived in. The countries told you whether to wear your hair straight or curly. Whether to tan or seek shade. The countries had plastic surgeons and the surgeons had stories too. The countries had priests or imams, and they had stories. The countries had colonizers and they had stories. The countries had revolutions and they had stories. Each story had a good body and a bad body. A body that did as it was told. A body that didn't listen. But each of these stories—after a while, they're yours. You don't remember ever not hearing them in your own voice.

✦

The theory of pregnancy cravings is inconclusive. Some say the body is signaling the need for certain nutrients. Some say the dopamine receptors get stimulated and trigger cravings. Or maybe it's as simple as scarcity: after a lifetime of restraint, an invitation to eat whatever you want. Sometimes, the pregnant crave soil. They crave clay, rocks, sand. There are theories, of course: iron deficiency, immune system changes. But sometimes the blood work comes back clear and the craving remains. Palmfuls of earth. The crunch of salt between your teeth. During my pregnancies, I've only craved nothing, a hush. I've longed for my mouth not to taste of itself, to smell nothing. But the first time I threw clay in a pottery class, I had to restrain the urge to lick that earthen red. I wasn't pregnant. I was crying.

✦

The years after drinking, my body was returned to me unceremoniously. I had no idea what to do with it. It took me months to notice I'd lost fifteen pounds. There was no more beer, no more blackout midnight meals. Instead, I started to notice things: the slices of cheesecake in café displays, pizzas through the window of Joe's, greasy and beautiful and whole. My appetite had run rampant when I was a drinker. I always had a stomachache. I wolfed down kebab wraps and cheeseburgers without tasting them, without remembering I'd eaten them. But now I was stone sober. I wanted sugar on my tongue. I wanted to taste everything on the menu. *But look where all that wanting got me*, I wrote in a journal in early 2011. My drinking years had rendered a steep cost, but it didn't feel high enough. I hadn't fallen out of a window. I was still walking around New York City in my worn sneakers, smoking cigarettes, writing poems. I felt like a criminal. There was punishment to dole out and, in the absence of the person who'd demanded the drinking, there was the body that had done it.

♦

I lost more weight. I admired my cheekbones, the slope of my waist. I lost and lost and lost. I'd let my body do what she wanted, and now her terrible reign was over: there would be no more messes, no more appetite. My body became tweakable, tunable as a guitar. I could skip breakfast. I could skip lunch. I had made myself manifest and I could make myself disappear. I could erase bit by bit, hear the clicking bone of an elbow, give myself something to want—at night, the feeding dreams grew: my hands tearing hunks of bread, licking yellow icing from cake— like keeping an animal just to not feed it.

♦

In Canada, my waiting is no longer waiting: Ulysses has been spotted. Scheherazade is near her triumph. The season is turning. There are no lists left. I feel myself slacken the rope of my attentive, cagey self. We order burritos every night and stay up late. Canada is another adolescence. Canada is the quiet before the storm, the storm before the sunlight.

♦

My first pregnancy ended in blood.

"The truth is," the doctor said after the ultrasound, "that this fetus likely wouldn't have been viable anyway. See this sac? See how thin it is?" I looked at the meaningless white curlicue.

"Should I just wait then?" I liked the idea of letting nature run its course. "I can just wait."

The doctor frowned. "We don't advise waiting."

She left the room and returned with a resident and a tray full of silver, immaculate instruments. The resident seemed very excited.

"Did she tell you about the sac?" she chimed.

"They don't advise waiting," I replied.

They gave me two Advils and a well-meaning blonde—"I'm the support coach!"—chirped in my ear about breathing. "Try to imagine the pain as a light," she'd say. "Breathe it out." She seemed so earnest I felt bad for her; she really believed she was helping. I played along, breathing deeply through my nose, nodding when she asked if it was better. It wasn't. Johnny asked if I wanted him to leave the room.

"You can stay," I said sweetly. I was seething. The whole time the tissue was being suctioned from my body, the same awful thought kept echoing: Let him see.

There was pain. There was a lot of pain. Later, I'd hear that other women were given anesthesia, put to sleep. This was a low-income clinic. There were no graham crackers afterward. I had to ask for water for the Advil. Afterward, I walked myself the ten blocks back to work, the forensic unit of a hospital. I was bleeding so heavily I had to change pads every hour. The smell of Clorox was reassuring. I didn't ask for a day off. I didn't tell anyone at work. I wanted it not to have happened, and so it didn't.

◆

One week after the procedure, I got an email from the clinic. There was an attachment and I opened it. It was an image of the sonogram. I'd not asked for it. Nobody had asked if I wanted it. But there it was: all that almost-something.

◆

Dee texts me about her body. The skin of her stomach is starting to tingle a little. Bud is kicking more than usual. There is a burning sensation in her belly button. With her other pregnancies, the burning meant the baby would come in a few days. I am the natural audience for these updates, but I still feel like an intruder. Like the witnessing itself is a transgression.

✦

If my body were a film, the montage would be repetitive and maddening. Me, biting my nails in the clinic. Me, checking a cyst in my breast thirty, forty times. It would be somersaulting between glut and restraint. Me, chewing cookies at a party and spitting them in a napkin when nobody's looking. Jiggling feet. Popping jaw. Fingers tapping across kneecaps. Even in sleep: mumbled words, gasped breath, a heartbeat that climbs above a hundred during dreams.

✦

Five years after the first sonogram, we are planning a trip to the Southwest. We'll be driving across the desert, stopping in little towns. I pick out sundresses and tights. At work, I flip through photographs of snow on cacti. I've been feeling low. I am moody and tired. My back aches. There's a twinge that travels from my right neck all the way down to my calves, and I take endless baths, submerging miserably into hot water. We throw a housewarming party and, afterward, I lie on the rug in the dark and tell Johnny something doesn't feel right. The next morning, I start spotting, even though it's a week after my last period. The ER visit feels like a lark. I feel the bloom of hope in my throat as the subway rushes toward Manhattan. The pregnancy test had shown two lines. It was happening.

The emergency doctors are rushed and full of rhetorical, terrible questions. Did I know I have a bicornuate uterus? I did not.

Has anyone ever mentioned something about a septum to me?

Have I had a miscarriage before?

The bloom of hope dissolves with the hours. My blood work comes back troubling. The doctor shakes his head. My pregnancy hormones are high, too high. I understand from his brow this is not a good thing. "It means we should be able to see something on the regular ultrasound. But we don't . . ." He doesn't finish the sentence.

I am sent for a transvaginal ultrasound. The room is entirely dark, save for the moonlike glow of the screen, and an Indian woman who asks if I am Muslim as she roots around inside me. I am, I tell her.

Alhamdullilah.

The question belatedly reminds me to pray. I silently recited the Fatiha as she looks. Her face is earnest as she searches. "It's empty," she says.

Was I sure I was pregnant?

She interrupts herself with a small sound. She clicks at the keyboard several times and tells me I can get dressed. "The fertilized egg wasn't in the uterus," she says. Did I know what an ectopic was? I say yes, but I'm not sure. Back downstairs, Johnny pulls out his laptop. He plays a movie while we wait for the doctor. It is the one about a famous ice skater. The actress playing her is blonde and beautiful and curses a lot. I discreetly google *ectopic* on my phone.

When the doctor comes, he looks somber. He doesn't greet us first. He doesn't apologize for the wait. "You have a cornual ectopic," he begins. I try to imagine what it must be like—to stroll into rooms and say things like this. It's bad dialogue, I think. "It's exceedingly rare. Quite critical if it ruptures."

"I have a flight tomorrow," I remember.

"Not anymore," he says steadily. The pressurized air in the plane would rupture it. This is how people die. He keeps speaking, but I can't stop hearing that word. He is ordering methotrexate, he says. It's a chemotherapy shot. "Why?" I manage to ask.

He misunderstands my question. "We need to stop the growth," he says and then pauses, gauging my reaction. Would I make a scene? Would I beg him to save my baby? I suddenly understand. Chemo kills things that are growing. There is something inside me growing. And it will kill me if it keeps growing. "This is not a viable fetus," he says firmly, as though he doesn't want me getting any ideas.

"We weren't trying," I say, hating myself as I say it, hating my desire to neutralize the situation, to comfort this stranger, this man who means nothing to me. "It was a mistake."

He nods, cheered. "Good," he says. "That'll make all of it easier."

✦

I return to the ER three times: eleven-, twelve-hour waits that end with another methotrexate shot as my pregnancy levels continue to rise. I see mostly male doctors, who speak in cool tones. They talk about my fallopian tubes and HCG levels. Did I know that I might be infertile? Had someone told me that if the sac ruptured, I'd probably lose my uterus? Their questions were runaway trains; they'd stop for nothing.

"Can I still go running?" I ask one. He is tall and handsome, with floppy, sandy hair.

"You run?" He leans against the ER bed. "What's your time? I just did a half-marathon."

I look around me. Is this really happening? "I jog," I amend. "For like thirty minutes."

"I ran ten miles this morning." He sounds like a boy flirting in a bar.

"That's amazing," I hear someone with my voice gush. A pause. "So. Can I run?"

"Oh, definitely not," he says. "That would be dangerous."

✦

The price for an answer is banter, being unhysterical, shaking my hair out. Attention is attention and I am in an unfamiliar wilderness, grateful for any scrap I can get. Later, I'd read a Leila Chatti poem and it would return me to the scene. *And what of the doctors' looking?* she writes. *Having looked so long, I think them gods. And anyway, I can't demand they avert their gaze—the looking's what will save me.*

✦

The story of a body is the story of what it gets you.

✦

The third visit was the worst. It stretched thirteen hours and Johnny was in Saint Louis for his brother's wedding. My brother and his girlfriend, Yara, spent hours with me. There was a woman handcuffed to the bed across from us, the cop next to her ignoring her cursing. When the nurse took my blood, a drop of it fell to the floor.

"Excuse me," I told a passing tech. "There's some blood on the floor."

"We'll get someone to clean it up," he replied. It stayed the entire thirteen hours, congealing into a half-moon. I lived seven lives in that fluorescently lit room. It was a Saturday and the emergencies kept coming. I was taken for an ultrasound and forgotten in the room for an hour. *Pay attention*, I told myself. *You'll write about this.* When the new doctor breezed by to update us on the pregnancy levels—a dip would mean my body was responding to the medication—he cocked his thumb toward the ceiling to signal the rise, like he was giving me a thumbs-up. I started weeping and couldn't stop.

In the street, it was nearly midnight; my brother held me by the shoulders. He kept whispering. My body was aching from the shot. I nearly collapsed on the L train home. My back was killing me. I could barely walk. Johnny called as I was hobbling out of the station. I couldn't even say hello.

"Baby," he said. "Baby, baby. Please don't cry. I'll fly home tonight."

"It'll end," I sobbed.

✦

There is a game I played with myself in the emergency room. I've always loved time-travel stories, the moment when the future self and the past self meet. How they contain all their hauntings: the longing for what will come, the longing for what has passed. How it turns out that the past self needs to keep being the past self, exactly as it is, or else it erases the future self out of existence. The future self hinges on the continuation of the past self. In this way, the future haunts the past as much as the other way around.

The game I played is an old one: I pretended I was no longer my present self. I was my future self. I had tapped myself out, a wrestling tag-team buddy, a coworker taking over my shift. I'd recognized the impossibility of the moment, and so the self that knew it would end stepped in. She endured it because she was proof it had been endured.

◆

Later, I find psychological writings around time and self: temporal self-continuity, temporal self-extension, the ways we build the connection between our past, present, and future selves. It is multidirectional: the sense that a past self's voices led to a better future, the motivation to veer a present self onto a different path. I'm most interested in the future self: the one that is soothing, cheering on, watching like a minor god from *just* up ahead.

◆

That night, I returned to a house of women. My sister, Miriam, was studying for a final. My mother had flown in the night before from Abu Dhabi. She was asleep, jet-lagged, when I entered the house. I took two steps, saw my sister, and my legs gave out from under me. I wailed on the floor. I saw my sister's scared brown eyes, her voice calling my name. I couldn't speak, couldn't say the strange thought I was suddenly filled with, how nostalgic I was for her babyhood—her tiny body against mine—how I didn't know when it had ended. I remembered how I'd tell her she held my heart in her hands, and when I'd ask where it was, she'd instinctively cup her fingers. For years we did this. For years she was my baby. And now she stood, taller than me and afraid. I wanted Beirut. I wanted the room we'd shared when I was a teenager, her hand against my arm asking me for water. I wanted to go home. The dog trotted up to me, licking my face anxiously. Miriam called for my mother, her voice shaking out, and she ran out, half-awake, and pulled me up.

"Ya rab, please," I heard her whispering. "Please." She pulled me into bed, and I settled against her body and she read sura after sura and played with my hair and every time I started crying, she told me to sleep.

✦

When I say I played a game with myself, I mean the story is what saved me. Knowing the story was coming. Knowing someday I would tell it. The story itself reminded me that I wouldn't always be in that room, in that light, staring at a drying smudge of blood.

✦

In Canada, Dee texts from the doctor's office. She is not in labor, but she is dilated. We pack a small bag, drive west to her town. There is a small house on a lake. The water is white. The trees are white. Everywhere, snow.

✦

The men that came for my body came later. I didn't develop early. I was nearly fourteen when I got my period. I remained relatively flat-chested. I got hips but stayed small on top, with a flat ass. I was never catcalled, my body never commented on. The men appeared in university class-rooms, in airport lines, in hotel lobbies. When the drinking started, I preyed upon myself. I used men the way a cutter uses knives; I used them to make marks, to draw blood. I woke to them mid-blackout. I pretended I remembered how I'd gotten there.

✦

During our honeymoon, we went to a hammam in Istanbul. They led Johnny to his scrub first, then a man came up to me. He said there were no more women left. I told him I'd wait, and he looked so forlorn I hesitated. "I will get in trouble," he said. "I promise, I scrub the best." I followed him to the hammam and ten minutes later left, my breath hitched, ran back out. I never told Johnny. I pretended I'd finished a little early. I pretended I had a headache. I never told him, and so I blamed him for not knowing. Then I blamed myself for protecting him at my own cost.

◆

The story of a body is the story of what protects it. What doesn't.

◆

They told me my uterus was a heart. I became obsessed with it. For months, for the months that would've been a normal pregnancy, I became obsessed with the ectopic. The literal sac of blood and tissue. Whenever I thought about my uterus, the right-hand corner obedienly ached. I would imagine the mass—the size of a sesame seed—pulsing as I walked or slept or read an email. I had dreams of ripping it out with my own nails. Years later, I still dream of it rupturing.

◆

I am the same with doctors and with love. I shrink. My voice gets girlish. I laugh too much, fidget with my hair, waiting to be told I'm okay, waiting to get eyes on me, waiting to be made safe, evaluated as worthy or not. They are both spaces of appraisal. I am chirpy, talkative, affecting a cool girl. I ask questions as though they just occurred to me, belying their polish, their careful rehearsal. In both, I wait for the looking, I wait for the looking to save me.

◆

My uterus wasn't a heart after all. It was a sealed mouth. I had a septum fastening it shut from tip to tip and I'd need surgery. Months later, once it was over, I woke up from the anesthesia in pain and thirsty. The doctor was speaking with one of the nurses, and in the haze, I heard the nurse ask, "How far along?"

It doesn't matter, I want to say. It's not real. I don't get to keep it.

"Few more months to go," the doctor said.

That's not right. That's not right.

That was the first time I noticed the swell under her scrubs. I'd been seeing her weekly without seeing it.

✦

I am gambling when Dee texts. We're at a small casino in Belleville, and Johnny is annoyed. I keep withdrawing another twenty from the ATM when he goes to the bathroom. I lose and lose, until I win, then keep winning. I'm at a slot machine, mesmerized like a child with the flashing lights and music, pulling the lever over and over and over. I win ten dollars. I win fifty dollars. My phone dings. It is 4:03 p.m. March 12th. *Think I'm having contractions.*

✦

Terror, delight. Delight, terror.

✦

A meditation teacher once told me about a passage by Adam Phillips. When a claustrophobic client says he might die if he goes into a crowded space, Phillips mentally retorts, *Why not agree to die and see what happens?*

✦

I have a photograph of the IVF needles. They are lined up like pencils or flowers. I have a photograph of my knees in the fertility clinic waiting room. I have a photograph of a vial of blood, one of dozens taken over the years at the clinic. I have a photograph of each bathroom before surgery, my hair in a pale green net, my eyes frantic. I am smiling in all of them, into the mirror, into the camera, for nobody.

◆

That first surgery, I was terrified of anesthesia. The thought of the body, emptied of consciousness, a cut from awake to awake. The second surgery, I've figured it out. It's like blacking out, I told my friend. That time, I follow the anesthesiologist down a drab hallway and into the operating room. When the panic comes, I have only one thought: *I've agreed to die. I've agreed to die.* I lie down on the operating table and this time, there is not a needle, but a mask, which smells like the inside of a beach ball and makes it hard to breathe.

"Don't panic," the surgeon says. "It'll feel like you can't breathe but you can."

This time my last thought is: *Even if I couldn't, I'm already here.* The world darkens.

◆

The story of a body is the story of those that love it.

◆

After one surgery, we stopped at a Duane Reade to get my pain medication. There was a long line. I felt a sear between my legs, so bad I nearly got on my knees. Above me, there were hands, Johnny's hands on my shoulder. Above me, there was a sound like nothing I'd heard before. There was a roar. *She's in pain,* Johnny bellowed. *Do you not see her.* The pharmacist said something, and Johnny kept repeating to nobody, *She's in pain. She's in pain.* The tiles were gray and uniform. I thought of Istanbul. I thought of that night in the baths, the steam, those hands on my body. I remembered the rain on our wedding day, both of our wedding days, the way he looked at our makeshift altar, his beautiful face. I thought of that moment, merging with the hot pain, how I'd thought getting married meant my body would become someone else's, that my whole self would. How what I meant was that I wouldn't be my own problem anymore.

♦

While we wait for Dee to arrive at our motel room, we speak nervously about nothing. I keep getting an uncanny sense of déjà vu. Like I'd already lived all this before. Like I was visiting, returning one last time to see this moment through.

♦

The most I've felt in my body was after that first surgery. Because I watched it recover. There was pain, then the pain was cozily muted by a Percocet. That first night after, I was certain I'd never feel okay again. Even peeing felt like fire. My throat hurt. I couldn't walk a few steps without panting. But then I watched my body—that question mark, that defector—mend, bit by bit. I could swallow the food Johnny made me. I was able to walk down the stairs, then down the block, then across the borough. My lungs got stronger. Mine, this body. Mine. I'd lose it again, in the coming years, with the IVF and miscarriages. But for a while, it was mine. For a while, I was nowhere else but inside it. With the healing came a peculiar, sheer joy: suffering charged a steep price, but on the other side of it lay survival.

♦

Bless the self that sat in the emergency room. Bless the self that waited for the doctor. Bless the self that waited for the doctor for three years. Bless the self that answered the phone. Bless the self that answered Hello, then yes, then oh, then thank you, thank you for the updated HCG numbers, thank you for confirming the miscarriage, yes, maybe next time, no, I'm okay, yes, I'll see you again on Monday. Bless the self that watched a half-moon of blood congeal on a tile. Bless the self that waited and waited and tried.

◆

Which self, then, walks up and down First Avenue? Which self waits for a knock at a Canadian motel door to change its life?

◆

"Where your fear is," Carl Jung says, "there is your task."

◆

The story of a body is the story of its fear.

◆

Anything buried is solely deferred. My hunger ignored was hunger deferred. It always came back with a wild ferocity: for love, for the window dressing of a life, for a child.

◆

Two years after the ectopic, a nurse named Carol sticks a syringe inside me and tells me her granddaughter's birthday is the next day. Fuck your granddaughter, I think, staring at the light fixture above us. The stirrups are cold. I am counting my breaths. Outside, it's the hottest day of the year so far, and walking down First Avenue in my N95 mask, I'd felt like I was underwater. She holds up the syringe of milky yellow.

"The semen's excellent," she sings out. "And your egg is looking nice and juicy." She doesn't have to tell me to part my legs. I already have.

She slides the speculum in me and I barely wince. I am distracted. I am distracted because I have that same weightless feeling as when I forget my keys, when I realize I'm not wearing my purse. It takes me a moment to understand. The thing that is missing is me. The self I'd been waiting for, the self who would lie down on this exam table. The future Hala, self-possessed, dignified.

The asshole never shows up. It's just me. This me: panting in my mask, swimming in dark thoughts, thanking the nurse as she slips her gloves off, scrolling through my feed as the sperm tries to swim toward my uterus. It's my feet in the stirrups. It's my hand on my belly. I let her die a little, that self, that delicious fiction, hybrid ghost of wish and expectation. In the absence of that magical self, I have to make do with this one. I shut my eyes and let what will happen happen. Which is another way of saying it works, then it doesn't. Then it works again. Then it doesn't. Which is another way of saying I die and I die and I die.

◆

There is a knock on a door in a small town in Canada. I am on the other side of that door. Suddenly, there she is: Dee. Tiny, and somehow filling up the space. Filling up the whole country. There are two queen beds and she sits on one. We talk shyly. Her stomach is enormous, her face young and round. I look at her belly and think of Meimei. I think, *That's Meimei's great-granddaughter in there.* That's the daughter's daughter's daughter. It makes me feel a little dizzy. This woman, this stranger, this life raft. This woman with her own story, who has intersected mine in this brief and enormous way. *Ah*, she winces a few times. The contractions are coming more often, but not often enough to go to the hospital. She has two daughters, she knows about these things. She is amazingly relaxed. We'd had a conversation the week before where she said, "I have loved having Bud in here, but I can't wait to see Bud in your arms." She told me a few minutes later she wouldn't ever want a third child. I understood what she was saying. I was grateful to her for saying it. She had a daughter who loved to draw, another who was a hell-raiser. She had nursed and burped and rocked and sung. She had things to love, and she didn't need more.

On the opposite bed, she smiles mid-sentence. Her hand flutters to her belly automatically, a gesture that's clearly happened hundreds of times. I feel my own automation, the hunger in my gut, the yearning for something so instinctive. But she is already speaking to me, grinning, "You want to feel?" My hand on her stomach feels otherwordly: it's harder than I'd expected, like a basketball, and the second I press my palm I feel the kick, the flurry of motion, a little fist or heel, a knock all of its own.

◆

I'd always had a knack for self-destruction, but there was a fail-safe button that only I knew about. I always knew when to stop, that step away from a precipice, at the last possible moment. The night before I took my GREs, I went drinking with my friend Jared in Beirut, shot for shot for shot, until he was done, and I kept going. My exam was in the morning. Everything hinged on it. It was one in the morning, then three. I flung down a street, calling out for him to hurry up, one more bar, one more stop. He finally blocked my way, begging me to stop. "Everyone's going to be mad at me," he said, and his voice was so distraught, so boyish, I agreed to go home. Please don't drink more in there, he said at my building, and I giggled and staggered up the stairs. But once I got in my apartment, my memory sharpens: I remember remembering the exam. I remember seeing the wine bottle on my kitchen counter. I remember washing my face. I didn't touch another drop.

◆

I always told myself during my drinking years: I'll stop drinking before it kills me, because I'll know when I've reached that line. But what stopped me was Daniel's fall, recognizing myself in that plummet, recognizing in that story that sometimes a thing can kill you before you've even known it's happened.

◆

What I'm saying is I've always chosen the seat—in restaurants, in gatherings—that faces the door. What I'm saying is I've always understood exits. I've always known that every suffering ends. Except in the days of the clinic, the hundreds of dollars on pregnancy tests, that endless walk up and down an avenue, the subway through water that returned me to a ghost, someone who wouldn't look me in the eye, someone who didn't lose what I lost, who turned away from my grief because he refused to make it his own. What I'm saying is I knew how to make a body obey. I knew how to make a body do what I wanted. When I didn't eat, my body whittled. When I drank, it disappeared. But I couldn't make it pregnant. I couldn't make it stay pregnant. I couldn't make it make a life.

◆

It's true: every time I wore a paper gown, I met my selves in our own consortium, all of us crowded on that examination table. Every time I lost a pregnancy, I met my selves again, all my almost-mothers. But it is like this with everything—every time I drank, touched, didn't eat, I summoned all the other times. Like this we show up to heal, even if we pretend to have lost hope. Like this we hold our breath. Like this we wait for this time to be different.

◆

There's a story of a Tibetan master Milarepa. One day, he returns to find that his cave has been taken over by demons. He tries everything. Lunging at them, pleading with them. Finally, he surrenders. He sits on the floor and sings, "It is wonderful you demons came today. You must come again tomorrow. From time to time, we should converse." The demons vanish.

◆

The early evening turns dark in the motel room. We order tacos and burritos. We talk about Dee's daughters. Her ex, our wedding day, my siblings.

We get into the beds, Johnny and I in one, Dee in the other. There is the giddy feeling of a sleepover, and I keep waiting for someone to enter the room, that uncanny feeling that there is someone missing. It's her, I finally realize. It's her. She's in the room right now. The simplicity of the thought knocks the air out of me. We turn off the lamps and Dee promises to time the contractions if they get stronger. We put on a superhero movie, one where children turn into adults when they say a magic word. We fall asleep, and before I do, I think, *This is the last movie I'll watch before.*

♦

In another version, Milarepa goes to the biggest, scariest demon of all and puts his head in her mouth. The demon bows deeply and disappears. I like that version best.

♦

We sleep and wake, tossing and turning. I have a dream about an airplane. I'm stepping on the tarmac when I wake up. There's a noise and that noise is coming from the fumbling dark. I forget where I am, I forget who the woman's voice is, a voice that moans my name like it's a question. That says, *It's time.*

♦

Johnny rushes us to the hospital. It's just me and her in the hospital room. I think about that hot August afternoon when I called her, her kindness: *We started this together, we'll continue this together.* I'm right here, I say to her after she changes into the gown. I'm going to be here the whole time. I don't change into a gown. I keep wearing my clothes, my earrings, my bra. What's about to happen isn't going to happen to my body. I stand in that room, the massive windows overlooking a river that I forget to look up later, a river that will remain unnamed forever in my memory, and the strangest thing happens: I can't summon all the other times. Because there is no other time like this.

◆

On the day of her birth, I think of the Mediterranean. I don't think of desert. I watch that unfamiliar water, the snow surrounding it, and I think of home. I hold another woman's thighs. I smell another woman's scent. It is sharp and beautiful. I think of the sea. I hear another woman make the sounds I thought I'd make someday. I look at the woman and the woman is in pain and beautiful and I pray for it to be quick and it is.

◆

I hold Dee's knee against my body and I don't stop looking at her until the doctor speaks. "Look," the doctor says. "Look," she says. "Look." "I am looking—" I finally start to say, but then she speaks louder, her voice a wave in my heart: *Look at your daughter.* Dee laughs through her grunting. *Look*, the doctor says. *Your daughter*, the doctor says. And I peer into that chasm of an almost-daughter, a daughter in becoming, and I see the crown of a skull, matted and dark. I am possessed. I cannot stop looking. For a moment, I see the blue of the Mediterranean, the blue of Nadia's thin veins, the half-moons of Seham's fingernails. And suddenly, I am in the room. My body is in the room. My body is not the body parting and opening, but still, it's there, it's here. My arm is looped through Dee's knee. The doctor tells us both to push: me the knee against my chest, her the daughter into the air. "Talk to her," the nurse whispers at my side, and I don't know if she means Dee or the almost-daughter, so I talk to both. "It's almost over," I tell Dee. "You're doing amazing. Look at me. Look at me," I say. She looks. I look back. This is almost over. Soon this will just be a memory. Soon this will be a story. This will be a story.

Perhaps I never left that room. Perhaps I'll leave that self in there, with her hoarse voice, her urging, her story of how this will end, so soon, so soon, just keep pushing. Perhaps time stopped in that room. Perhaps time saw what was happening and quietly let us be.

✦

She pushes and we all die. She pushes and we are all different people at the end of that pushing. She pushes and you are here. You are here, wet and filmy and mewling. You open your eyes almost immediately.

Johnny makes it just in time to cut the umbilical cord. He stops when he sees you. No matter what happens after, this is the truest moment I know: I watch him see you. I watch the breath leave his body for a moment. He lifts you, he touches your ears. This is the first thing he says: *They're yours*, meaning her ears. They're yours.

✦

I am possessed by something when I see you.

✦

I knew your name all along. I said it with my eyes closed months earlier, while my brother filmed me. A night. Dusk beauty. Of course—you are born in the morning. You are born the morning of daylight savings. The day we get an hour of sunlight back. Right before noon. The sun streaming through the windows like milk.

✦

For years, I'd repeat the same line. At dinner parties, at bars. When the topic turned to children. *I want something to matter more than myself.* I said it because I liked how it sounded. Because it sounded like something that might be true. To somebody. Someday. I had a vague sense of what it meant: something about less ego, a different kind of disappearing. I knew what it was to lose myself in the other. But even that losing was still about me. I wanted to forget I was in the room. To be in the service of something else.

✦

Sometimes you tell a story so that you can hear the story. Sometimes you tell a story so that someday, you'll recognize its happening.

◆

When I see you, everything changes. There is no future, or it is only future. There is no future or, if there is, it is screaming in my arms, pulling me into the moment. My life snaps into focus. The future is no longer mine or it is no longer only mine. It is yours now too. It is more yours than mine. It is a possession of self. I'm not shaking. I'm still. I'm not consumed with love; I'm enlivened by it. I'm silenced by it. I sit in the hospital room and hold you. The little squeak of your suckling. I can't nurse you, and I spend minutes trying to think of a joke to whisper only to you, something about a dry bar, but then you blink and I forget what I was saying.

◆

Leila means night. In Arabic, "a thousand and one nights" is *alf layla w layla*. When you name a thing you are giving a future, but you are also giving a past. A place in the order of things. Leila for dusk. Leila for night. Leila for ornament. For the glitter of possibility. Not for alleyways or blackouts or secrets. For all the roads not taken. Not for hiding. For cover. For safety. For shelter, for all that leads you to dawn. I name her for all the stories that can change when you're not even looking, in the darkest hours. I name her for all the things that can happen, the joyful, unexpected things, before morning.

Postpartum

After. After, every night lasts a week, but the first week is over in the length of an exhale. I read a book about an apocalypse, then fall asleep for one hour, two, waking to her mewling. We are kind to each other, Johnny and I, even in the fumbling dark. We are confronted every hour with this creature, this animal of sound and hunger and heat. We let each other sleep. "Wake me at five," we tell each other, only to be shaken awake past nine, by a delirious hand.

◆

I don't see Dee again after the birth. The hospital policy keeps us in our respective rooms because of the virus. When she returns home, she sends pictures of her daughters, her recovering on a couch. I send her pictures of Leila and she sends back heart emojis. There is no map for this *after*. Some people have no contact after the baby is born. Some exchange cards for the rest of their lives. There is no right way. No template for this relationship: a woman who changes your life, who gives you what you couldn't give yourself. Who gives what cannot be repaid. There is almost a freedom in this: the enormity, the absolute impossibility of reciprocation.

✦

I ask you a question, in the middle of the night, waking to every cry with a start, already reaching for you in the bassinet before I've fully woken. I'm terrified of sleep, afraid I'll sleepwalk, keep having dreams of losing you in the tangle of sheets, somewhere in the comforter. But once I'm awake, the two of us alone in the dark, your eyes gleaming and unfazed, I calm. Whose baby is this? I whisper to you. *Inti bint meen.* Whose daughter. Where did you come from, little duck? Little bird. Little one.

✦

In the mornings, I take her on cold Canadian walks. I tell her story after story. The curtains are always drawn in the rented apartment now. The television loops. We are exhausted, wired. There is no time to ask questions. There is no time to ask about happiness or depression or marriage. I walk in the cold air and I hold a daughter and I remember whose daughter she is. Mine. I tell her stories. I tell her the stories I know I won't be able to repeat when she's older. Stories about nights in Beirut, fights I overheard between my parents. I tell her dumb jokes. I ask her advice about a job offer. At night, I sing Courtney Love songs. I recite poetry. I talk to her about my sister, my cousin, I tell her about my first weeks in America. I hum the songs Meimei used to sing to me. I read Quran. I don't know what to offer this tiny squawking being, so I offer it all, the cacophony of a life. I almost like the mid-night wakings. The night a velvet cloak around us, the street lamps gleaming like a dozen moons. I'm the worst Sheherazade in this way: the stories I tell are to get me through the night, not her.

✦

Darwish: *No night is long enough for us to dream twice in it.* And yet:

◆

The sounds come back to me in dreams. Even though I know it's not *hearing*. It's remembering. They aren't sounds, they're auditory impressions. Echoes. No matter: I hear what I remember. I sleep in brief fits, even on the nights Johnny is with the baby. I sleep and I jolt to noises that aren't there: The click of prayer beads. The stray cats of my old neighborhood in Beirut. The sound of their timorous fucking. The fruit vendors. The cab drivers yelling at each other. And everywhere— the adhan. The land is my body. The downtown emptied of its people is my body. I rise with the ocean. It comes for me.

◆

We leave Toronto like thieves leaving a heist. The very morning we get her final signed birth certificate, we pack the suitcases, cajole the dog with a Dramamine-laced treat. The car is piled with things: her cot, her stroller, diapers, formula, a bottle-cleaning machine. We drive ten hours straight to my mother's house in Connecticut. We only stop once, long enough to eat burgers and a handful of fries.

◆

It is the tenth day of Ramadan. The twelfth. I play the adhan for Leila, an app on my phone, and she turns her head toward the sound.

Adhan from *announce*. Adhan from *listen*. Adhan a call to all that can hear, announcing the time for prayer. I love thinking of the auditions for becoming a muezzin. I love when there are several of them at once, within seconds of each other, like one bird calling after the other. How an entire city can orient to that call. You pause your sentence, your thought. Even for just a second. You are reminded. You are perpetually asked to return. You are perpetually called home.

✦

One day, a woman catches my eye crossing the street, smiling, and says, *Hang in there, Mama.* She is gone before I can explain what nobody had asked me to explain. I want to explain the love I'd felt for her the second she was born. That I couldn't remember a time when she hadn't been there, even though it had only been weeks. I want to explain that I hadn't suffered enough, that I was afraid someone would spot it, name my mothering a brand of tourism. A game of house.

Whenever I found myself in small talk with a new mother—the park, the grocery store—I felt like my years of subterfuge had finally caught up with me. I told the truth compulsively, before it was even asked of me. *Eight weeks,* I'd say, then rush: *She was born via surrogate. She's biologically ours. I couldn't carry her.* The same three lines, sometimes in different order, as though casual, unrehearsed: *So she's biologically ours, but I couldn't carry her and she was born via surrogate. I couldn't carry her actually, but she's biologically ours. Born via surrogate.* They carried three vital truths: I wanted it known she was mine. I didn't want undue credit. I wanted it known I had tried.

✦

And yet:

If I trail my forefinger between her eyebrows, she shuts her eyes. If I hum close to her ear, she sleeps. If I open and close my mouth against her cheek like a fish, she turns toward the warmth of my breath.

✦

"Actually,

✦

you seem to be forgetting," my friend says, "that your body had a part in all of this." Called into the room, that old thing, my body: I am embarrassed all over again.

✦

And yet:

✦

We sit, me rocking her, her pensively blinking in the darkened room. Our idea of safety comes from our early days and months. What of this will endure? A hand rubbing circles on her back, the sound of washing machines, the same murmuring voice hour after hour.

✦

And yet:

✦

She coos in the dark. You're a bird, I like to tell her. Not a baby. Only I say it with fake consternation. "I believe I asked for a daughter. But they've made a mistake! Someone's brought me a bird instead." She stares solemnly at me for a second, then squawks. The other sound is a little engine. A-gha. A-gha. When I coo at her, she coos back, two birds in the dark.

✦

And yet. And so.

✦

I wanted to explain to the woman on the street everything. *Hang in there, Mama.* I wanted to tell her about the wall above Leila's crib, how she followed my voice with her little face, about our house with the machine that mixes formula and the machine that makes white noise and

245

the machine that answers our questions, and the backyard where all the birthday parties are held. I want to tell her there is always tinsel in the backyard, that it has been several years of winter and, suddenly, everything is in full bloom. That yesterday I'd eaten a fig from the neighbor's tree, the branch low into our yard, and fed half to the dog. To tell her that Leila had made a little humming sound as I sang, her body held close to mine. That, latent in me: waking—a mother.

◆

The first things Leila knows of the world: light. Our voices. Femme hands. My mother. My sister. The motif of sisters and mothers and aunties in fairy tales: the guiding lights, that which brings you home. The women that help us: one from the Caribbean, then one from Tibet. My aunt. My cousin. They show me how to fold onesies, the perfect temperature for milk. They tell me when it's time to unswaddle her, the best way to cradle her neck in the bath. It's a new country. The men will leave or they won't. There is no waiting for them anymore. It's the women that save us.

◆

The stories of *One Thousand and One Nights* weren't assembled by Scheherazade. They were gathered over centuries and dozens of countries, by authors and philosophers and magicians and teachers. Then they were given the frame of a woman, given the voice of a single woman.

◆

In Arabic, the highest blessing to a parent and child is *Allah khaleekom la ba'ad.*

May Allah keep you to each other. May you keep each other. May you get to keep each other.

◆

Three weeks after Leila is born, my cousin Layal sends me an email. *This poem has been waiting to be sent to you.* Inside, a piece dated two years earlier. It's a poem to Leila, written after one of my miscarriages. It begins: *Hey kid / We missed you again.* It ends: *She is always waiting for you / A miracle of love / She is always waiting / She wants you to know / she loves you already.*

+

The women in my family are beasts when it comes to love. Savages. They will tear this whole city to the ground searching for it. Protecting it.

+

When I overhear Miriam singing to Leila about stars and spiders, when Layal whispers to her, *Your mama says you're not named after me, but you are.* When Reem lifts her and they both giggle, when Mama prays above her little crown. My heart shatters and is somehow reassembled at the same time. I realize, over and over, what I somehow didn't before: These are the women in her family. Their perfume. Their velvety jewelry boxes. Their mended hearts. Their stories. These are her elders. May they be kept to each other.

+

I read her stories. Dozens of them in those first few months. My favorite is one about cows and wolves and sheep and ants. Like this I love you, the book says. Like this I love you. *I'll love you till the cows come home. I'll love you till the frogs ride past. I'll love you till the yaks come back.* The premise, of course, is that there is no end to the love. It keeps going and going.

+

Sometimes, at night, humming with exhaustion, your name becomes the song. Sung over and over again: *ba-by Lei-la, ba-by Lei-la.*

✦

Every day, I forget then remember to speak to you in Arabic. I am a child in Arabic. I am Fatima's granddaughter, Mama's child. How faulty the language is in my mouth, how erratic. Years of living in this country, years of living with someone who doesn't speak it. She will speak it if you speak it, my aunt Reem tells me, so I speak it. I speak it badly. I forget the words for certainty, pear, apology.

✦

When she'd visit us in America, my grandmother refused to speak in English. Anytime I said something to her, she'd say: *In Arabic, in Arabic!* Now, decades later, when my parents speak to you in English, I rush into the room like a comet. *In Arabic! In Arabic!*

✦

My friend Ghinwa brings me mahalabia. It's the traditional food to celebrate babies. Boiled rice pudding with almonds and cinnamon and sugar. I finish all four jars in a single day. After the first bite, I go into the nursery and fall to my knees, like I'm going into prayer, but instead I lower my face onto the white, fluffy carpet, press my open mouth against it like it is snow. I cry while you sleep.

✦

When I'm with you, my body remembers. My body knows how to change you, how to cradle you. It knows what it learned two decades earlier. Miriam nestled against my body. Sometimes, in the nighttime delirium, everything gets confused. Upside down. It is the past and future all at once. I am changing Miriam. I am thirteen years old, holding you to my chest, my girl-arms tremulous. You coo and I am undone. I am waiting for my mother to take me home, to come take you, to let me sleep.

✦

I wanted to have one final story for you. I wanted the story to be so good, so magnificent, so perfectly resonant that it summarized everything. I wanted to tell you a final story about your father and me, a simple ending, a binary code that we landed on like birds perching on wire. I wanted to become fused with him or to never see him again. In the end, it is neither. We are bound for the rest of our lives. We cannot rescue each other, though we tried, we tried harder than we've tried at anything, and goddamn if that isn't its own kind of rescue.

✦

Let me return to you for a second. This morning you head-butted us both. The want of your mouth trying to find my chin, my nose, my teeth. You cried like I'd done it and I apologized, but only pain can teach us about pain. When you are falling asleep, I press my nose against your nose, our breath fluttering against each other. I let my eyelashes sweep against your forehead. Eyes blinking open.

✦

I stay up at night and worry. I worry about the land. I worry about what I will give you. What I can pass down. My paltry jewelry box. I cannot give you Latakia, Gaza, Akka, al-Majdal. I cannot give you Iraq Sweidan. Baby, it doesn't exist anymore. Baby, you can't find it on a map.

✦

The part that longs for a resolution: a boxer getting ready for the ring. A performer bowing to an applauding crowd. It functions for the audience, not the one experiencing it. The part that is hungry for resolution is the part that is hungry for certainty. That part keeps asking for it, and I keep urging her to try waiting instead. It's an acquired taste, I'll say, but trust me, and perhaps someday she will. I understand if it takes a long time. I understand why she doesn't trust me yet. After all: the person that has abandoned her most of all, most consistently, for the longest periods of time, has been me.

✦

In the early evenings, right before bedtime, when Johnny is at work, I play Fairuz for you and pretend I know all the lyrics. The only song I have memorized is *Nassam Alayna El-Hawa* and so I sing that one over and over. I sing and twirl you around until you giggle. *Take me to my country*, Fairuz says. Only the direct translation is: Take me to my countries. All of them.

✦

Our children do not owe us antidotes, though sometimes, unexpectedly, they bring them anyway. Sometimes they incite a humbling, sharp love. It is a love that asks little, that doesn't need to be returned, that is replenishable. Like anything of quality, it raises the caliber of all other love. It makes us wonder if we've been calling the right thing by the right name all this time.

✦

You, pale as a moon on the playground. Twice I'll be asked if I'm your nanny. But I bore you, didn't I? I bore you out of want and want and want, and in the end someone else bore you and I loved just the same.

✦

I sit in the dark and sing. *Ya rab, jibli baby*. My father's song, revised: Bring us a baby named Leila. Let the baby be nice.

✦

Miriam is the person I trust Leila with the most. I don't know why. Then one day, I suddenly know: she is the closest thing to myself, which is the first moment I realize I am trusting myself.

◆

I'm trying to say: for so long, I couldn't forgive myself.

◆

I'm trying to say: there is no resolution. Who cares. I leave my marriage or I don't. I'm left or I'm not. There are two apartments or one. There is a daughter. There is a house. There is love. There is no great reckoning. There have already been ten million small ones.

◆

I have remade myself many times: in the image of different cities, partners, addictions, recoveries. I am hungry for origin stories, and to be hungry for an origin story is to be hungry for a story of return. To retrieve whatever I can from the stories I swam in for decades: stories about where I'm from, stories about place, stories about my own remakings. With every recovered piece, I reclaim something for the ones that came before me too. I remake the self, again and again, that thing which cries out to be remade. I learn from my land, the history of those cities, the way their stories were told. For so long, their stories were told back to them like gospels. A land, prehistoric. A land, cut up like bread. A land, erased and erasing. What gets us back to it but a story? They'll tell you it doesn't count, but don't listen: the machinations of a return can happen in your imagination first. It begins with becoming tired of letting the past govern you, of letting history govern what made you. The myth of scarcity is dismantled first by the daydream of abundance.

◆

There's something we forget about Scheherazade: she came after the stories. The stories preceded her. She was invented to give them a home: a vase for water, so that they may be carried. She does not exist outside of them. But the rest of us do.

✦

In you is the glittering Beirut pavement after rain. The ports of Boston. In you are both my grandmothers' rebellious blood, following men, escaping wars, from one country to another, my mother's leavings, my aunts'. The rage and humiliation and exile. In you is the harm and rejoicing and help of generations of women. In you live the people that made you. All of them. I wouldn't give you another story even if I could, for this is the one that bore you, and it is heavy and dazzling and the truth. In you is your father's wanderlust, his father's loneliness, his father's father's heart giving out on a tiled floor. In you is the story of sailors, occupiers, the occupied, the people who never left, people who were made to. You will learn to live within this, as we all do. You come from people that love the way moons pull tides, or else the way tides are pulled by the moon, and someday you will have to reckon with your own, unruly heart. I have no advice to give, save one thing: Don't exile anything. Turn the sun of your attention—briefly, sometimes, briefly—on all that awakens your love.

✦

This is your birthright, Leila. You will have to hunt for many things. Excavate them in others or yourself. But not your mother's truth. I'll leave that right in the open for you to see.

✦

One day, I'm bathing my baby and she blows a bubble into the water and I instinctively look around to see who else saw but no one else is there. I'm struck by a particular longing, for the moment to be seen by those who no longer can. And so I am left to look for all of us. I look for Mei-mei. I ache for Meimei. Meimei who bathed my mother, my uncles, my aunt, then me, my brother, my cousins. How many times had we been made clean by her hands. How many hands had she touched. How many crowns of heads. What a beautiful life. What a beautiful way to have spent one's life. Now, I touch my child with my hands and think of her, of how we are made of the same thing.

◆

And I sit in the dark. In that room with the furry rug. In that room with the olive branch on the wall. In that room in the house with the happiness and sorrow and bottles and music. I sit and I hold Leila and I hold Layal and I hold Miriam, her elders. Her living ancestors. I hold the ones that taught me how to hold. Even Fatima wasn't Meimei once. I always forget that: she became it because we named her so. We named her so because we needed her to be that for us. We named her so and so she became. Who knows what Leila will call us, what she will be called. *Allah ykhaleekom la ba'ad.* In this lifetime and whatever ones might come after. I sit in the dark. I sit in the dark and I sing. I hold her and I am holding them. I am rocking them, her, all of us, to sleep.

Acknowledgments

This book exists because my communities exist.

◆

Thank you to the incredible team at Avid Reader Press and Simon & Schuster, particularly Lauren Wein for midwifing this book from fragments and dream-scraps.

◆

Thank you to Amy Guay, Meredith Vilarello, Alexandra Primiani, Eva Kerins, Caroline McGregor, Kayla Dee, Katya Wiegmann, Ruth Lee-Mui, Allison Green, Amy Medeiros, Alicia Brancato, Cait Lamborne, Jessica Chin, Alison Forner, Sydney Newman, and Clay Smith.

◆

Thank you to Michelle for the endless support over the years. I will always be grateful.

✦

Endless gratitude to Jenny Xu and Naomi Klein.

✦

Thank you to Meredith for new paths.

✦

Michael, Dalea, Andre, Colin, Jared, Sahar, Kiki, Lola, Alexis, Beth, Karam, Olivia, Sara—I love you beyond measure.

✦

To the brilliant beloveds: Sarah, Zeina, Ashna, Jon, Peter, Ghinwa, Hamed, Kamelya, Randa, Fady, Marwa, Susan, Kate, Miguel, Zein, Remi, Sepideh, Simone, Hannah, Iris, Madeline, Nawal, Ro, Michelle, Mira, Safia, Mira, Etaf, Rumaan, George, Jason, Courtney, Zahra, Fady, Mahogany, Theo, Amatan, Natasha, George, Cherien, Karl, Zaina, Safia, Darine, Megan, Sarah A., Lara, Fati, Sana, Noorah, Sharifah, Nicole.

✦

Thank you to Tenzin, to Jen, to Hannah, to Pauline, for the gorgeous acts of care.

✦

Thank you to my Mama and Baba, a thousand times.

✦

Thank you to my aunts and uncles, and the legacy of your stories. Your lineage is an honor. Your survival is how I got here. To Meimei, Teta, my grandfathers, for all the sacrifice and grace you showed this life, which allowed life to continue generations later.

✦

To Reem, Layal, Omar, Talal, Miriam, Yara—Leila is as lucky as I am to have you.

✦

Thank you to the incredible woman who carried life for nearly a year. I will never be able to fully articulate what you've given.

✦

Thank you to the team at the Langone Fertility Center, especially Shannon.

✦

Thank you to my clients and students.

✦

Leila, my heart: I love you in the moon, I love you in the dirt. B7ibbik kteer kteer kteer.

About the Author

HALA ALYAN is the author of the novels *Salt Houses*—winner of the Dayton Literary Peace Prize and the Arab American Book Award, and a finalist for the Chautauqua Prize—and *The Arsonists' City*, a finalist for the Aspen Words Literary Prize. She is also the author of five highly acclaimed collections of poetry, including *The Twenty-Ninth Year* and *The Moon That Turns You Back*. Her work has been published by the *New Yorker*, the Academy of American Poets, the *New York Times*, the *Guardian*, and *Guernica*. She lives in Brooklyn with her family, where she works as a clinical psychologist and professor at New York University.

Avid Reader Press, an imprint of Simon & Schuster, is built on the idea that the most rewarding publishing has three common denominators: great books, published with intense focus, in true partnership. Thank you to the Avid Reader Press colleagues who collaborated on *I'll Tell You When I'm Home*, as well as to the hundreds of professionals in the Simon & Schuster advertising, audio, communications, design, ebook, finance, human resources, legal, marketing, operations, production, sales, supply chain, subsidiary rights, and warehouse departments whose invaluable support and expertise benefit every one of our titles.

Editorial
Lauren Wein, *VP and Editorial Director*
Amy Guay, *Assistant Editor*

Jacket Design
Alison Forner, *Senior Art Director*
Clay Smith, *Senior Designer*
Sydney Newman, *Art Associate*

Marketing
Meredith Vilarello, *VP and Associate Publisher*
Caroline McGregor, *Senior Marketing Manager*
Kayla Dee, *Associate Marketing Manager*
Katya Wiegmann, *Marketing and Publishing Assistant*

Production
Allison Green, *Managing Editor*
Jessica Chin, *Senior Manager of Copyediting*
Amy Medeiros, *Production Editor*
Alicia Brancato, *Production Manager*
Ruth Lee-Mui, *Interior Text Designer*
Erika R. Genova, *Desktop Compositor*
Cait Lamborne, *Ebook Developer*

Publicity
Alexandra Primiani, *Director of Publicity*
Eva Kerins, *Publicity Assistant*

Subsidiary Rights
Paul O'Halloran, *VP and Director of Subsidiary Rights*
Fiona Sharp, *Subsidiary Rights Coordinator*